LOSING TO WIN

Studies in American Political Institutions and Public Policy
General Editor: James W. Ceaser, University of Virginia

Presenting works on contemporary American politics that address the question of how institutions and policies can best function to sustain a healthy liberal democratic government in the United States.

LOSING TO WIN

The 1996 Elections and American Politics

JAMES W. CEASER
and
ANDREW E. BUSCH

ROWMAN & LITTLEFIELD PUBLISHERS, INC.
Lanham • New York • Boulder • Oxford

ROWMAN & LITTLEFIELD PUBLISHERS, INC.

Published in the United States of America
by Rowman & Littlefield Publishers, Inc.
4720 Boston Way, Lanham, Maryland 20706

12 Hid's Copse Road
Cummor Hill, Oxford OX2 9JJ, England

British Library Cataloguing in Publication Information Available

Library of Congress Cataloging-in-Publication Data

Losing to win : the 1996 elections and American politics / edited by
    James W. Ceaser and Andrew E. Busch.
        p.   cm.
    Includes index.
    ISBN 0-8476-8405-9 (cloth : alk. paper). — ISBN 0-8476-8406-7
(pbk. : alk. paper)
        1. Presidents—United States—Election—1996.   2. Elections—
United States.   3. Presidents—United States—Nomination.
4. Republican Party (U.S.)   5. United States—Congress—Elections,
1996.   6. United States—Politics and government—1989–   I. Ceaser,
James W.   II. Busch, Andrew E.
JK5261996a
324.973'0929—dc21   97-1579
                                                              CIP

ISBN 0-8476-8405-9 (cloth : alk. paper)
ISBN 0-8476-8406-7 (pbk. : alk. paper)

Printed in the United States of America

⊚ ™ The paper used in this publication meets the minimum requirements of
American National Standard for Information Sciences—Permanence of Paper
for Printed Library Materials, ANSI Z39.48-1984.

To Mindy and Blaire

Contents

Acknowledgments

The authors would like to thank the following persons for their assistance in preparing and editing this manuscript: Josh Dunn, Mike Cairo, Andrew Hall, Blaire French, Richard Skinner, and Robert Stacey. Julie Kirsch, managing editor at Rowman & Littlefield, guided the manuscript through production with remarkable speed and efficiency. Finally, our appreciation goes to the Rowland Egger Fund of the Department of Government and Foreign Affairs at the University of Virginia for financial assistance in preparing the manuscript.

Chapter 1

Greater Dooms Win
Greater Destinies

The American electorate of the nineties stands out for its willingness to experiment with alternative political lifestyles. Call it a penchant for majority shopping, or perhaps merely a succession of cases of buyers' regret, but American voters have tried three of the four possible partisan combinations for arranging power in Washington: a Republican President with a Democratic Congress, a Democratic President with a Democratic Congress, and a Democratic President with a Republican Congress.[1] To the Republicans' dismay, the one option that has been neglected is a Republican President with a Republican Congress. In only two periods in the last century has there been a comparable series of shifts, between 1888–1896 and between 1946–1954, when the electorate batted for the whole circuit and went through the cycle of all four combinations.

The current decade—let us start in 1988—began with a Republican President (George Bush) elected with a Democratic Congress. This configuration appeared with such frequency during the previous twenty years that many political scientists considered it the statistical "norm" for modern American politics. Under the daunting title of the theory of "split-level realignment," Republicans were said to hold a lease on the presidential suite on the top level, while Democrats were the permanent tenants of Congress, certainly of the House. As Byron Shafer succinctly put it, "The Republicans, being the party of cultural traditionalism and foreign nationalism, control the presidency. The Democrats, being the party of economic liberalism and service delivery, control the House."[2]

Divided government ended in 1992, when the Democrats main-

1

tained their control of Congress while ousting the Republicans from the presidency, albeit with only 43 percent of the national vote. Although this election violated the recent statistical norm of a split-level result, many interpreted it as a return to the deeper historical equilibrium condition of unified party government. According to James Sundquist, divided government was accidental and dysfunctional, leading to policy incoherence, nondecisions, standoffs, checkmate, and deadlock.[3] The election of 1992 broke this stalemate. Although it was perhaps not a great realigning election, many argued that it tapped a real domestic majority that had been obscured for some time. According to Wilson Carey McWilliams the 1992 election signaled the public's "demand for an active government engaged to relieve America's discontents and reclaim the future."[4] Left unsaid, although widely understood, was that unified government for the immediate future would have to take place under the Democratic Party, because Republican control of the House was at best a project for the next decade. All that Republicans could reasonably hope for was a return of divided government with a Republican presidential victory in 1996, along perhaps with a Senate majority in 1994 or 1996.

No sane individual in 1992, unless it was Newt Gingrich, foresaw the Republican congressional sweep in 1994. The unexpectedness of this victory, together with the breadth and depth of GOP gains in the governors' mansions and state legislatures, made 1994 no ordinary midterm takeover of Congress. Many analysts called 1994 a full-scale realigning election. For Walter Dean Burnham it was "one of those rare elections from which bearing will have to be taken for a long time to come."[5] The historical analogue of 1994, in this view, was the congressional midterm elections of exactly a century before, when Republicans seized control of the Congress from the Democrats and went on to win the presidency in 1896. Republicans then held both branches of the government uninterrupted for the next 14 years. In this scenario Bill Clinton's fate was to play the part of the portly Grover Cleveland, who was left to preside helplessly and haplessly over the decline of his party's fortunes.

So favorable a view for the Republicans was bound to inspire a counter-interpretation to buoy the Democrats' flagging spirits. A quick search through the history books yielded another potential analogy: 1946. Some observers, whose numbers increased starting in late 1995, argued that 1994, like 1946, represented no more than a brief burst of public protest by "angry white males" that would be erased in the next presidential elections. As in 1948, Republicans in 1996 would awaken the day after the election to face unified party government under the Democrats. In this scenario Bill Clinton was asked to play the role of the sprightly Harry Truman, fighting valiantly to lead his party back to power.

In the end the clash of interpretations for 1996 proved disappointing to both sides. The President turned out to be neither Bill Cleveland nor Harry S Clinton, but quintessentially himself. He won his own reelection handily, but he left congressional Democrats largely on their own, and they were unable to recapture either house. The improbable result of divided control between a Democratic President and a Republican Congress was not only confirmed in the election of 1996, but it began to produce new theorizing of continued Republican control of Congress together with a Democratic "lock" on the presidency. The "normal" split-level of 1988 had been reversed. Democrats vacated their premises on the ground level and moved upstairs, while Republicans moved downstairs and took over the Democrats' digs. From the perspective of 1988, it seemed that we had entered an era of permanent deviance. But in 1996 this all somehow seemed so natural.

If a pattern underlies these extraordinary swings of the pendulum, it was foreseen long ago by the famous pre-Socratic pollster and philosopher Heraclitus: "Greater dooms win greater destinies." In modern parlance this is the theme of losing to win. A precondition—and more likely a cause—of the Republicans' congressional victory in 1994 and the Democrats' presidential victory in 1996 was the decisive defeat that each party suffered in the previous election. The idea that a party must lose to win was advanced, somewhat facetiously, by Thomas Mann in 1991, when George Bush's reelection seemed certain. Asked by the magazine *Roll Call* to project a scenario under which Republicans could ever capture the House, Mann responded that it could occur only if Republicans would lose the White House. Otherwise House Republicans might continue wandering in the wilderness for as long as thirty years.[6]

Mann's modest proposal for the GOP to sacrifice the presidency was based on the insight that big party victories in American politics are only possible when a single party is clearly in control and when things go poorly on its watch. National party accountability is then possible, and a campaign can be run on a "throw the bums out" theme. (The last, almost successful, campaign conducted on this basis was in 1980, when the Republicans took the presidency and the Senate and made impressive gains in the House.) The logic for this kind of development is simple. Broad party changes rest not only on the public's attachment to the program being proposed by the out party, but also on its rejection of the policies of the in party. Epochs and cycles of American electoral politics are defined nearly as much by the negative symbols that are evoked as by the positive alternatives that are offered. Electoral mobilization on this negative basis is nothing new, beginning from the time of the Jeffersonians' demonization of Hamiltonian monarchism, to the Republicans' post-Civil War reminders of Democratic treachery, to the many Democratic New Deal elections run against Herbert Hoover, to the three Reagan-style campaigns (1980 thru 1988) run against a cocktail of the liberalism of George McGovern and Jimmy Carter.

But like everything else in our age, the process of negative symbolization has sped up tenfold. And it was enhanced by the practice of "morphing," the computer-assisted transformation in political advertisements of one's opponent into a demonized national target. In 1994, Republicans "morphed" their Democratic congressional opponents into Bill Clinton. In district after district, centaur-like figures appeared on the television screens sporting the body of a Democrat and the head of Clinton. Clinton served as the symbol of unified Democratic government, even as Republicans targeted Democratic Party control of Congress with its special problems and scandals. Republicans also offered a positive alternative program under the title of the "Contract with America." Ultimately, however, as Gary Jacobson argued, "it was Bush's failure to win reelection that gave Republicans the opportunity that Gingrich and other Republican leaders exploited so effectively."[7]

But less than two years later, the tables were turned. To the musical question "Who's morphing now?" the answer was the Democrats. The new morphees were Republican congressmen, whose fragile necks were asked to support the ample head of an unshaven Gingrich. Democrats swaggered about with an attitude of he who morphs last morphs loudest. Although Republicans did win both houses of Congress, the Democrats' campaign to connect Republican candidates to Gingrich and the Republican majority helped in some degree, as shown by the distance that many Republicans tried to put between themselves and the Speaker. Far more telling was the rhetorical morphing employed in the presidential campaign. A central element of the President's strategy was to link Bob Dole to Newt Gingrich. As far as Democrats were concerned, the Republican ticket was not Dole-Kemp, but Dole-Gingrich.

One of the most unusual aspects of the 1996 presidential race was the extent to which it became a referendum on the performance of the

Congress and not just the President. The election looked back to 1994 even more than 1992. The ordinary rule of thumb on campaigns involving an incumbent is that they turn on the public's judgment of the President's performance. But Bill Clinton managed to turn the election in part into a judgment of the Republicans' performance in Congress. Clinton had it both ways: the Republican Congress was responsible for everything bad, while the President was responsible for everything good. Blaming Congress in a presidential race has not worked in recent American politics, but it was a plausible approach in 1996 after the Republicans had so visibly claimed and exercised the agenda-setting function in 1995. "Losing" for Clinton in 1994 became a chief cause for his winning in 1996.

The phenomenon of losing to win may be empirically observable, but why exactly did it occur? Three explanations have been offered, each with some evidence to support it. The first is that the winners proved incompetent and squandered their opportunities, managing to turn victory into defeat. The story of American politics from 1992 to 1996 is a tale of two overreachers. In Bill Clinton and Newt Gingrich, both men of huge political appetites, there is all the material for a classic chapter in Plutarch's *Parallel Lives*. In their respective periods of failure, these two leaders made similar misjudgments of constitutional form and political strategy. In 1992–94 Bill Clinton seemed almost without a compass in behaving presidentially. His manner, his lack of discipline, and his annoying practice of blaming things on everyone else left many with the feeling that there was a profound mismatch between the person and the office. In addition, in his political policies Clinton had gone much too far in the direction of governing as an "old Democrat" after having campaigned as a "new Democrat." By the time he launched his health care plan, according to Colin Campbell and Bert Rockman, the "discrepancy between Clinton's policy ambitions and the constraints of his policy and political environment" had become patently clear.[8]

Newt Gingrich's reign that followed the 1994 election displayed a comparable set of errors. If there were risks attendant to a president's strategy of "going public," then there were hazards in a Speaker of the House who carried himself as if he owned the bully pulpit, expatiating daily on anything from cybernetics to organizational theory. Gingrich seemed constitutionally incapable of letting actions speak louder than words. He did not know how to be "speakerish," continually claiming prerogatives for the position that went well beyond its powers. For most of 1995, as Norman Thomas and Joseph Pika remarked, Gingrich seemed to be "usurping roles previously reserved for Presidents: he claimed an electoral mandate, pledged to adopt provisions of the House Republicans' Contract with America within the 100-day-time period traditionally associated with new Presidents, conducted daily briefings with the press, and presented a prime-time address to the nation."[9] Politically, he proceeded as if a great Realignment had already occurred in 1994. A program to balance the budget by making some potentially unpopular reductions was risky, although it might have proven popular if it could have been enacted. But this was just the point. Control over its enactment did not lie in the Republicans' hands, and in the end Republicans received the blame for proposing cuts while winning no credit for balancing the budget.

The second explanation is that it was the losers' skill that enabled them to take advantage of new opportunities in their situation. Here we see the other qualities displayed by Gingrich and Clinton— qualities that earned them both the honor of *Time Magazine*'s person of the year. Stumbling in victory, they proved adept in defeat. After the Republicans' defeat of 1992, Newt Gingrich seized the occasion of operating in the mode of full opposition, unencumbered by the responsibility of having to protect a Republican president, to mobilize Republican forces. Almost alone Gingrich fought an attitude among House Republicans of resignation at being the minority party. By his energy, will, and strategy, he did more than any other individual to engineer the Republican victory in 1994.[10] After what amounted to a personal defeat in 1994, President Clinton (following a long period of self-doubt bordering on depression) picked himself up and began to learn from his previous misjudgments. He seemed to discover the presidency, making a conscious effort to appear more presidential and using the formal powers of the office, from the veto to his broad discretion in the conduct of foreign affairs, to reassert his powers. He also began to recenter himself on the political spectrum, embracing the strategy of "triangulation" fashioned by his Republican strategist Dick Morris. The Democratic Party in Congress also learned a lesson. Backed into a corner after 1994 and needing the presidency if they were to have any influence whatsoever, Democrats rallied around Clinton and allowed him a free ride to renomination.

The third explanation is that during this period there was a structural advantage to losing. Losers were able to escape responsibility for assuming the initiative in governance at a time when neither party had a formula to win majority approval, at least not with the amount of power it had. This explanation is arguably the most important of the three. American leaders can be punished for either of two different things: implementing measures that prove to be unpopular or failing to pass a legislative program. Both Bill Clinton and Newt Gingrich ran afoul of the second problem. Both had programs—one for national health care, the other for balancing the budget—that were not only stopped because they were unpopular but also grew more unpopular because they were stopped. Neither leader had the power to force through highly charged policy changes, and both were punished for trying and for failing. At a time when a negative majority could be mobilized, but a positive majority was lacking, exposure in leading proved a liability. The electorate was neither in favor of "Big Government" nor was it ready to embrace a "revolution" to dismantle the welfare state. The best offense was a good defense. Having both begun by prizing the right to initiate, Clinton after 1994 and Gingrich after 1996 both sought to surrender it to his opponent. The once vaunted power of agenda setting became the hot potato of American politics.

In the end Clinton won reelection by engaging in a two-step rehabilitation program that was made possible by the results of the 1994 election. Forced to the right by Congress, Clinton neutralized the negative coalition of 1994 that had been based on stopping liberalism. And freed from association with Congress, he created a negative coalition of his own in 1996 based on opposition to a perceived extremism in dismantling the welfare state.

Losing to win is an observation of political science, not a recommendation for conducting campaigns. But in a capital city starved for new ideas of electioneering, it could not be long before some would propose this theme as a new, high-stakes form of political strategizing. To play this game, a political party must know when and how to lose in order to cash in at the bottom of the market. (All such strategizing presupposes, of course, that the opposition will never succeed while in power.) For example, there were Republicans who regretted their victory of 1994, preferring instead to have come close in preparation for going over the top in 1996 along with a Republican presidential victory. Carrying this subtle kind of analysis a step further, the conservative *Weekly Standard* featured an article in the fall of 1995 recommending a Republican defeat in the presidential race in order that Republicans might strengthen their hand for 1998.[11] Under this strategy the Republican Party's aim would be to seek out presidential candidates who make good losers and then hire political consultants skilled at producing defeat—a line the party has recently been following anyhow. The party would embrace a new political Protestant ethic of saving up for more power but never actually exercising it. Losing, it would seem, should ordinarily be an easy objective to accomplish, at least where the other party is foolish enough to want to win. But if the opposition is intelligent and also tries to lose, competition would be as stiff as it is today, although no doubt with far less negative campaigning.

Losing to win is connected with a new relationship in the interplay between presidential and congressional campaigns. The complicated connection between these two campaigns has been described up to now according to the models of "attraction" or "separation." Attraction is characterized by a direct (or positive) effect exercised by candidates of the same party on each other. Usually this has assumed the form of the winning presidential candidates helping congressional candidates of their own party producing what was known in a more polite age as coattails. (Occasionally, in a reverse coattail effect, an especially strong congressional or gubernatorial candidate might help a presidential candidate from his own party.) The same thing, of course, holds on the downside. A weak performance of the presidential candidate tends to pull down the other candidates of the same party on the rest of the ticket. Underlying this model is the idea that a significant part of the electorate perceives the national party as a team to be rewarded or punished across the board.

The descriptive power of the model of attraction has diminished greatly since the 1950s, supplanted by the tendency of separation. Under this model, presidential and congressional candidates run separate and disconnected campaigns that have minimal impact on one another. Party labels for many in the electorate are incidental, and the candidates—often the incumbents—work to keep it that way. Neither the presidential nor the congressional campaign really helps or hurts the other very much. In the extreme, it is even a misnomer to speak of *a* congressional campaign because all the candidates run on their own: All politics is local. Congressional campaigns are de-nationalized and disassociated from the presidential campaign and even from each other.

A third model came to the forefront in 1996 that was framed by the context of losing to win: "repulsion." In this model, as under attraction, the presidential and congressional campaigns influence each other, but that relationship is negative or inverse. As a party's presidential candidate rises its prospects for winning the Congress fall, and as its congressional candidates rise the prospects for its presidential candidate dims. The way to win one institution is to lose the other.

This model was at the core of a large part of the strategizing in the 1996 elections. The Clinton campaign early on gained from the perception that the Republicans would keep control of Congress, while the Republican campaign for Congress gained at the end from the perception that the Democrats would capture the White House. Neither winner did much to dispel these perceptions, but rather sought to use them to their advantage. Such was the new code of partisan honor in 1996.[12]

The elections of 1996 produced a result that, despite the odd configuration of a Democratic President paired with a Republican Congress, kept with the "norm" of American government since 1954: a government of divided partisan control. But on closer inspection, the more things stayed the same, the more they seemed to change. For if the fact of divided government was confirmed, its place in political discourse and in the campaigns was different. The concept of divided government began to go from negative to positive. As the presidential scholar Charles Jones has shown, although divided government has become the statistical "norm" of American politics, elites who comment on politics have usually regarded it as not only harmful but also a violation of a deeper wish of the American people.[13] But scarcely anything of this attitude was found after the 1996 elections. There were none of the usual chorus of laments in the press against divided government, and within the political science profession no one was seen raising the old Schattschneider banner for responsible political parties. No doubt this change of heart rested on something more than just a reevaluation of institutional capacities. With Congress now in the hands of Republicans, a call for united government might somehow be interpreted as promoting Republican Party control, a result at odds with the wishes of most inside the high priesthood of national journalism. Still, the accumulated weight of political science studies on the normalcy of divided government was beginning to take its toll.

Of the elites Jones discussed, he necessarily exempted the politicians whose role is never to concede publicly the inevitability, let alone desirability, of divided government. But even the politicians in 1996 seemed to be softening. President Clinton, who campaigned in 1992 on the pledge to "end gridlock," asked voters in 1996 to allow him to be the agent of gridlock, checking the Republican extremists in Congress. For their part, Republicans came to conclude that Bob Dole's bid for the presidency was doomed and began arguing that a Republican Congress was necessary to prevent Bill Clinton from having a "blank check." In this way, both sides were running on a "losing to win" theme. Clinton's argument depended on losing Congress, the Republicans' on losing the presidency.

Finally, there is the question of what the voters themselves wanted. Was a critical portion voting for divided government? For some time now certain analysts have suggested that voters have been engaging in a form of strategic voting and consciously seeking to divide party control, although this argument has not been proven at the national level.[14] The more conventional explanation has been that divided government was not something intended, but a result of many people preferring one party in the presidency and the other party—or rather a particular person from the other party—for Congress. If the political strategies and campaigns of 1996 are any indication, a decisive set of voters, whose number might be small but whose impact was great, were now choosing divided government because they wanted it. And they wanted it less because they liked both parties than because they feared the excesses of each.

Who's On Top?

After the succession of the different partisan configurations in the last decade, what changed in American politics? Who won? Listening to the different answers after the election only seemed to increase the confusion. Although many made self-serving claims, no one quite knew whether Americans had voted for one majority in the vital center, for two majorities hostile and suspicious of each other, or for no majority at all. The idea of a coherent or purposeful majority in the vital center became a convenient fiction for those trying to chart a centrist governing course, but no one has discovered such a majority as a positive force. The more reasonable explanation is that there is no real majority, but rather two distinct negative coalitions each represented in a different part of the government. The "majority" found in Congress represents the negative coalition against the big government Democratic ideas of 1993 and 1994; the "majority" held by the President represents a negative coalition against the Republican "revolution" of 1994 and 1995. These two negative coalitions cannot be classified as real majorities because the last two elections reveal that there is no clear positive majority for big government, nor a clear positive majority for an assault on government. Of course, the larger part of each coalition has a positive objective—there is a core of liberals who wish to maintain or expand government and a core of conservatives who wish to limit and reduce it. But in neither case can this "positive" part stand by itself to make up a majority. To create a statistical majority, each needs the "anti" block on its side.

If there is no clear majority, it is still possible to ask who has gained or lost ground over the past cycle of changes. To speak in such terms implies a benchmark against which gain or loss can be measured over a long period. The two benchmarks usually offered are partisanship and ideology. For partisans, if the attitude of officials after the election offers any key, there was a kind of shared contentment reminiscent of 1956, when Eisenhower was handily reelected but Democrats held on to the narrow congressional majority they had gained in 1954. The ambivalent feelings of both parties were best reflected after the election, when both sides claimed a victory of sorts. For Democrats the "comeback kid" had done it again, while Republicans could feel much relief that the election of 1994 had not been repudiated and that the party won both houses of Congress. In fact, the answer to who won in 1996 depends on the base year from which one begins. If 1994 is the point of reference, the Democrats can now claim to be gaining ground. Republican hopes for a full-scale takeover were thwarted in 1996, as Clinton was reelected by an impressive margin and as Democrats made some gains in the House and at the state level. All in all the Democrats found themselves not only with the presidency in their hands but also in a stronger position at the other levels (See Table 1.1). On the other hand, if 1988 is the base (or any year earlier back to the 1950s) the Republicans can claim to be moving forward. While they fell back slightly from where they were in the House in 1994, they gained ground in the Senate. And they moved forward over the whole period, trading a more modest presidency for a resurgent Congress and for a much improved position in the states. If the major event in this cycle is the 1994 election, the Republicans can claim that they held on and did not relinquish their huge gains of that year. The shift of a certain segment of voters toward the Republicans in 1994 indicates that there has been a realignment of strength in favor of the Republicans. (This idea is distinct from the notion of a Realignment with a capital R, which implies a preponderant majority for one party.)

Movements of realignment among certain groups in one direction tend to produce countermovements by other groups. The politics of mobilization and polarization attracts new adherents but also loses old ones. This process may not take place in one election, but over a cycle of elections as voters observe how a party acts when it is in power. The current change of strength in Congress to the Republicans over the past

TABLE 1.1
Party Strength, 1988–1996

Year	President percent of vote		Congress Senate		Congress House		Governors		State Legislatures	
1988	45.6	D	55	D	250	D	29	D	67	D
	53.4	R	45	R	175	R	21	R	30	R
									1	Tie
1990			56	D	267	D	27	D	69	D
			44	R	167	R	21	R	25	R
					1	I	2	I	4	Tie
1992	43.0	D	57	D	258	D	28	D	64	D
	37.4	R	43	R	176	R	20	R	31	R
	18.9	I			1	I	2	I	3	Tie
1994			48	D	204	D	19	D	47	D
			52	R	230	R	30	R	50	R
					1	I	1	I	1	Tie
1996	49.2	D	45	D	207	D	17	D	51	D
	40.8	R	55	R	227	R	32	R	46	R
	8.5	I			1	I	1	I	1	Tie

decade has owed much to a regional shift in which the South has become much more solidly Republican. Conservative Democrats in the
South turned into conservative Republicans. The countermovement
began to take place after the 1994 elections as Democrats made solid
gains in the Northeast (See Table 1.2). A similar kind of action and
reaction has occurred in the realm of interest group activity. The Christian Coalition, which has played such an important role in mobilizing
Republican voters, especially in 1994, was met by a reenergized organized labor movement, which played a much stronger role in the 1996
elections than at any time since 1968. And the so-called "angry male"
who swung to the Republicans in 1994 was countered by the reverse
movement of the concerned female in 1996.

A movement on ideological grounds is more difficult to measure,
because candidates do not run as liberals or conservatives and because
the meaning of these terms is always changing. But conservative analysts have been much bolder than Republicans in claiming progress, if
not outright victory, for their position. Their contention is that in the
realm of "public philosophy," meaning the ideas that dominate the

TABLE 1.2
Regional Party Strength in South* and Northeast**, 1980–1996

Year	President percent of vote South		N.E.		Congress Senate South		N.E.		House South		N.E.		Governors South	N.E.		State Leg. South	N.E.	
1980	44.7	D	42.3	D	14	D	7	D	79	D	38	D	8 D	6	D	26 D	8	D
	51.3	R	45.8	R	11	R	7	R	46	R	26	R	5 R	1	R	0 R	6	R
	11.9	I	11.9	I	1	I	1	I										
1988	41.5	D	50.1	D	14	D	8	D	85	D	35	D	7 D	4	D	26 D	10	D
	57.7	R	48.4	R	11	R	6	R	46	R	23	R	6 R	3	R	0 R	4	R
1990					16	D	8	D	87	D	37	D	8 D	2	D	26 D	9	D
					10	R	6	R	45	R	20	R	5 R	4	R	0 R	4	R
														1	I		1	T
1992	41.5	D	47.2	D	14	D	8	D	87	D	32	D	9 D	3	D	25 D	10	D
	41.9	R	32.8	R	12	R	6	R	53	R	21	R	4 R	3	R	0 R	4	R
	16.1	I	19.4	I										1	I	1 T	1	T
1994					11	D	7	D	69	D	21	D	7 D	1	D	23 D	8	D
					15	R	7	R	71	R	22	R	6 R	5	R	3 R	6	R
														1	I			
1996	46.6	D	58.9	D	8	D	7	D	59	D	36	D	5 D	2	D	18 D	11	D
	46.0	R	31.8	R	18	R	7	R	81	R	15	R	8 R	4	R	7 R	3	R
	7.4	I	9.0	I							1	I		1	I	1 I	1	T

*The South includes the following states: Alabama, Arkansas, Florida, Georgia, Kentucky, Louisiana, Mississippi, Missouri, North Carolina, South Carolina, Tennessee, Texas and Virginia.

**Northeast here includes the following states: Connecticut, Maine, Massachusetts, New Hampshire, New York, Rhode Island, and Vermont.

discourse on public policy, 1996 demonstrated (or reconfirmed) that America had entered what George Will called "a conservative era" in which "voters produced another advance for conservatism."[15] Bob Dole may have lost the election by eight points, but—so the argument goes—conservative ideas won, and there has been a realignment to conservatism, even if there has not yet been a full-scale partisan realignment. Proof of this realignment is that conservatives succeeded in imposing a public standard against which to measure liberalism and conservatism—"big government"—and then got President Clinton to embrace their side of the argument. Clinton's most memorable phrase of his first term was not the oxymoronic "forcing the spring" of the 1993 Inaugural, but the simple declaration from his 1996 State of the Union Address that "the era of big government is over." At least rhetorically Clinton raised the white flag on the core public philosophy of modern liberalism. And unlike other recent Democrats who were merely wary of embracing liberalism, Clinton explicitly disavowed it, protesting during the campaign that he did not qualify as a "closet liberal." If, in a reversal of Samuel Lubbell's analysis of the 1950s, the Democratic Party has become the moon to the Republican sun, it is largely because of the gravitational pull exerted by the conservative ideas animating Republican politics. In this sense, the politics of the 1990s have seen the further development (though hardly the completion, which may or may not come) of a process set in motion by Ronald Reagan.[16]

To the extent that ideological self-identification of voters is a valid indicator of the relative strength of the different ideological groups, conservatives gained ground between 1992 and 1996, although they were only making up ground they had lost in the Bush years. But the more important point is that conservatives have long outnumbered liberals by a significant margin in voter self-identification, even though moderates make up by far the largest group.[17] The continuing preponderance of self-identified conservatives over liberals coincided in the congressional elections of 1994 and 1996 with an increasing tendency of more ambivalent voters, in whom a "philosophical conservatism" coheres with an "operational liberalism," to vote on the basis of the former. The Republican congressional victory of 1994 was not so much founded on an upsurge of new conservatism as on a mobilization of existing but previously latent conservatism.

But liberals also enjoyed a measure of victory in 1996. If rhetorical symbols are the criterion, liberals could claim that they forced conservatives to retreat by making them abandon the symbol of the Contract with America and to cease all talk of a "revolution." Conservatives made deals with Clinton throughout the summer of 1996, sometimes on his terms, and they defended themselves against liberal attacks by pointing out how *much* money they wanted to spend on Medicare and how much they, too, "cared." And during the 1996 campaign, Clinton managed to load up his bridge to the twenty-first century with a fairly large agenda of tiny liberal proposals. If Clinton and many liberals were forced to the right over the long term, Republicans and many conservatives were forced to the left in 1996. Conservatives have ample cause for satisfaction over the course of events since 1992, but little excuse for triumphalism.

There is obviously much overlap between the partisan and ideological dimensions, especially in the recent period. Since Ronald Reagan's election of 1980 the Republican Party has become more and more the vessel for conservatism, while liberals have traditionally found their home in the Democratic Party, even if many liberals felt uncomfortable wearing Clinton hats and badges in 1996. Still, ideology and partisanship are not identical, otherwise there would be no "Reagan Democrats" or "Rockefeller Republicans." The importance of the distinction is twofold. For those who believe that ideology is more important, they can try to measure winning and losing in ideological terms and downplay the significance of partisan votes. For those who put partisanship higher, candidates and the parties can relocate themselves on ideological grounds in order to keep their base in changing times and conditions. The party then lives on to fight other battles. Ideological tides are always shifting in politics; there is nothing new in that. The important thing is to maintain the power of one's group and party in order to prevail in any future contest.

A change in ideological self-presentation and direction was precisely what Bill Clinton sought and managed to accomplish in 1996. His switch in time that saved one was the centerpiece of his strategy for revival after the Republican victory of 1994. Clinton presented himself as a far more conservative figure than he had been in 1994 (and perhaps even 1992). Journalist E. J. Dionne called Clinton a "liberal Republican" who swiped the Republicans' lyrics.[18] Indeed, on some issues that divide liberals and conservatives he managed to position himself to the right of Bob Dole. As for the Democratic Party, beneath its facade of unity at the Chicago convention, where all swayed together to the beat of the Macarena, there were obviously deep divisions and much consternation among liberals over Clinton's move to the center. But Clinton was not all alone by himself in the center, with the entire congressional wing of the party on the left. The Democratic Party leadership in the Congress moved a long way to the center, and a large number of Democratic congressional challengers ran as "Clinton Democrats." While Clinton prodded them and provided the example that they copied, these Democrats chose of their own volition to move to the center, betting that they could survive the nation's ideological move by repositioning themselves. As minority leader Dick Gephardt commented in 1996, "I've said many times that we are all 'new Democrats' now . . . . we have to be. Times change."[19] Ironically, it was the moderate wing of the Democratic Party in Congress that was decimated in 1994, only to be revived in 1996.

Given the shifting meanings of liberalism and conservatism, measurements of ideological movement within the government are at best suggestive. Table 1.3 makes an attempt at such a measurement. It follows the simple procedure of locating our estimate of the ideological positions of the Democratic and Republican presidential candidates and of the parties' respective congressional party leadership since 1988. (No claim is made that congressional leaders have been representative of the majority in their bodies; the concern here is only with the views of those responsible for trying to define the initial agendas of action.) Table 3 then calculates an average ideological score for the choice presented to the electorate and for the victorious partners or what we call the "governing coalition." A higher point total is more liberal, a lower more conservative. Table 1.3 shows the quite liberal (and perhaps exposed) position of the Democratic governing coalition between 1992–1994, after which there has clearly been a movement in a conservative direction. The governing coalition after 1996 is clearly the most conservative of the cycle.

If these trends on the dimensions of partisanship and ideology were the only factors operating on the American electorate, the analysis would be complete. But there is another segment of the American electorate that is beyond partisanship and ideology. This floating or dealigned element lacks a fixed or meaningful orientation on these dimensions. No long-term benchmark for measuring the direction of this segment has been defined, so the supposition is that it is responding to short-term influences of personality, mood, and issues. Of course all voters respond to such short-term factors, but for the floating segment these responses are not influenced or structured by commit-

TABLE 1.3
Liberalism and Conservatism of President and Congress, 1988–1996

Year	President Liberal 6 5 4 Conservative 3 2 1			Congress Liberal 6 5 4 Conservative 3 2 1			Average Liberalism of Governing Coalition
1988	D		R*	D*		R	4
1990			(R)	D*		R	4
1992	D*		R	D*		R	5.5
1994	(D)			D		R*	3
1996	D*	R		D		R*	2.5

*Winners.

ments of partisanship or ideology. For the pure floating voters, every election is a new event without connection to the past (other perhaps than as an assessment of the performance of incumbents), and the electorate is like a mayfly, existing for one election only.

For some time now analysts have been asking what is the size of this segment and whether and by how much it may have increased in recent years. A view of the period from 1988 to the present indicates that this segment has increased, though unevenly.[20] Although the percentage of self-declared independents in the voting electorate has remained about the same (a little more than a quarter), the rise of the outsider phenomenon as evidenced by the Perot campaign in 1992 showed clearly the potential size and strength of this segment as a force prepared to act not just by floating between the parties but moving beyond them. Outsiderism clearly lost much of its appeal from 1992 and 1994, but it remains at higher levels than in 1988. Americans' continued interest in other possible third-party or independent alternatives was again manifest in the attraction to General Colin Powell throughout the summer and fall of 1995. As for the Perot vote in 1996, even though it fell off dramatically from 19 percent in 1992 to 9 percent—and therefore has tended to be ignored—it was still impressive by the historical standard of third-party performance. But by now a new question has arisen about how to conceive at least part of the Perot vote. Perot campaigned in 1992 as a pure outsider against the idea of political parties as such; in 1996 he institutionalized this appeal and sought to link it to the establishment of a new and permanent third party. Should the Perot vote therefore be thought of as embodying a new set of partisan voters, or is it still to be classified as unanchored and dealigned?

With the electorate now so closely divided in partisan terms, the non-aligned or floating voters in 1996 held the balance. In the presidential race this group responded to short-term factors that operated in favor of Bill Clinton. But it was also ticket-splitting among members of this group that enabled the Republicans to retain control of Congress. The outcome of future American elections will likely continue to be determined by the judgments of this swing group.

At the end of the 1988–96 period, it was therefore impossible to speak of a single coherent majority being on top. There were signs of both realignment and dealignment. Realignment was manifest in the relative gain of Republicans and conservatives in the decade. But a gain is not the same thing as a majority even among partisan voters. And in today's electorate, with a large segment of dealigned voters, a majority of partisan voters is not even close to constituting a majority of the voting public. Trends favoring dealignment could be seen in the growing importance of the floating and nonattached vote, the growing space for third-party candidates, and the positive embrace of divided party control. The alternating negative coalitions over this period were pieced together between partisans and ideologues who were firm in their long-term commitments and dealigned voters who were reacting to the politics of the day.

Institutional Change and the Politics of Permutation

The most significant institutional transformation in the series of permutations from 1988 to 1996 was the change of majority control in the House (and the Congress as a whole). Far more important than the Republicans' gaining a majority was the fact that the forty-year hold of one party on the House of Representatives had been broken. Single-party control for so long a period—it could have been by either party—did more than any other factor in the modern era to confuse political analysts about some of the fundamental properties of America's political system. Something that had previously been a variable (the majority party in the House) began unconsciously to be considered a constant, with the consequence that a generation of political analysts imputed to the political system features that in fact derived from one-party control of the House.

Almost immediately after the 1994 elections, many of the patterns of organization in the House that had long been considered permanent were now exposed as characteristics only of the Democratic House. The elections of 1994 themselves disproved the adage that "all politics is local." This adage in fact reflected in large part the system of permanent one-party control. Democratic incumbents generally ran ahead of their presidential candidates during this period. A form of incumbent "corruption"—in the sense of using power to grant policy benefits in order to keep power—became the standard way of operating. The whole system was erected in order to build dikes to protect the House majority from the tides of national politics. The 1994 elections finally broke through these dikes. The Republicans demonstrated the capacity of congressional parties, under the right conditions, to "nationalize" congressional elections around a set of programmatic issues and themes. Following in this line the minority Democrats, with their anti-Republican appeal and their Families First agenda, ran a thematically more nationalized congressional campaign in 1996 than the Republicans.

Loss of the House also dramatically changed congressional Democrats and their understanding of the place of the political party. Democrats were reminded that their majority was not guaranteed. Prior to 1994 they had come to think that holding the majority was a providentially ordained fact and that individual members could therefore seek their own well-being without regard to the party as a whole. Collective action, either in cooperation with fellow House Democrats or with a Democratic President, was unnecessary—hence the whole system of committee "barons" and subcommittee chiefs, each presiding over their own domain. This decentralized arrangement, which Republicans modified after 1994, now appears not as an intrinsic part of Congress that could only be changed by "reform" but as a product of years of Democratic dominance. Now that Democrats are in the minority, they too have been compelled to begin thinking and acting in less individualistic ways. Their loss made congressional Democrats more prone to follow the direction of a Democratic President and, in the Senate, discouraged the more prominent among them from launching a primary challenge.

A change of a congressional majority, especially when it is based on mobilization by a national theme, generates a center of active and visible power in American politics. To be sure, analysts knew full well that during the whole modern period of Democratic House control, Congress was always a powerful institution. Presidents might preen and receive most of the media's attention, but Congress still exercised much of the control of American domestic politics. Yet it was possible for the American people to think otherwise, because of the President's prominence in foreign affairs and because congressional power was exercised without the visibility that accompanies a changing majority. Proof of the invisibility of House power in this period was that no Republican President was able successfully to blame Congress for the nation's situation. The 104th Congress showed that, following a turnover of the majority, congressional leaders can openly assert a role for Congress in setting the national agenda.

Finally, the change of congressional party majority resulting from the 1994 election has altered the prospects of the term limits movement for members of Congress. Although the term limits movements has a number of objectives, it has perhaps been concerned most with the problem that congressional incumbency had become too strong to permit a change of majority inside the Congress. It is not that the movement was ever merely partisan in character. Rather, it was responding in part to conditions perpetuated by one-party dominance that were considered endemic to the system itself. The term limits movement continues to have many supporters, and it is too early to say whether it will now begin to die out. But clearly some of its urgency has been lost.

The manifestation of these new institutional capacities of Congress occurred during a period of adjustment in the power of the presidency. Rather than clarifying the properties of the American system, the changes in Congress in 1994 may have contributed initially to further misjudgments about the presidency. But events in the end brought politicians and analysts back to a truer understanding of that institution's constitutional properties. Presidential scholars have long argued that the President's power in a given epoch depends on three factors (besides, of course, a President's personal adroitness and public standing): the office's enduring constitutional powers, a prevailing doctrine or idea of the President's proper role, and the salience of foreign affairs and international politics. Of these three, foreign affairs clearly declined dramatically in importance for the American electorate in the aftermath of the Cold War, with the result that the presidency became diminished somewhat in its aura and influence. This change began under George Bush's tenure, although it was temporarily obscured by the Gulf War, and continued under Clinton's presidency.

It is one thing to speak of a modest readjustment of presidential power in accord with longstanding theories, but something quite different to proclaim a dramatic "miniaturization" of the presidency and a reversion to a supposed constitutional norm of congressional government. Yet it was just this Whiggish idea of an incredible shrinking presidency, championed by the columnist George Will, that began to win favor in many circles in Washington at the beginning of the Clinton presidency. According to Will, America has been witnessing a "marginalization" of the presidency; "Congress is the center of our government" just as the founders wanted.[21] Temporary support for this idea came from the attitudes of many Democrats in the 103rd Congress (who under the long period of one-party rule had come to think of Presidents, especially Democratic ones, as interlopers), and by the extraordinary character of the 1994 mid-term elections, which generated the new congressional majority that claimed its prerogative to define the national agenda. Clinton seemed to have all but acquiesced in this view when he plaintively sought in a news conference in early 1995 to remind Americans of the presidency's "relevance" to the American political system. Suddenly, the once mighty imperial presidency looked like an emperor who had lost his clothes.

But reports of the presidency's demise proved greatly exaggerated. Beginning late in 1995 Clinton showed the enduring power of the presidency, not just in the overused and often overvalued influence of the "bully pulpit," but more importantly in the irreducible power of the veto and the President's inherent discretion in the conduct of foreign affairs. The veto meant that far-reaching policy change of the sort Republicans proposed was impossible without control of the presidency. The presidency was downsized by the change of international politics, but the notion of full-scale "miniaturization" was a misreading of both the Constitution and American history. Nourished in part by this idea, Republicans entertained illusions that Congress could govern without the President and that sixty years of welfare state liberalism could be put in sharp reverse without an ally in the White House. Clinton almost literally took Republicans to school on this point in 1995. Clinton's power here may have been mostly defensive, but this was no different than the situation other Presidents had encountered when faced with a hostile congressional majority. And by summer's end in 1996, Clinton worked with his Democratic allies in Congress and was able to dictate terms on a number of policy issues.

The experiences of the changed partisan configurations in the national government provided a reeducation in certain constitutional realities, not only for the American people but also for its leaders. "Chastened" was a term frequently heard from 1994 to 1996, first to refer to Bill Clinton and then to Newt Gingrich and some of the freshman Republicans. Clinton had learned that the textbook model of the dominant presidency on which he operated in 1993 and 1994 vastly overestimated the powers of that office. Gingrich, who in 1995 thought that "being Speaker of the House . . . you can have an enormous impact on the Capitol and you don't have to go to the White House," was singing a very different tune a year later, when he made a conscious effort to lower his own profile.[22] When he was renominated for the Speaker by the Republican Conference after the 1996 election, Gingrich noted: "We find ourselves here with a Democratic President and a Republican Congress and we have an absolute moral obligation to make this system work."[23] Rather than this process being driven by moral obligation, he might have said that it reflected the inexorable effects of the Constitution itself.

The American system of separation of powers is premised not just on a balancing of the powers of the offices but also on the effect that this power relationship exerts on those who hold these offices. The practical maxim that "ambition must be made to counteract ambition" was meant to teach politicians who work in this system a certain moderation in what they can expect to accomplish on their own, given the limits they face on their powers. This lesson was one that, for different reasons, both Clinton and Gingrich had to relearn. Moderation does not necessarily mean that on all matters there must be an unending compromise. But it does mean that political leaders will have a more complete and accurate understanding of the limitations within which they operate.

The Campaign That Wasn't?

If there was a consensus among political observers on any point in 1996, it was that the campaign itself—meaning the effort to mobilize and change voters' minds—did not seem to matter. There was both a strong and weak version of this observation. The strong version held that the race was simply not winnable for Bob Dole. "Structural" conditions, chiefly the performance of the economy, all but dictated a Clinton victory. The weak version was that, whether winnable in theory or not, nothing much in fact happened during the campaign. There was almost no change from the conventions (or even from March) until two weeks before Election Day. Bob Dole kept waiting for Godot, but he never showed. The graphs of the polls during the fall campaign were almost as flat as the electronic lines of a dead man on a respirator monitor. After some tightening in August, the Republican convention "bounce" subsided and the race remained remarkably stable. After Labor Day, Clinton did not fall below the high 40s and Dole did not rise above the low 40s; most of the time, the gap was even larger. Dole could never change that elusive "dynamic," or "momentum," or whatever.

One point is certain. Few presidential campaigns have been as lacking in suspense and drama as that of 1996. Even many of the landslides, like 1964 and 1972, possessed some excitement because of the intensity of the arguments. And the recent election to which this one was most often compared, Ronald Reagan's "Morning in America" campaign of 1984 (which served as the explicit model of the Clinton team), contained at least one moment of suspense when the President faltered in his first debate with Walter Mondale. To find a campaign anywhere near as phlegmatic, one would have to go back to 1956, but even then the comparison is unfair to 1956: Eisenhower's health was a factor, the Hungarian/Suez crises erupted days before the election, and Adlai Stevenson gave long speeches that awed the intellectuals. Nothing remotely similar occurred in 1996. Americans ended by tuning out the campaign, aided by the vaunted Fourth Estate. Only about half as many people claimed to be following the campaign closely as in 1992, and the major network news programs ran only about half as many campaign stories during the month of September.[24] The lack of public interest was evidenced in the 48.8 percent turnout, which was the lowest in a presidential election year since 1924. And to be fair to 1924, women had just been guaranteed the right to vote in 1920 and were only beginning to be counted nationally as part of the electorate (1920 also saw turnout almost as low as 1996). Excluding this period, 1996 marks the lowest turnout of any election in American history since the advent of mass suffrage in 1828.[25]

The low interest in the campaign might be attributed to a number of factors besides its sheer boredom. One was the length of time that the nominees were known in advance of the election, which resulted from the scheduling of so many primaries so early on in the nomination process. Another was President Clinton's large lead, which was continually broadcast to the American public through an unprecedented number of polls. Finally, for Republicans at any rate, there was the eerie similarity of the 1996 campaign to that of 1992, making many of them think of the adage "first time tragedy, second time farce." There was Ross Perot, quirky as ever, Bill Clinton, glib and ingratiating as before, and another inarticulate establishment Republican, unable to deliver the message of the party.

And yet it would be hard to think of a national campaign in which so much of importance was determined in such a short period of time, right at the last moment. History is made by the movement of deeper causes and the occurrence of accidents. Accident, which merged into a deeper cause, played its part in the form of the revelation late in the campaign of large and suspicious campaign contributions to the Democratic Party. Questions were immediately raised about the ethical level of the Clinton White House, with the story this time being pushed as much by the national media as by the Republican campaign. The evasive behavior of the White House and the President's campaign—hiding officials, issuing conflicting explanations, and stonewalling—fit the profile of earlier White House scandals. Although this affair was not to be the scandal that broke the President's back, the revelations had an important effect. Perot's support climbed. (As in 1992, when he identified the budget deficit as the central issue, Perot proved again his ability to be in the right place at the right time, for he had sought from the outset to make foreign campaign contributions and influence a primary issue in the campaign.) And Clinton's lead over Dole also slipped. Much to Clinton's dismay he finished with less than 50 percent of the popular vote, denying him his elusive search for the approbation of a popular majority.

The more important effect, however, was on the congressional elections. As late as two weeks before Election Day both houses of Congress appeared to be within the Democrats' reach. Aided by the damage from the campaign financing scandal as well as by a late infusion of well-targeted resources, Republicans mounted a comeback and managed to hold on. The scandal not only reduced Clinton's personal popularity and hence the positive effects of any coattails, but it also gave added meaning to congressional Republicans' argument in favor of divided government and against handing Clinton a blank check. Although the difference in absolute numbers of votes between the actual results and a narrow Democratic victory in one or both houses would have been very small, the consequences of a Democratic victory would have been enormous. Nothing less than the fate of the 1994 elections was at stake. Had Democrats captured even one house of Congress to go along with their huge victory in the presidential race, the election results would almost certainly have been interpreted very differently. Instead of everyone marveling over the wonders of divided government and celebrating bipartisanship and the politics of the center, many would have been proclaiming the rejection of 1994. And the Democrats who would have made up the majority in the House would have believed, quite rightly, that they owed their election to Bill Clinton.

The significance of a national election, as Alexis de Tocqueville pointed out, inheres not just in occupying the offices or institutions, but in moral power and authority that attaches to the claim that one's party holds a majority. The last minute denial of that claim to the Democrats and the preservation of a claim to the legitimacy of the majority of 1994 made the closing two weeks of the 1996 campaign one of the most important political moments of the decade. So in a curious way the little campaign that couldn't turned out to be the little campaign that did.

Notes

1. In fact, because Congress consists of two houses, each with its own majority, a further subset of permutations is possible with a different majority in

each house. The complete range of possibilities is charted and discussed in Charles O. Jones, *The Presidency in a Separated System* (Washington, D.C.: The Brookings Institution, 1994), 12–15.

2. Byron Shafer, "The Notion of an Electoral Order," in Byron Shafer, ed., *The End of Realignment* (Madison, Wisconsin: The University of Wisconsin Press), 62.

3. See James Sundquist, "Needed: A Political Theory for the New Era of Coalition Government in the U.S.," *Political Science Quarterly* 103 (1988): 633–34.

4. Wilson Carey McWilliams, "The Meaning of the Election," in Gerald M. Pomper, ed., *The Election of 1992* (Chatham, N.J.: Chatham House, 1992), 194.

5. Walter Dean Burnham, "Realignment Lives: The 1994 Earthquake and Its Implications," in Colin Campbell and Bert Rockman, eds., *The Clinton Presidency: First Appraisals* (Chatham, N.J.: Chatham House Press, 1996), 363.

6. Glenn Simpson, "Democrats are Well-Ensconced on the Hill," *Roll Call*, September 5, 1991.

7. Gary C. Jacobson, "Divided Government and the 1994 Elections," in Peter Galderisi, ed., *Divided Government* (Lanham, Md.: Rowman & Littlefield, 1996), 61.

8. Colin Campbell and Bert Rockman, "Introduction," in *The Clinton Presidency: First Appraisals* (Chatham, N.J.: Chatham House, 1996), 2.

9. Norman Thomas and Joseph Pika, *The Politics of the Presidency*, 4th ed. (Washington, D.C.: Congressional Quarterly Press, 1996), 11.

10. See David Broder and Haynes Johnson, *The System: The American Way of Politics at the Breaking Point* (Boston: Little, Brown, 1996). This book, which shows clearly Gingrich's skill, is ungenerous in its assessment of the Speaker. For a more favorable treatment, see William F. Connelly and John J. Pitney, *Congress' Permanent Minority? Republicans in the U.S. House* (Lanham, Md.: Rowman & Littlefield, 1994).

11. Byron York, "Why a Second Term Might be Good for Republicans," *The Weekly Standard*, October 2, 1995, 29–32.

12. This claim is not controverted by the declining number of ticket splitters in 1996. Much previous ticket splitting was a product of campaigns of separation, whereas this time it may have been a product of repulsion. Furthermore, ticket splitting is not the only thing that may contribute to repulsion. Repulsion can result from the mobilization or demobilization of partisans and from voters selecting a straight ticket but still basing their vote on trying to create a split result.

13. Jones, *The Presidency in a Separated System*, 9–12. Jones makes no judgment about the merits of these normative claims, but he urges these elites to put aside childish things and begin to analyze modern American politics from the perspective of what is actually happening.

14. See Morris Fiorina's *Divided Government* (New York: Macmillan, 1992).

15. George Will, "Keeping Lame Duck on Short Leash," *Washington Post*, November 7, 1996, A21.

16. See Michael Barone, who argued that "Ronald Reagan is looming over

the politics of 1996 much as Franklin Roosevelt loomed over the politics of 1960" ("A Conservatism of the Head," *U.S. News & World Report*, August 26, 1996, 29), and Gary Wills, who agreed while deploring the fact ("It's His Party," *New York Times Magazine*, August 11, 1996, 30–59).

17. The national exit polls from the previous four presidential elections show the following breakdown. 1984: Liberal 16%, Moderate 44%, Conservative 33%; 1988: Liberal 17%, Moderate 45%, Conservative 33%; 1992: Liberal 22%, Moderate 50%, Conserative 29%; 1996: Liberal 20%, Moderate 47%, Conservative 33%. See CNN/TIME AllPolitics Vote '96, November 6, 1996; William Schneider, "A Loud Vote for Change," *The National Journal*, November 7, 1996, 2542.

18. E. J. Dionne, "Clinton Swipes the GOP's Lyrics," *Washington Post*, July 21, 1996, C1.

19. Dan Balz, "Party Has Learned Its Lessons," *Washington Post*, September 16, 1996, A1.

20. See Regina Dougherty, "A Most 'Independent' Electorate," *The Public Perspective*, October/November 1996, 47–51.

21. George Will, "The Charlie Rose Show," November 17, 1994. See also Will's book, *Restoration: Congress, Term Limits, and the Recovery of Deliberative Democracy* (New York: Free Press, 1992).

22. Katherine Q. Seelye, "Why Gingrich Trots for Presidency: Its Publicity," *New York Times*, July 26, 1995, A12.

23. John Yang, "Gingrich Reelected Speaker Despite Defections," *Washington Post*, January 8, 1997, A1.

24. Howard Kurtz, "Americans Tuning Out Campaign '96," *Washington Post*, October 10, 1996. The data here are based on surveys taken by the Pew Foundation and the Markle Foundation.

25. For a review of voting turnout trends through American history, see Ruy A. Teixeira, *The Disappearing American Voter* (Washington, D.C.: Brookings Institution, 1992), chapter 1.

Chapter 2

The Two Clinton Presidencies

As Bill Clinton looked ahead to his reelection campaign in March of 1996, many Americans might have been excused if they thought he was about to violate the Twenty-Second Amendment. For in many ways Clinton had already served two terms as President—one before the elections of 1994 and one after. In his first term Clinton modeled himself as a Kennedyesque agent of change, ready to "force the spring" and build new frontiers. In his second term he emerged as the great guarantor of stability, prepared to protect the public from the revolutionary changes proposed by a Republican majority in Congress. Paradoxically in President Clinton's first term, in which he assumed the burden of legislative leadership, his public standing reached its low point, whereas in his second term, in which he operated largely without an agenda, he rebounded significantly. In a very real way Clinton won in 1996 by losing in 1994.

Even two-term presidencies contain elements of continuity, and Clinton's was in this respect no exception. An important factor of constancy that worked to Clinton's benefit was the state of the economy, which continued the recovery that began in 1992. By March 1996 the Clinton administration had compiled a record of twelve consecutive quarters of slow but generally steady economic growth. Unemployment had come down considerably since 1992, inflation remained in check, and the bull market continued its run. By the time of the President's 1996 State of the Union Address, Clinton could boast that the economy had produced in three years the eight million new jobs he had promised in four.

But the recovery was weaker than previous ones, and there were widespread fears as late as the winter of 1995 of a return to recession. The four percent GNP growth rates of late 1992 had been replaced

27

with two percent growth rates, incomes remained stagnant, income inequality (supposedly a product of the "greedy 1980s") continued growing, and rates of job creation lagged well behind past recoveries. By some estimates, at least one million males had dropped out of the labor market entirely, and sizable increases were recorded in the number of Americans taking second jobs. "Corporate downsizing" became the dominant euphemism of the 1990s, which Pat Buchanan made a central theme of his campaign for the Republican nomination. On balance, academic analysts ranked Clinton's economic performance seventh of the ten postwar Presidents on a composite index of 18 key economic indicators.[1] Throughout Clinton's administration, economists, politicians, and citizens debated whether he should be given credit for a growing economy or blamed for a sub-par recovery. Clinton himself for a long time attributed the economic difficulties to the old order, for which he claimed his policies were supplying the remedy. But at a certain point, which came surprisingly late, Clinton began proudly to claim the economy as his own. This moment arrived at about the same time that Americans became convinced that the economy was definitely in good shape.

Along with the steady economic growth came declining federal deficits. In fiscal year 1996, the actual deficit was $109 billion, down from $290 billion in 1992. Supporters of the President credited his 1993 deficit reduction package, while opponents countered that the package envisioned a deficit of $220 billion in 1996 and argued that most of the additional reduction came in spite of Clinton's preferences. (Included here were the President's proposed stimulus spending package of 1993 and his health care reform proposal, as well as many of the discretionary spending cuts imposed by the 104th Congress.) No matter. President Clinton was able to say—and therefore did say—that he was the first President in the postwar period to preside over a deficit that declined four years in a row.

A second element of constancy in Clinton's presidency, this one working to his detriment, was the persistence of the "character" issue. As the nation's economic performance put a floor under Clinton's public approval rating (it seldom dropped below 40 percent), so the character issue seemed to impose a ceiling above it (it seldom went above the mid-fifties).[2] Sometimes simmering and sometimes boiling to the surface, the character issue took several forms that reinforced doubts about Clinton that had been raised during the 1992 presidential campaign. The character issue now expanded to include Clinton's demonstrated protean ability to change positions almost overnight with no apparent discomfort, as well as a complex of scandals that went by such names as "Whitewater," "Travelgate," "Filegate," and the accusations of sexual misconduct made by Paula Jones. The character issue was never eliminated, only overshadowed from time to time by compensating successes in other areas.

Linked to the question of character was Clinton's struggle to appear "presidential," a quality that calls for a careful balance between a capacity for empathy (at which Clinton excelled) and a projection of dignity (which he found so elusive). Clinton's difficulties here were emblematic of the 1960s culture from which he emerged; he craved power yet was uncomfortable with authority, including his own. From the jogs to McDonalds to the half-salutes to the briefs versus boxers MTV dialogue to lascivious comments directed at a 500-year-old Peruvian mummy, Clinton never fully won this struggle, although by the end he had clearly become more careful and was widely seen to be "growing" in office.

Many wondered why Clinton's character and stature problems never took a much greater toll on his presidency. Trying to resolve this puzzle became a virtual obsession of some presidency watchers, especially those who made so much of his shortcomings. Indeed, President Clinton—very much like President Nixon—inspired a constellation of observers whose lives seemed to center on chronicling his deficiencies and exposing his contradictions. And, like the Nixon haters, these observers managed to convince themselves up until the very last moment that their exposés would bring him down. A variety of explanations have been offered for why this fall did not take place in 1996. For one thing, character in the sense indicated is not the sole foundation for the voter's choice of President. While the total of Clinton's flaws as known in 1996 might well have disqualified him as a first-time nominee—the character issue nearly sank him in the 1992 nomination race—he was going to be his party's nominee; and the question presented to the nation was not just whether it wanted to change the person in the White House, but whether it wanted to change the policies and political party of the President. If Clinton could adequately manage the character issue while focusing the public on other issues, he could prevail. No doubt the character issue lowered his margin for error, but it did not disqualify him. Plus there were compensating aspects to Clinton's character. Although displays of "I feel your pain" sympathy may have compromised the President's stature, they also provided a kind of substitute for it. As President Reagan became known as the Great Communicator, so President Clinton became the Great Empathizer. In a nation of Barney lovers and Sally Jesse Raphael fans, empathy covers a multitude of sins.

Clinton also appeared to benefit from widespread public cynicism about politicians. A majority of Americans had reservations about Clinton's basic honesty, but they believed that he had sufficient integrity to serve as President. The sheer number of scandals and gaffes—assessed in the new metric of whether the President experienced a "bad week" or a "good week"—contributed to public lethargy about such matters. Taking a cue from the cultural theme of "defining deviance down," columnist Charles Krauthammer wrote of "the normalization of Nixonian ethics" that led not to a belief in Clinton's innocence but to a conviction that nothing more could be expected.[3] Clinton may have been aided here by lowered expectations for the presidential office in the aftermath of the Cold War. The public could perhaps be more forgiving of a President who was not being asked to carry all the burdens of the leader of the free world. The presidency began to look more like a governorship. As Clinton was growing to meet the demands of the presidency, so the presidency was shrinking to meet his attributes. By 1996, it seemed that the all-important "comfort level" between the office and the man had finally been reached.

Bill Clinton's First Term: 1993–1994

Although these strands of constancy were important, Bill Clinton's presidency—and the elections of 1996—cannot be understood without telling a story of two radically different terms within the same four-year period. Bill Clinton entered office in January 1993 as the first Democrat to win a presidential election in 16 years. Since Democrats retained control of Congress, Clinton's inauguration also ended a period of divided government that had begun in 1981. Yet underlying weaknesses were observable in the Democratic victory: Clinton had won with only 43 percent in a three-way race, Democrats had actually lost 10 House seats, and there was no clear public clamor for more activist government, with majorities continuing to say that they favored smaller government over larger.[4]

Clinton faced some crucial decisions. After winning as a "New Democrat" and an outsider agent of "change," he had to choose between operating in the center to try to forge a bipartisan consensus or to move to the left to reward his base, and he had to choose whether to stake out an independent and "outside" position or whether to tie himself to his party in Congress. He and his advisers decided fairly quickly to move left and to court Congress, which meant taking a partisan stance and jettisoning most of his campaign talk about campaign finance reform and other governmental reforms. Within a few weeks of the election Clinton held a much-publicized "summit" meeting with the Democratic leadership in Congress, after which it became clear that the President and an already unpopular Congress were operating as a team. The marriage to Congress and the move leftward were inextricably linked.

Clinton's first one hundred days began in confusion and ended in humiliation. His first two major acts were to announce a new policy admitting open homosexuals to the military, which he was soon forced to withdraw, and to shelve the middle-class tax cut that had been promised in the campaign, replacing it with a substantial tax increase. The increase included an energy tax that would have cost the average middle-class family $400 a year. The President also proposed a $20 billion economic stimulus package that was filibustered to death in the Senate. The administration was also plagued with embarrassing problems in making certain appointments, most notably for the posts of Attorney General, where two nominees ran into difficulties, and for Assistant Attorney General for Civil Rights, where Clinton pulled the plug on his old friend Lani Guinier because of her views on race-based political representation. The low point of this period was marked by a highly publicized incident in June in which follicle engineer Christophe of Beverly Hills gave the President a $200 haircut while Air Force One closed two runways at Los Angeles International Airport for nearly an hour.

Accompanying the public's reaction to the first hundred days was the sense among journalists that the administration was too clever by half, chronically disingenuous and yet consistently arrogant. One illustration was Clinton's announcement in abandoning his middle-class tax cut that "I've worked harder than I've ever worked in my life" to preserve it but could not, because he had just discovered that deficit estimates were worse than expected—a fact he must have known since the previous August.[5] Over the next two years other trends and events in domestic politics contributed to Clinton's difficulties. But it was the equivocations and reversals in foreign policy that did the most to contribute to an image of a less than forceful leader. "Incoherent" and "vacillating" were the tag words that seemed attached to every assessment of the Clinton international record from Bosnia to Haiti to Somalia to North Korea.

There were two defining moments for the administration in 1993–94, both of which involved programs for substantial expansion of federal authority. Clinton lost one of them by losing and one of them by winning. The first was the struggle over the 1993 budget and deficit reduction plan, which Clinton developed in close coordination with congressional Democrats but without consulting congressional Republicans. This plan contained a projected $496 billion in deficit reduction over five years, split more or less evenly between tax increases and spending "cuts" (actually, for the most part, reductions in planned rates of increase). About $170 billion was to be added to domestic spending programs. At first, the program was sold as a well-balanced economic program, yet it soon was discussed almost purely in terms of deficit reduction. The debate became radically polarized. Republicans attacked it for containing the largest tax increase in American history and for hiding a major expansion of government under a phony deficit reduction plan. Indeed, the lowest deficit predicted under the Clinton plan was $220 billion in 1996—half again higher than deficits at the end of the Reagan administration—after which they would begin to rise again. The Democratic Senate rebelled against several aspects of the program, killing the energy tax, insisting on a greater proportion of spending cuts to tax increases, and refusing to fund many of the President's new domestic initiatives.

As the focus shifted from an overall economic program to the deficit, Clinton was caught in a trap. Many of his spending provisions had been stripped out, leaving a massive tax increase that satisfied bond traders more than his natural constituency. Clinton was reported to have told his advisers in frustration that "I hope you're all aware we're all Eisenhower Republicans. . . . We're Eisenhower Republicans here, and we are fighting the Reagan Republicans. We stand for lower deficits and free trade and the bond market. Isn't that great?"[6]

Public support for the plan dropped from over 60 percent in February to 33 percent in August, when the final vote was taken. A televised presidential address failed to turn the tide. One Democratic consultant later said, "The program wasn't a life preserver, it was an anvil."[7] Only frantic presidential lobbying saved the plan, which passed by one vote in the Senate (cast by Vice President Al Gore) and by only two votes in the House. Democrats suffered 41 defections in the House and 6 in the Senate. Not a single Republican in the House or Senate voted "yes." In one sense the victory was critical for Clinton, because failure to secure passage of his central priority of 1993 would have been a disastrous display of political weakness. But the victory was pyrrhic. It marked

Clinton as a tax-raising apostle of big government, the agenda was shifted to budget-balancing in a way that made future domestic spending increases or new programs problematic, and Republicans were unified and on the offensive. Not least, the close margin of the votes enabled Republican challengers in 1994 to target every Democratic incumbent who had voted for the program as "the winning vote for Bill Clinton's tax increase."

The second major issue of Clinton's leadership was the health care initiative. Health care reform was a key element in Clinton's 1992 presidential campaign, and Clinton had promised to introduce a plan promoting universal coverage within the first one hundred days. But on taking office the President became immersed in the budget battle, and the general outlines of his health care proposal were not available until September. The plan accordingly did not become a legislative priority until after the passage of the North American Free Trade Agreement (NAFTA) in November, which inevitably brought health care into the election-year politics of 1994.

As with the budget proposal, public response for Clinton's general proposal was initially favorable. But it gradually turned against the plan as details became known and as opponents of the plan sharpened their attacks. Known by some as "Clinton Care," the proposal began with some marks set against it. First, important details of the plan were formulated by a task force headed by First Lady Hillary Rodham Clinton and adviser Ira Magaziner. The task force had worked in private meetings that were shielded from public scrutiny, which raised issues of propriety and even legality. This fact only accentuated the role of Hillary Rodham Clinton, who was put "in charge" of the medical plan proposal. Lionized by feminists and those who saw in her the role model of a strong modern woman, Mrs. Clinton was an unusually polarizing figure who was attacked by others for her allegedly devout liberal views. Fueling this hostility were numerous incidents, such as Travelgate and quick profits in the cattle future markets, that led her critics to charge that behind a mask of sainthood Mrs. Clinton bore a greater resemblance to Rasputin than to Mother Theresa. The controversy over Mrs. Clinton's role went back to the 1992 campaign, when Bill Clinton promised voters "two for the price of one" if they elected him and then objected when opponents sought to scrutinize her views, saying that he was the one running for President, not her. Was she to be the supportive political wife who would stand by her man, as she did at a critical juncture in 1992 to deflect charges of Bill's womanizing? Was she to become the world's advocate of the cause of women or adopt a standard First Lady's role of working for the well-being of children? Or was she to be, as her activities on health care reform now suggested, a virtual co-President entrusted with the administration's most ambitious policy initiative, the task of redesigning one-seventh of the American economy? Widespread public concerns over an unelected and unaccountable figure taking that role ultimately hindered the administration's proposal.

Second, liberal supporters of universal health care differed considerably among themselves about how to achieve their objective. Despite Clinton's proposal Senator Ted Kennedy (D-Mass.) and Representative Pete Stark (D-Calif.) pushed forward with their own plan for completely nationalized health insurance. Aggravating this ideological infighting was the jurisdictional fragmentation of Congress, which meant that health care was referred to three competing House committees and two Senate committees. Finally, and most importantly, the 240,000-word bill that was ultimately produced appeared to require a massive expansion of the federal bureaucratic apparatus and of federal control. Republicans displayed a Rube Goldberg-style diagram purporting to show the organizational structure necessary to implement Clinton Care. While most could agree on the two primary objectives of health reform—expanded coverage and cost containment—those goals were largely contradictory. All other things being equal, expanded coverage would naturally *increase* health care costs, by increasing demand. The only way to square this circle was by imposing substantial rationing and regimentation of health care, a sort of redistribution by which some would gain coverage by others losing. Ultimately, Americans were simply not prepared to accept either the prospect of rationing or the federal control that the plan entailed.

The loss of momentum experienced by the health care proposal was palpable. At first wary, Republicans and insurance companies went on the attack as public support weakened. The insurance industry launched a costly series of television ads—the so-called "Harry & Louise" spots—opposing the plan. Objections were bolstered when the Congressional Budget Office estimated that Clinton Care would swell annual federal outlays by $566 billion by 2004.[8] Conservative analyst William Kristol advised Republicans against compromise, circulating an influential memo arguing that health care could be turned into "liberalism's Afghanistan," an example of overreach leading to total defeat. As the months passed congressional Republicans came increasingly to adopt that stance. Democrats, meanwhile, lost their nerve. At the beginning of 1994 it was a foregone conclusion that something resembling the Clinton plan would pass. By late summer the Democratic congressional leadership had jettisoned the Clinton plan and offered their own alternative. In September Senate Majority Leader George Mitchell announced that health reform was dead for the year.

In the end Clinton Care did not so much die as just fade away. No vote was ever taken on the floor of either chamber; support evaporated and time ran out. The Democratic Congress had been caught in a bind: polls showed that most Americans opposed Clinton Care as a big government social scheme but also that Democrats would bear the brunt of public blame if no health care reform passed. Two months later, some voters punished the Democrats for having failed, others punished them for having tried, but in any case health care added a second albatross to the tax increase already around the necks of congressional Democrats. Clinton would later admit, "I overestimated the extent to which a person elected with a minority of the votes in an environment that was complex, to say the least, could achieve a sweeping overhaul of the health care system when no previous President had been able to do it for decades and decades."[9] The health care battle was the pivotal event leading to the Republican congressional takeover of 1994.[10]

For most of his first two years in office Bill Clinton appeared to the nation as someone far to the left of the man who had won the 1992 election. Even his hard-won victories on issues like the budget and the crime bill did not bring him the credit he desired, partly because majorities came to disapprove of those measures and partly because his victories seemed so tenuous. And when voters did approve of his actions and when his successes were unambiguous, Clinton still derived all too little acclaim, at least at the time. The Brady Bill, motor-voter registration bill, and Family and Medical Leave Act—all popular measures—passed in 1993 after years of presidential obstruction, but they offered limited help to Clinton's sagging public standing. Overall, Clinton's measures passed Congress 86.4 percent of the time in 1993–94, a near record, but his public approval rating seldom breached the 50 percent mark.[11]

Setting aside the President's tactical blunders and self-inflicted wounds, his problem with the public centered on the discrepancies between the principles he professed in the 1992 campaign and his actions in office. As his pollster Stanley Greenberg said, "The mandate he ran on was not necessarily the one he executed. . . . The cultural conservative side of Bill Clinton disappeared in the first two years."[12] The disappearance of cultural conservatism was best exemplified in the struggle for priority between welfare reform and health care reform. If health care was important to the 1992 campaign, welfare reform had arguably been at its very center. It was the pivotal issue that convinced swing voters that Clinton was really a "New Democrat." Yet Clinton subordinated welfare reform to health care reform early on, against the advice of Democrats like Senator Daniel Patrick Moynihan (N.Y.) who urged that welfare be tackled first. By fall 1994 a half-hearted welfare reform measure weakly promoted had gone nowhere, and there was little defense against the charge that the President had played bait and switch with the voters.

Clinton's difficulties here had their roots in the coalition he forged during the 1992 campaign, when Clinton appealed to two broadly divergent constituencies: moderates and "Reagan Democrats" who wanted a real move to the right, and liberals who were willing to tolerate a cosmetic move to the right as the price of victory. As long as no action was required these constituencies could be kept together. That luxury ended once concrete steps had to be taken, such as setting the priorities between welfare reform and health care reform. A liberal Congress pushed Clinton to choose the options on the left, which contributed to his first-term difficulties. In a nation in which, for presidential politics, right has for some time been better than left and outside has become better than inside, Bill Clinton found himself on the left and the inside.

It may not be a coincidence that Clinton's peak of popularity during his first "term" came in the winter of 1993–1994. During this period he abandoned his liberal congressional base and forged in its place a bipartisan coalition to score a major legislative victory on NAFTA. In contrast to the highly partisan approach pursued by the White House in the budget and health care battles, Clinton was forced to build a coalition from the center in order to overcome the opposition of left-labor Democrats to NAFTA. Starting in September with what appeared to be slim odds of success, Clinton skillfully applied both public persuasion and the private tools of the presidency to shift popular opinion and congressional votes. The turning point came when Vice President Al Gore engaged in an unprecedented nationally televised debate about NAFTA with Ross Perot. Gore won the debate handily, and polls showed public sentiment shifting in favor of NAFTA. Congressional sentiment followed. For his part, then-House Republican Whip Newt Gingrich delivered most of the Republicans. If the health care and budget battles were textbook cases of how to lose or nearly lose when starting out ahead, NAFTA was a classic example of how to win after starting out behind. The NAFTA victory temporarily burnished Clinton's credentials not only as a moderate but also as a competent legislative leader with principles he was willing to fight for.

Shortly after the NAFTA win, Clinton delivered a highly acclaimed "New Democrat" speech on moral values at the annual convocation of the Church of God in Christ in Memphis, Tennessee, in which he gave some indication of returning to the themes of community and moral responsibility that had punctuated his 1992 campaign. He called for people to provide "structure, discipline, and love" to children mired in a culture of drugs and crime. Government must play a role, he said, along with business and churches, but government's efforts would fail "unless we say some of this cannot be done by government because we have to reach deep inside to the values, the spirit, the soul and the truth of human nature."[13] Unfortunately for the President, this combination of bipartisan coalition-building and cultural centrism was the exception rather than the rule in 1993–1994. As the elections of 1994 approached, it became clear the Democrats would suffer losses. Few, however, could imagine how serious those losses would be.

The Elections of 1994

The President's party has lost seats in Congress in every midterm election since 1934. Yet not since 1946 had so dramatic a change taken place. Descriptions of the 1994 election fixed on geological and meteorological metaphors, with the results variously being likened to a tidal wave, a tsunami, an earthquake, a volcano, or a tornado. When the dust (or waves, fault lines, lava, or trailer park) had settled, Republicans had gained 52 House seats and eight Senate seats, enough to seize control of both chambers for the first time since the election of 1952. Republicans also gained almost 500 state legislative seats and made a net gain of 11 governorships; they held 30 governorships, including the governorships of seven of the eight most populous states. The realignment of the South toward Republican dominance was confirmed and extended. Major Democratic figures like House Speaker Thomas Foley, House Ways and Means Committee chairman Dan Rostenkowski, New York Governor Mario Cuomo, and Texas Governor Ann Richards went down to defeat. Not a single Republican incumbent senator, House member, or governor lost a bid for reelection. Within a few months, these successes were bolstered by the defection of two Democratic senators, five representatives, and scores of local officials to the Republican Party.

These results confounded most observers who predicted much smaller Republican gains, even though a Republican tide was presaged by state and local elections in November 1993 in which Republicans swept the governorships of New Jersey and Virginia and the mayorships of New York and Los Angeles. Republicans naturally claimed an ideological mandate in favor of smaller government and dared to speak openly of national realignment. Democrats were more divided about the meaning of the election. Some blamed it on visceral anti-Clintonism fueled by "angry white males"; others saw the problem in the excessive liberalism of the President and the party as a whole. And others still, like Jesse Jackson, faulted Clinton's inability to inspire the Democratic base because of his unwillingness to embrace a genuine liberalism.[14] For its part an understandably shocked administration offered a bewildering and conflicting array of interpretations. The President's initial explanation was that voters were not repudiating his administration but simply wanted "change" as they had in 1992; somehow, the vote represented a reaffirmation of the mandate of 1992, with voters continuing to express frustration with gridlock. Other (sometimes contradictory) explanations were offered, including a desire by voters for smaller government, a desire by voters for divided government, poor communication of the President's program, and mistakes by Congress. In his post-election news conference, Clinton simultaneously accepted personal responsibility and blamed voters for not sufficiently understanding the benefits of his tenure in office.[15]

What factors led to this Democratic debacle? First, the economy, while growing, was weaker than in the average economic recovery. Job creation, GNP growth, and incomes were all relatively low. Indeed, incomes were actually falling in 1994, despite the recovery. Polls immediately before and after the election showed that 59 percent believed the nation was still in a recession and only 21 percent thought their standard of living was getting better.[16] Second, Clinton's continued unpopularity depressed Democratic fundraising and turnout and stimulated Republican mobilization.[17] The intensity of disapproval of President Clinton may have been more important in this respect than the overall numbers, which were not unusually bad until late in 1994. Clinton's low level of approval appeared to be more damaging than usual to his copartisans because it tended to be concentrated among swing voters.[18] President Clinton's pollster, Stanley Greenberg, even advised Democratic candidates to separate themselves from Clinton.

Third, the Republicans benefitted from several structural advantages that usually helped Democrats. Democratic retirements created a large number of open seats, many of them in districts that leaned Republican despite having had a Democratic incumbent. For the first time in recent memory more Republican incumbents were uncontested than Democratic incumbents, and the quality of Republican challengers, measured in terms of previous political experience and fundraising capacity, increased substantially from 1992.[19] (Some of these structural developments were clearly indirectly traceable to Clinton's unpopularity.) Finally, the full effects of the post-1990 redistricting, which many thought would prove helpful to the Republicans but which had been obscured by Bush's defeat in 1992, finally became apparent when Republican congressional candidates ran on their own.[20]

But these three factors fall short of explaining the sheer magnitude of the electoral change in 1994. The new and critical element was the national, thematic, and ideological nature of the 1994 campaign. It had become something of a commonplace in recent accounts of congressional elections to argue that these were largely local events, and midterm elections particularly so. Although this generalization remained true in many districts in 1994, the most striking feature about the 1994 elections was the degree to which Republicans succeeded in overcoming this localistic bias. Republicans effectively tapped into three broad sets of national concerns that had been simmering for years: big government, loss of individual responsibility, and social/moral decline.

To many Americans government seemed to have grown increasingly out of control—a Leviathan that taxed too much, spent too much, and regulated too much. It was government run increasingly by bureaucrats and unelected judges that had lost all connection to the constitutional vision of the Founding Fathers. Similarly, a variety of issues ranging from crime to welfare reform to tort reform to affirmative action to social services for illegal immigrants swirled around the theme of individual responsibility. For many Americans, the therapeutic state was producing a therapeutic society in which responsibility for one's own life—presumably a fundamental precept of a free society—was being supplanted by an ethic of self-appointed victimhood, entitlement, and irresponsibility. Finally, to a large and growing number of Americans, the country they saw before them was no longer the country in which they had grown up, but an increasingly alien society in steep moral and ethical decline. To make matters worse, to these voters, government at all levels had not only accepted but accelerated this decline by adopting countercultural themes as official policy: handing out condoms in school while banning prayer; promoting homosexuality as a positive alternative lifestyle; funding obscene "art" produced by radical dilettantes; imposing abortion on demand through the courts; and subsidizing illegitimacy through the welfare system.

These concerns congealed into a powerful general theme that was able to anger and mobilize the millions who formed the negative coalition of 1994. The record of Clinton and the Democratic Congress over the previous two years touched a nerve that brought out the electorate's "philosophical conservatism" at the level of national issues, which analysts of public opinion have long argued has been obscured by the "operational liberalism" found in voters' tendency to support particular programs that benefitted their special interests. The Republicans' great success in 1994 lay in their ability to nationalize the elections, bringing the philosophical conservatism of voters to the fore. Republicans in 1994 were able to make the elections more like the presidential elections of 1968 through 1988 than like the typical congressional elections of this period. They were assisted in this campaign—in fact, it was only made possible—by their loss of the presidency in 1992, which set the stage for a midterm backlash against unified liberal government.

The primary symbol of nationalization was the "Contract With America," devised by Newt Gingrich and signed in September 1994 by over 300 Republican House candidates. They pledged to bring to a vote a ten-point program of balanced budgets, tax cuts, welfare reform, tort reform, term limits, ballistic missile defense, and a series of congressional reforms. While only a minority of Americans knew the details of the Contract, majorities supported the essence of most of the planks.[21] It drove the debate, ultimately provoking President Clinton to denounce the Contract as a throwback to Reaganism. Freed from the constraints of either congressional control or possession of the presidency, Republicans were now able to seize the mantle of outsiders and reformers, defenders of the people against big government, and representatives of the "country party" against the "court party."[22] They won two-thirds of Ross Perot's voters.[23]

The Republican victory in the elections of 1994 abruptly ended Bill Clinton's first "term," eviscerating his policy agenda and putting him on the strategic defensive for the next year and a half. But it also proved the key to his political rehabilitation. As the Republicans' triumph would not have been possible without their loss of the White House two years earlier, so President Clinton's reelection is much harder to imagine without the Democrats' loss of Congress in 1994.

Bill Clinton's Second Term: 1995–1996

The second "term" of Bill Clinton's presidency saw a vastly different President, one who was on the defensive and increasingly conservative, but also one who gained in public popularity and stature. From a success rate of 87 percent with Congress in 1993–94, Clinton's rate dropped to 36 percent in 1995, the lowest on record.[24] And on issues such as a seven-year balanced budget, middle-class tax cuts, unfunded federal mandates, school uniforms, the v-chip, and homosexual marriage, Clinton moved right—sometimes endorsing Republican legislation, sometimes just signing it, and sometimes merely positioning himself in the realm of words. As a consequence, public perceptions of Clinton shifted considerably. In January 1994, 45 percent of the populace considered Clinton a "liberal" and 32 percent a "moderate"; by mid-1996, the image was reversed, as 43 percent judged him moderate and 37 percent liberal.[25]

But while moving to the right, Clinton took pains to distinguish himself from the Republicans on other issues. Here he made vigorous use of the veto, which he had never employed in the previous Congress. Sometimes the veto helped establish "wedge issues" for the electorate at large, like the veto of Republican-proposed Medicare reform, while on occasion it served to consolidate the President's interest group base, as when he vetoed lawsuit reform legislation opposed by the Trial Lawyers Association. Overall, Clinton sought to mute or coopt the social issues and size-of-government proposals while emphasizing pocketbook issues. This eclectic strategy of cooption and confrontation was called "triangulation" by controversial presidential adviser Dick Morris, and it seemed to be modeled on Harry Truman's strategy of rehabilitation during the 80th Congress. Contrary to subsequent mythology, Truman's recovery had little to do with a "do-nothing" Congress (in fact, the 80th Congress passed a major tax cut, the Marshall Plan, and the Taft-Hartley Act that has governed labor relations for half a century) but much to do with an effective presidential strategy that combined modest adjustment with artful confrontation.[26] Clinton largely followed this prescription for the next two years, although the conservative nature of the times altered the prudent ratio in favor of greater adjustment. Clinton also deviated from Truman by leaving Democrats behind and developing a strategy for a personal comeback, which was predicated not on overthrowing the Republican Congress but on promising to check it. This individualistic strategy of separation and repulsion, Clinton explained, was necessitated by the changing character of the times, in which a less partisan electorate would respond adversely to openly partisan appeals.

For the first half of 1995 the new Republican Congress held the nation's attention and seemed to win its approval. The House spent its opening day in a widely viewed marathon session that instituted numerous House reforms, including a ban on proxy voting and a ban on exempting Congress from regulatory measures. In the next three months the House went on to pass nine of the ten Contract items, falling short only of the two-thirds necessary to pass the congressional term limits amendment. While numerous measures were slowed and modified in the Senate, progress on Contract items was maintained by the Republicans well into the summer. The low point for Bill Clinton came in mid-April of 1995, when Republicans were completely dominating the news and when Clinton felt compelled in a news conference to defend his relevance: "The Constitution gives me relevance, the power of our ideas gives me relevance. . . . The President is relevant here, especially an activist President."[27]

But the first important stirrings of presidential recovery came in the very next week, in the aftermath of the terrorist bombing of the Alfred P. Murrah federal office building in Oklahoma City in which 168 people were killed. This tragedy strengthened the President in two respects. It provided an opportunity for Clinton to act as the head of state, the ceremonial unifier in a time of national grief. Oklahoma City was the first step in Clinton's adoption of the role of national healer, which he was to play so frequently and artfully in the next year and a half. And because the bombing was apparently carried out by Americans with vague ties to the burgeoning militia movement, anti-government rhetoric of all shades was declared suspect by numerous commentators, including the President himself (somewhat contrary to his theme of healing). Anyone calling for tax cuts, deregulation, or decentralization of government—or anyone opposing gun control—was thus associated with the crime. The bombers were linked to the militias, the militias to the gun nuts, the gun nuts to the National Rifle Association, the NRA to Newt Gingrich, and Newt Gingrich to the Republican Party. President Clinton later invoked the tragedy in his 1996 State of the Union Address when he pointed to a survivor of the blast sitting in the gallery as his guest as an example of why future government shutdowns should be avoided. The Oklahoma City bombing marked the beginning of a readjustment, abetted by the President, of Americans' view of the Republican victory of 1994. For many Americans the Republican "revolution" now had a more ominous sound to it, and the feelings evoked by the disaster in Oklahoma City probably contributed to the "gender gap" that haunted Republicans through November 1996 and helped to seal their loss in the presidential election.

Another factor that contributed to Bill Clinton's resurgence was a string of important if tenuous foreign policy successes. The invasion of Haiti, undertaken weeks before the 1994 elections, proved over time not to have been the disaster critics had predicted. Brokering peace agreements in Bosnia, the Middle East, and northern Ireland also improved Clinton's standing, or at least deprived his opponents of the target they had enjoyed in 1993–94. By 1995 Clinton clearly enjoyed his foreign policy role and to some extent found refuge in it. Indeed, his willingness to forge ahead with unpopular actions in Haiti and Bosnia and his ability—at least through 1996—to make them work added to his general stature. And, in contrast to his first term, Clinton and his administration began claiming credit for the economy's strength instead of bemoaning its weakness.

But the key to Clinton's comeback revolved around his interaction with Congress. The Republican takeover of Congress both posed a dilemma and offered an opportunity for Clinton. His dilemma was whether to be confrontational or conciliatory in his dealings with the Republican majority. His opportunity was that he was now freed of the responsibility of trying to hold together the disparate elements of his coalition. Indeed, Clinton was the first modern President to be relieved of the burden of appearing to set the agenda. As words were often the only tool available to the President after November 1994—he had virtually ceased trying to lead—the tension between words and deeds largely subsided. Bill Clinton reaped three broad benefits from the loss of Congress: he was forced to move in a direction that neutralized the anti-Clinton coalition of 1994, he was given a target against which he could build a negative coalition of his own for 1996, and he was spared a primary challenge that enabled him in 1995 to begin what amounted to a "permanent campaign" for the presidency.

Conventional wisdom holds that President Clinton gained from the Republican takeover of Congress because the Republicans went too far, promoting an extremist agenda that left open the center for Clinton to fill. Bill Clinton clearly built much of his comeback on the pledge to serve as a check on the Republican Congress, and the opportunity to put himself in opposition to the Republicans, who were in charge of setting the national agenda, was crucial to the formation of the "negative coalition" that ultimately led to his reelection. The 74 House Republican freshmen with their unyielding conservative program were particularly indicted, and Newt Gingrich unwittingly offered himself as the demon du jour, with a disapproval rating that reached 70 percent in January 1996. The Republican budget plan clearly served as a lightning rod of criticism, with its tax cuts and limitations on entitlement spending. Polls from the 1996 election would later show that 15 percent of voters considered Medicare the most important issue in casting their vote, making it the second-ranked issue among all voters. Attempts to cut back federal spending on education, eliminate Cabinet departments, repeal the assault weapon ban, and put greater checks on environmental regulation also became grounds on which Republicans were attacked.

But the reaction against Republican extremism was often more the product of effective political rhetoric than a reflection of the policies that had been approved. Some of the proposals attacked as extremist were substantively little more than attempts to do things that Bill Clinton himself had once called for, including a seven-year balanced budget (Clinton had once promised a five-year balanced budget), welfare reform, and reducing the rate of growth of Medicare. In fact, after Democrats had successfully sown the seeds of the image of extremism in the public mind, Clinton went on to take credit for some of these same measures.

Much of the political controversy in 1995 also centered on the effects of the two government shutdowns, which many argued exemplified Republican extremism. The reaction of voters at the time suggests that matters were more complicated. The first shutdown, lasting approximately one week in late November of 1995, ended when President Clinton capitulated to Republican demands for a seven-year balanced budget based on Congressional Budget Office numbers, receiving in return only a vague assurance that his priorities in Medicare, Medicaid, education, and the environment would be "protected." Poll data showed no consistent gain for the President through the shutdown, and administration insiders conceded that the decision to end the stalemate was made when polls showed the President's support evaporating.[28] By the end of the second, longer shutdown in January 1996, Clinton's approval dropped to a one-year low of 42 percent, and Clinton and congressional Republicans were viewed as having acted equally responsibly (or irresponsibly). Bob Dole even briefly took the lead in some polls.[29]

Clinton's decline in the polls at this time accordingly casts doubt on the idea that the shutdowns alone were responsible for Clinton's rehabilitation. Clinton's comeback rather had to do with the interpretation he managed to impose on the shutdowns, as well as on a string of blunders committed by congressional Republicans. Clinton took advantage of the Republicans' exposure. The Republicans, acting in their self-chosen role as the nation's governing party, stepped up to the plate and—as they saw it—did the responsible thing by proposing tough measures that would bring the budget into balance. Chief among these were curtailments in the projected growth of Medicare spending. Responsible proposals of this kind, without the power to implement them, were what led the Republicans into a political trap. Seizing the opportunity, Clinton labeled these curtailments in growth "cuts" that would endanger senior citizens and the poor. He made the Republicans pay dearly, just as Democrats had made President Reagan pay dearly in 1982 for proposals that dared to touch Social Security. Republican efforts to fight back and claim that they were only saving a program slipping into bankruptcy were met by Democratic counterclaims that the cuts were only needed to finance a Republican-sponsored tax plan that would assist the wealthy. So began what Republicans called Clinton's "Mediscare campaign," a public opinion offensive that Republicans, as well as a large part of the national media elite, openly labeled as "demagoguery." Never one at this time to mince words, Newt Gingrich charged that Clinton was engaging in "one of the most interesting and potentially dangerous experiments ever undertaken by an American President . . . a conscious strategy of falsehood."[30]

But if Clinton was nimble in turning the tables on his foes in Congress, Republicans proved adept in making matters worse for themselves. Republicans were operating on the assumption that if the government were shut down, the blame would automatically be affixed to the President, as it had been—at least by the media—in the cases of Presidents Reagan and Bush. But this assumption was flawed in two ways. First, even in the earlier cases the public (unlike the media) tended to blame Congress more than the President.[31] Second, in contrast to the earlier periods, it was now the congressional majority, not the President, that claimed to be running the government. All other things being equal, blame attaches more readily to the leaders who are viewed as being in charge. In addition, it was the Republicans who appeared to be pushing the process toward a shutdown, saying that it might prove how little the public needed government anyhow. In contrast, Clinton and the Democrats, as the pro-government party, could properly show their concern for those who suffered disruption from the crisis. Cavalier acceptance of (and sometimes even eagerness for) a shutdown thus shifted public responsibility from the President (who vetoed the appropriations and budget reconciliation measures necessary to keep government operating) to the Congress.

Republicans also gave in to the temptation to personalize the political struggle. Policy disputes were embodied in the clash between Newt Gingrich and Bill Clinton. Seldom have two men been so despised by their respective oppositions. Gingrich's early confidence, which at first worked in his favor, seemed to push him too far. He and his allies boasted all along that the President would cave in to their demands and virtually suggested that the President lacked the fortitude to bring the government to a halt. Bill Clinton's willingness to stand and fight, whether for reasons of politics or principle, was severely underestimated, and Republicans thus stumbled into the shutdowns by picking a fight they mistakenly thought Clinton would avoid. They then lost confidence and let Clinton off the hook at the very moment he was beginning to suffer damage and before they could extract a deal that might have inoculated them against charges of extremism on Medicare. Newt Gingrich's low point came in his admission that the failure to reach a budget deal with the President may have owed something to his having been forced to sit at the back of Air Force One during the trip to Israel for Prime Minister Yitzhak Rabin's funeral.

Yet not all of the Republican mistakes were tactical. There were two grand strategic errors as well. The first was the assumption that a party realignment had already taken place, that history was already set, and that Congress could lead almost without regard to the President. Because of this confidence, Republicans felt that they could proceed with a balanced budget plan even without the political cover that would have been provided by a balanced budget amendment.[32] Second, Republicans became fixated on a balanced budget to the exclusion of other policy objectives. Like Clinton's 1993 plan, the Republican plan was meant to accomplish several goals: balance the budget, reduce the role of government in society, provide tax relief to families, and promote economic growth through targeted tax incentives. Like Clinton's 1993 plan, the Republican budget was ultimately reduced by both its friends and its foes to a bean-counting exercise. The Republican willingness to bank all on the budget-balancing theme, and to justify all spending cuts on the balanced budget argument, put off for another day the tougher job of making the political, social, and moral case for smaller government.

It was not only Congress's move to the right that enabled Clinton to look moderate, but also his new-found independence and freedom of action. Clinton positioned himself as not quite part of the government, but rather as the defender of parts of the public against a Republican-led government. He was able to reacquire a partial "outsider" status, which he had been forced entirely to abandon under a Democratic-controlled unified government. Vetoes could prevent enactment of policies that were anathema to his liberal base and preserve a liberal status quo, but these could be justified in terms that did not undercut his revitalized "New Democrat" message. When Clinton twice vetoed welfare reform, he was able to argue that he was not against welfare reform per se but simply against those particular versions of it, which were "too extreme." Clinton used the same strategy to perfection in the budget minuet, when he was able to profess fidelity to a balanced budget while making minimal real concessions on the entitlements. He refurbished his image in this dance by showing that he was ready to stand up for a set of core beliefs while at the same time not having to say, in a specific and positive way, what they were.

The Republican congressional takeover not only provided Bill Clinton a target to attack but also played an important role in his reelection by neutralizing the negative coalition of 1994 for the presidential race. The Republican Congress both forced Clinton rightward and allowed him to move rightward, thus enabling him to accomplish some of the objectives he had discussed in the 1992 campaign. Numerous federal executive agencies moved rightward after 1994 to accommodate new congressional realities, relaxing regulatory burdens on individuals and business.[33] And a Democratic Congress would not have passed the welfare reform legislation Clinton ultimately signed, nor would it have made the cuts in discretionary domestic spending that forced the deficit well below earlier projections. Clinton was thus able to make virtues out of two major issues that would otherwise have been liabilities. His revival probably owed less to the shutdowns and alleged "extremism" of the 104th Congress than to the way Congress forced him and his administration rightward, placing him in the mainstream and defusing popular concerns about runaway government. Only after establishing his credentials as a true "centrist" was Clinton able to attack the GOP effectively for "going too far."

Often Clinton never had to leave the realm of words at all, but was able to quell rising discontent by carefully timed speeches that promised rightward movement without requiring any real action. School prayer and affirmative action were at least partially defused as issues in this manner. His sudden reversal in summer 1995, when he abandoned his previous budget for a balanced budget, allowed him to shift the debate from the unfavorable terrain of whether to balance the budget to the question of how to do it. Even his much-noted declaration in January 1996 that "the era of big government is over" was ambiguous, lending itself to both center-right and center-left interpretations. Did the end of big government entail cutting government back, reducing its bureaus, its budgets, and its revenues? Or did it simply entail not making government any bigger? Altogether, as *New York Times* reporter Alison Mitchell pointed out, "What is instructive about many of Mr. Clinton's speeches is what they allow him not to do."[34]

Clinton's rightward move was abetted by his growing influence over his party's congressional contingent. Relations between Clinton and his party remained strained at times—as when Clinton revised his budget to include Medicare cuts in June 1995, when he told a fundraising audience that he had raised taxes too much in 1993, and when he intimated in early 1996 that it would be "self-defeating" to push for a Democratic Congress. But after their defeat in 1994 weakened congressional Democrats were eventually forced to look to Clinton as a party leader far more than they did during Clinton's first "term." Once Clinton's political revival was underway, he took the opportunity to try to remake the Democratic Party in his image to an extent unimaginable after 1992. There were tentative signs he had made great headway. Incumbent Democrats increasingly took their cues from the White House, both on policy and tactics; most Democrats running for Congress for the first time faithfully repeated the presidential line on the budget, Medicare, taxes, the death penalty, gun control, and a variety of other issues. The 1994 elections created a vacuum in the Democratic Party that only Bill Clinton was positioned to fill.

The final benefit Bill Clinton derived from the Republican congressional victory in 1994 was the positive effect it had on his renomination and reelection campaign. Clinton was able to return from a posture of governing, which he had found consistently uncomfortable in his first "term," to a posture of campaigning, at which he excelled. He could avoid responsibility for the real actions of government while claiming credit for benign national conditions largely beyond either party's political control. Rendered unable to govern by circumstances, he made the most of his situation. Clinton and his administration engaged in what was essentially a permanent campaign throughout his second "term," with the dual purpose of preparing for the general election and discouraging any serious primary opposition. Ads touting Clinton's crime record began airing in July 1995, "the earliest campaign ads in history."[35] The Democratic National Committee began to run advertisements against the Republican budget in the fall of 1995; throughout the fall, Democrats spent $1 million per week on Medicare attack ads. By May 1996 Democrats had spent upwards of $40 million.[36]

This media blitz was critical in establishing the political context and boundaries of the 1996 election for both the presidency and for Congress. Democratic consultant Bill Knapp expressed astonishment at the Republicans' failure to answer the Democrats' charges: "Every week that went by [without a response], we'd look at each other blankly."[37] Republican pollster Frederick T. Steeper later acknowledged that "I don't think anybody [on the Republican side] fully appreciated how critical it was to do something" about the Democratic attacks.[38] For his part, Newt Gingrich later conceded that the Republicans' unwillingness to respond in 1995 hurt them badly in 1996, calling it "our biggest failure."[39]

The President's campaign was also organized much earlier than usual for an incumbent. By June 1995 the White House had already done extensive campaign work in more than a dozen states, had established informal "Clinton family" discussions with party leaders in 15 to 20 key states, and had proceeded with what a senior aide called "a controlled sense of urgency" to nail down commitments from Democrats nationwide to support Clinton. Later that summer, the campaign devoted $10,000 to organize Iowa. And by Thanksgiving, the Clinton-Gore campaign had met its fundraising goal of $24 million.[40] This extraordinary preparation stood in stark contrast with George Bush's dilatory reelection effort four years earlier, when Bush had shown great reluctance to go into "campaign mode." Ann Devroy of the *Washington Post* noted that President Clinton put in place "one of the earliest and most aggressive reelection campaigns ever." This campaign ultimately had its sights on the general election, but "its first goal seems to be to scare off—or to beat—a Democratic challenger."[41]

The prospect of a challenge to the President was quite real. Throughout 1995 several names were mentioned as possibilities: Senators Bill Bradley (N.J.) and Bob Kerrey (Neb.), former Pennsylvania governor and pro-life spokesman Bob Casey, and Jesse Jackson, whose dissatisfaction with Clinton was made clear at the May 1995 convention of the Rainbow Coalition. Bradley, Kerrey, and Jackson all had the stature to pose a serious threat; a run by Casey, though doomed, would have exposed the Democratic divisions on abortion that, though obscured, run far deeper than is generally acknowledged. That no challenge ever materialized was largely due to the aggressiveness of the Clinton campaign, which was made possible by the fortuitous new circumstances the President faced. These circumstances proved helpful in another respect. The Republican takeover of Congress and its dominance in setting the national agenda posed a threat that served as a bond to hold together a party that might otherwise have continued fraying. Labor unions, environmental groups, and other key elements of the Democratic coalition were forced to put aside their dissatisfactions and mobilize for Clinton, or at least against Congress. As 1995 progressed, intra-party criticisms of Clinton abated and the AFL-CIO pledged $35 million to help Democrats retake Congress.

The importance of avoiding an intra-party challenge cannot be overstated. Any challenge would have split the party, drained campaign resources, and provided fresh ammunition on the character issue. And in the context of the politics of 1996, a challenge from the left, perhaps by Jesse Jackson, might have made Clinton's rightward shift, which was so important to his political recovery, more difficult. Primary challenges from within the President's party almost always hurt the incumbent. It is no coincidence that of the five incumbents who have lost reelection in the twentieth century, four faced a major primary challenge, while no winning incumbent ever fought primary opposition.[42]

All three of the theories explaining "losing to win" found support after the 1994 congressional elections: the winners made blunders, the losers learned, and the ambivalence of the American electorate, which lacks a clear majority, was obvious. The factors that worked to lift Bill Clinton's standing in his second "term" involved a complex mixture of Republican mistakes, his ability to use fluid new circumstances to his advantage, and an almost-inevitable liberal countermobilization in which even skeptical Democrats rallied around their President. Clinton disabled the coalition of 1994, created his own coalition for 1996, and launched into a permanent campaign that secured easy renomination and that set the stage for a successful reelection effort. Absent the Republican congressional victories of 1994, it is difficult to imagine how Clinton might have pieced together this scenario. It is easy to imagine instead another two years of foundering, continued inability to avoid the talk-action dilemma, and ultimately a serious primary challenge. Indeed, Clinton strategists said in the midst of the presidential campaign, "The '94 election was a total blessing in disguise. If the President wins re-election it's in no small part due to our losing the Congress."[43]

Heading into the Election

The election of 1996 was as much a referendum on 1994 as it was on 1992. A central question of the campaign was whether the Republicans misinterpreted the elections of 1994. And the answer nicely predicted the ambiguity of the results in November: yes and no. Republicans did not make a mistake in believing that Americans were revolting against the general idea of big government, and in this respect the electoral results of 1994 were nothing more than a case of congressional elections catching up to where presidential elections had been since 1968. Yet the 1994 elections revealed only one face of the American electorate: a "majority" patched together from the right to the ambivalent middle, in which many short-term political factors helped the coalition to form. But that coalition is clearly not a firm or consistent majority. Americans do want smaller government, but they do not want to lose the benefits of the welfare state. The philosophical conservatism of the American electorate is real enough, but Republican success in appealing to that conservatism in 1994 did not mean that operational liberalism was dead. In truth Americans were and remain collectively divided about the welfare state.

The Republican Congress did not share that ambivalence. By 1996, on the other hand, President Clinton did. Republicans had long assumed that Bill Clinton's flip-flops and inconsistencies were weaknesses. During his first "term" they almost certainly were, but during his second "term" they often proved a source of great strength. When Bill Clinton told Americans that "the era of big government is over," they could feel that their President was somehow attuned to their abstract conservatism, yet they also knew that he would not act precipitously. Clinton's triumph in the budget battle lay in his ability to persuade Americans that under his stewardship government was shrinking but not too fast.

If the forces and tendencies of the American electorate are in rough equilibrium, with both sides well entrenched and those in the middle ambivalent, the blitzkrieg envisioned by Newt Gingrich after 1994 (or by Bill Clinton in his first "term") could not easily succeed, at least not without a more solid governmental majority. American politics in the 1990s had entered a phase when, as in the early battles of World War I, the defense had an intrinsic advantage over the offense and the offense shattered itself time and again in large-scale assaults against superior fortifications. As one analyst remarked, Clinton's political successes during the 1995–96 budget battle reflected "how much harder it is to explain and defend complex initiatives—such as Republicans' Medicare proposal in 1995 or Clinton's health care plan in 1994—than it is to attack them."[44] This national ambivalence, which under American political institutions usually manifests itself as an advantage for those playing defense, was at the heart of the phenomenon so much in evidence in the 1990s: losing to win.

After three years in the presidency Bill Clinton looked ahead to a reelection campaign that would be fought on a terrain defined by losing to win. Many of the underlying forces that drove the fall campaign were already set by March 1996. Clinton had many strengths, but some weaknesses as well. Gone were the whispered rumors of a shell-shocked President. Clinton began to regain confidence as his approval ratings edged up toward the upper limit of his normal band and the intensity of those who disapproved abated. Democratic election victories in November 1995 and January 1996 indicated that the Republican tide had stalled. Many skeptical Americans concluded that Clinton had grown in the job, was "trying hard," and was protecting them against Republican excesses. The economy continued to grow, even to speed up, while unemployment and inflation remained low. The Democratic Party was united, at least on the surface, and all of the considerable advantages of incumbency lay in Clinton's hands.

Yet fundamental problems remained. The economy was perhaps still not what it ought to have been in a normal recovery. The character issue was a permanent fixture of life at the White House. The President's twisting and weaving presented a variety of potential future pitfalls; a person who had won election in 1992 as an advocate for "change" would be running for reelection as the sturdiest defender of the status quo in Washington. Pluralities continued to indicate in polls that, as an abstract proposition, Clinton did not deserve reelection, leading Clinton strategists to state that they could not allow the election to be turned into a referendum on Clinton's first term: "The election can't be about the last four years—it has to be about the future, the 21st century."[45]

Thus, the imponderables loomed large. Would the economy hold up? Would the scandals resurface, and if so, could the damage be contained? Would the foreign policy juggling act explode? Could Congress embarrass Clinton by forcing him to veto popular measures? Would a third-party or independent candidate enter the scene, and if so who and with what effect? Would Dole run a skillful campaign? Would he unite Republicans, exploit Clinton's continuing vulnerabilities, choose a vice presidential candidate who would add to the strength of the ticket, turn his own prosaic nature into a strength of solidity, a positive contrast with Clinton's blow-dried slickness? And, not least, would the Clinton campaign make mistakes born of overconfidence? The answers would have to wait for the final events of the fall campaign.

Notes

1. See Richard J. Carroll, "Clinton's Economy in a Historical Context, or Why Media Coverage on Economic Issues is Suspect," *Presidential Studies Quarterly* 26 (Summer 1996): 828–834.

2. Clinton's approval ratings remained remarkably constant throughout the first three years of his presidency. There were, of course, variations, from a low of 38 percent to a high of 60 percent. But he kept returning to a range from the mid to high 40s, and his average showed less variation than any President since Franklin Roosevelt, though Roosevelt's average was much higher (cited by Lyn Ragsdale, "Roundtable: The 1996 Presidential Election," annual meeting of the Western Political Science Association, San Francisco, California, March 15, 1996).

3. Charles Krauthammer, "A President for Our Time," *Washington Post*, July 5, 1996, A15.

4. See Kenneth T. Walsh, "Coming of Age," *U.S. News & World Report*, September 2, 1996, 22–27; Michael Barone and Grant Ujifusa, *The Almanac of American Politics 1996* (Washington, D.C.: The National Journal, 1995), xxxvii.

5. "Transcript of President's Address on the Economy," *New York Times*, February 16, 1993, A14.

6. Quoted in Bob Woodward, *The Agenda: Inside the Clinton White House* (New York: Simon & Schuster, 1994), 165.

7. Michael Barone, "His Problem: Indifference, Not Hate," *U.S. News & World Report*, August 16, 1993, 37.

8. Robert Pear, "Congress Asserts Health Proposals Understate Costs," *New York Times*, February 9, 1994, A1.

9. Alison Mitchell, "Despite His Reversals, Clinton Stays Centered," *New York Times*, July 28, 1996, A11.

10. Theda Skocpol, "The Rise and Resounding Demise of the Clinton Plan," *Health Affairs* (Spring 1995): 67.

11. Jon Healey, "Clinton Success Rate Declined to a Record Low in 1995," *Congressional Quarterly Weekly Report*, January 27, 1996, 193.

12. Mitchell, "Despite His Reversals," A10.

13. See Douglas Jehl, "Clinton Delivers Emotional Appeal on Stopping Crime," *New York Times*, November 14, 1993, A1; "Excerpts from Clinton's Speech to Black Ministers," *New York Times*, November 14, 1993, A24.

14. See Dale Russakoff, "Gingrich Vows Cooperation," *Washington Post*, November 9, 1994; Dan Balz, "Clinton, GOP Leaders Offer Cooperation," *Washington Post*, November 10, 1994; David Broder, "Vote May Signal GOP Return as Dominant Party," *Washington Post*, November 10, 1994; Edward Walsh, "Democrats Wonder Whether Sea Change Is Plea for Centrism," *Washington Post*, November 10, 1994.

15. See David S. Broder, "Sharp Turn to the Right Reflects Doubts about Clinton, Democrats," *Washington Post*, November 9, 1994; Walsh "Democrats

Wonder Whether Sea Change"; Ruth Marcus, "Clinton Reiterates Vow to Pursue New Democrat Agenda," *Washington Post*, November 11, 1994; "News Conference November 11, 1994," *Weekly Compilation of Presidential Documents* 30, November-December 1994.

16. Philip Klinkner, "Court and Country in American Politics: The Democratic Party in the 1994 Elections," in *Midterm: The Elections of 1994 in Context* (Boulder: Westview, 1996), 71.

17. See Theodore J. Eismeier and Phillip H. Pollock, "Money in the 1994 Elections and Beyond," in Klinkner, ed., *Midterm: The Elections of 1994 in Context* (Boulder: Westview Press, 1996), 81–97.

18. Gary C. Jacobson, "The 1994 House Elections in Perspective," in Klinkner, ed., *Midterm: The Elections of 1994 in Context* (Boulder: Westview Press, 1996), 5.

19. Jacobson, "The 1994 House Elections," 9–20; Eismeier and Pollock, "Money in the 1994 Elections."

20. Bob Benenson, "GOP's Dreams of a Comeback Via the New Map Dissolve," *CQ Weekly Report*, November 7, 1992, 3581.

21. Thomas B. Edsall, "Revolt of the Discontented," *Washington Post*, November 11, 1994, A31; Richard Morin, "Voters Repeat Their Simple Message About Government: Less is Better," *Washington Post*, November 10, 1994, A1; Larry Hugick and Andrew Kohut, "Taking the Nation's Pulse," *The Public Perspective*, November/December 1994, 3–6; "A New 'Contract With America?,' " February/March 1995, 28–29.

22. See Klinkner.

23. Jacobson, "The 1994 House Elections," 6.

24. Healey, "Clinton Success Rate Declined to a Record Low in 1995."

25. Mitchell, "Despite His Reversals," A11.

26. See Susan M. Hartmann, *Truman and the 80th Congress* (Columbia: University of Missouri Press, 1971).

27. Press conference of April 18, 1995.

28. Everett Carll Ladd, "Don't Believe the Hype," *The Weekly Standard*, December 4, 1995, 13–14; Charles Krauthammer, "Beyond Cynicism," *Washington Post*, November 24, 1995, A29.

29. Richard Benedetto, "Clinton approval falls amid budget fight," *USA Today*, January 8, 1996, 1.

30. Mitchell, "Despite His Reversals," A11.

31. See Ladd, "Don't Believe the Hype," 14.

32. The failure of the Senate to pass a balanced budget amendment in March, due to the defection of Republican Senator Mark Hatfield as well as six Democrats who had earlier pledged to support it, marked a key turning point. Had the amendment succeeded, Republicans could have presented their program of budget cuts as a constitutional necessity. After the amendment's failure, Republicans might have been well advised to wait for a chance to win the presidency before proceeding with the potentially unpopular cut in entitle-

ments. Instead, in an excess of responsible behavior, they proposed to make these cuts on the basis of their own political initiative.

33. Jonathan Weisman, "The Impact of GOP Congress Reaches Well Beyond Bills," *Congressional Quarterly Weekly Report*, September 7, 1996, 2515–2520.

34. Mitchell, "Despite His Reversals, Clinton Stays Centered," A10.

35. Ann Devroy, "Clinton Reelection Machinery in Place—Already," *Washington Post*, August 3, 1995, A9.

36. Ben Wattenberg, "Presidential Race Over? No, It Hasn't Started Yet," *Rocky Mountain News*, June 27, 1996, 52A; Alison Mitchell, "Stung by Defeats in '94, Clinton Regrouped and Co-Opted G.O.P. Strategies," *New York Times*, November 7, 1996, B1.

37. Mitchell, "Stung by Defeats." See also James Bennet, "Liberal Use of 'Extremist' Is the Winning Strategy," *New York Times*, November 7, 1996, B1.

38. James A. Barnes, "Too Little, Too Late?," *National Journal*, November 2, 1996, 2335.

39. Francis X. Clines, "Dismissing Image in Attack Ads as 'Fantasy,' Gingrich Stresses Need for Diplomacy," *New York Times*, November 6, 1996, A11.

40. Devroy, "Clinton Reelection Machinery in Place—Already," A9; Ann Devroy, "The Traveling Salesman," *Washington Post*, June 11, 1995, A8.

41. Devroy, "Clinton Reelection Machinery in Place—Already," A9.

42. Taft faced Roosevelt and LaFollette, Ford faced Reagan, Carter faced Kennedy, and Bush faced Buchanan. Only Hoover did not have serious primary opposition. In addition, two other incumbents who were eligible to run for reelection—Truman in 1952 and Johnson in 1968— were driven from the race by the spirited opposition of Estes Kefauver and Eugene McCarthy.

43. Mitchell, "Despite His Reversals, Clinton Stays Centered," A10.

44. Healey, "Clinton Success Rate Declined to a Record Low in 1995," 193.

45. Kenneth T. Walsh, "Taking the Offensive," *U.S. News & World Report*, January 29, 1996, 32.

Chapter 3

The Republican Nomination

In selecting Robert Dole as its nominee in 1996, the Republican party bowed to the inevitable. Or so everyone would say after the race was over. The case for Bob Dole's inevitability is admittedly a strong one. Dole was the Republican Party's senior national leader, having a stature akin to a sitting vice president. He was Mr. Republican—a five-term senator, the Senate Republican Majority Leader, a past Republican Party national chairman, the party's vice-presidential nominee (1976), and a second-place finisher for the Republican presidential nomination (1988). Although Dole's advanced age was clearly a concern—at 73 he would be the oldest first-time nominee of either party—it also helped to soften a longstanding image as a partisan "hatchet man." Dole could now appear as an elder statesman and the last war hero on the political scene from a generation that knew something about honor and country. Nor was this all. After the Republicans' congressional victory of 1994, Dole had situated himself in the center of the party's conservative range, moving right as the party moved right. He made himself acceptable to a wide range of interests inside the party, including the leadership of the Christian Coalition. By the beginning of 1996, Dole had collected the endorsements of a huge number of Republican elected officials, far exceeding that of any of his rivals. He had raised more money than any of the other candidates, and he was far ahead in the polls. Dole in short was the clear winner of the "invisible primary," the contest for popular support and money that precedes the actual selection of the delegates. And as political scientists have shown, winning the invisible primary has been a good predictor of who will win visible primaries and the nomination.[1]

Still, for a candidate heralded as the inevitable winner, Dole experienced a hazardous journey to the nomination. To launch his campaign

Dole opted to deliver the Republican reply to President Clinton's State of the Union Address in January. The speech was by all accounts a disaster, with Dole looking like a piece of petrified wood. Confidence in his candidacy began to wane. By the end of January, just before the visible campaign was officially to begin, Dole began to slip in the polls in Iowa and New Hampshire and was running neck and neck with Steve Forbes, a man who a few months before was almost unknown to the American people. Dole barely won the caucuses in Iowa—virtually a home state for the Kansan—and he then lost the New Hampshire primary to Patrick Buchanan, narrowly averting a third-place finish to Lamar Alexander. Inevitability should be made of sterner stuff.

The Schedule

The nomination contest in 1996 was conducted under the same national party rules as in 1992. The Democratic national party, which several times since 1968 had forced a remodeling of the nominating process, was content in the aftermath of Clinton's 1992 victory to keep the existing arrangement. There were accordingly none of those funny sounding party reform commissions to meddle in the states' delegate selection procedures. But the nomination system in 1996 nevertheless differed significantly from that of 1992. The change came about not from the top down but from the bottom up—from an uncoordinated movement of various states to place their primaries or caucuses nearer to the front of the primary season. This movement, known as "frontloading," goes back to the 1980s, especially to the advent of "Super Tuesday" in 1984. The logic operating in favor of frontloading is fairly simple. States with contests near the end have usually found themselves holding contests when the race has already long since been decided. In an effort to achieve greater influence some of these states (combining sometimes into regional blocs) began to move nearer to the start of the campaign. What was a gradual creeping forward of the states turned by 1996 into a stampede, as the big buffaloes—New York and California—both moved their contests into the month of March.

There was also a breech in the jealously guarded frontline of the starting point for the campaign. Traditionally, Iowa held the first caucus and New Hampshire the first primary. For these two states, being first was a matter of influence, pride, and (not least) big business. Professors write books about these states' contests. Candidates who otherwise might pause only to tip a wing of their airplane as it entered these states' air space spend months courting their voters. And the national journalists make their quadrennial sojourns into the snowy landscape to inform Americans what "real" Iowans or New Hampshirites are thinking. In an effort to encroach on the privileged position of these two states, some states began to experiment with so-called "straw polls" at their state conventions in advance of the delegate selection process. But despite some hoopla surrounding these contests (especially in Florida)—and despite the money and time some candidates put into them—they never quite measured up to the real thing. In 1996 the Republican Party of Louisiana (at the urging of Senator Phil Gramm) broke tradition and scheduled a caucus in the week before Iowa's.[2] Republicans in Iowa were so upset at this affront that they solicited and secured pledges from most of the candidates not to compete in Louisiana. Only Gramm, Alan Keyes, and Pat Buchanan entered the race, making it a contest between right, righter, and rightist. The Louisiana race nonetheless was critical in narrowing the field, as Gramm's loss to Buchanan proved to be a damaging blow from which the Texan never recovered. A similar, if less egregious, challenge was made to New Hampshire, when Delaware scheduled a primary in the same week (although after) New Hampshire's. Fearing a dilution of their state's influence, New Hampshire in a battle of the Titans threw its weight to try to stop the candidates from actively participating in the Delaware primary.

While some thought this new schedule might lead to deadlock, most predicted that it would produce a rapid decision. This result was all the more likely in the Republican contest, where most of the delegates are awarded under some form of a winner-take-all, rather than a proportional, system. Compared to the nomination races of the 1980s, the Republican contest would proceed like a videotape on fast forward. Campaigning for the Iowa caucus, Dole told an audience that it "will all be over by the end of March." Although this comment was offered to reassure nervous supporters when fears were mounting over his campaign, Dole's prediction turned out to be a huge understatement. The race in fact was all but over on March 2, and certainly no later than March 7. The decisive contest in 1996, as in the Republican race in 1992, was probably South Carolina, where Dole decisively bested Buchanan and Alexander. By the time Super Tuesday came along on March 12, many of the candidates had already dropped out (Gramm, Lugar, Alexander, and Taylor), and the contest held about as much excitement as most Super Bowls. The high-brow weekly *The Economist* called it

"Stupor Tuesday." By the next week, the primaries in the key heartland states (Illinois, Michigan, Ohio, and Wisconsin) scarcely merited mention in the evening news.

Many citizens and legislators in the states that had moved up their primaries were clearly frustrated at once again conducting a Soviet-style election where only one viable candidate was running. But it takes no mathematical genius to realize that states' scheduling an earlier primary date does not matter very much if the other states hold their primaries earlier as well. States that once considered themselves to be near the front of the process—like all those on Super Tuesday—found themselves slipping further back in the pack in 1996. In states like Montana and New Jersey that have kept their old dates near the end (in May or June), many citizens have probably forgotten that they have a voice in the nomination of the President.

The Events

Although remarkably short in duration, the Republican nomination contest was filled with drama, genuine conflict, and important consequences. If there was any period of genuine political excitement in the entire 1996 presidential campaign, it occurred during the brief six weeks of the Republican race from the Louisiana caucus to the South Carolina primary. It was then, and only then, that an expected outcome was in some doubt, and then, and only then, that candidates threw down gauntlets and declared themselves ready to fight for the "heart and soul" of something. After early March the nomination quickly faded from view, and the presidential race, the most sleep-inducing of modern times, began slouching its way to the numbing conventions of San Diego and Chicago.

The events of nomination campaigns typically rank among the more forgettable of American politics, especially for the party that loses the White House. Just to remind everyone of what happened, it will be helpful at the outset to list the six steps to Dole's nomination.

1. The withdrawal of Colin Powell. The great story of the summer and fall of 1995 was the potential candidacy of former General Colin Powell, who consistently scored at or near the top in preference polls for the Republican nomination and who was the most formidable rival to President Clinton. Powell's decision in early November to forgo a

TABLE 3.1
Early Republican Caucus and Primary Results, 1996

State/Date		Turnout	Alexander	Dole	Buchanan	Forbes	Keyes	Gramm	Other
CAUCUS:									
Alaska	Jan. 27-29	9,172	.6	17.1	**32.6**	30.7	9.8	8.6	.6
La.	Feb. 6	22,846	---	---	**44.4**	---	4.0	42.0	10.0
Iowa	Feb. 12	96,451	17.6	**26.3**	23.3	10.2	7.4	9.0	6.0
PRIMARY:									
N.H.	Feb. 20	208,993	22.6	26.2	**27.2**	12.2	2.7		9.1
Del.	Feb. 24	32,773	13.3	27.2	18.7	**32.7**	5.3		2.8
Ariz.	Feb. 27	347,482	7.1	29.6	27.6	**33.4**	0.8		1.5
N.Dakota	Feb. 27	63,374	6.3	**42.1**	18.3	19.5	3.2		10.6
S. Dakota	Feb. 27	69,170	8.7	**44.7**	28.6	12.8	3.4		1.8
S. Car.	Mar. 2	276,741	10.4	**45.1**	29.2	12.7	2.1		0.6
Colorado	Mar. 5	247,752	9.8	**43.6**	21.5	20.8	3.7		0.6
Conn.	Mar. 5	130,418	5.4	**54.4**	15.1	20.1	1.7		3.3
Georgia	Mar. 5	559,067	13.6	**40.6**	29.1	12.7	3.1		0.9
Maine	Mar. 5	67,280	6.6	**46.3**	24.5	14.8	1.8		5.9
Maryland	Mar. 5	254,246	5.5	**53.3**	21.1	12.7	5.4		2.0
Mass.	Mar. 5	284,833	7.5	**47.7**	25.2	13.9	1.8		3.8
R. Island	Mar. 5	15,009	19.0	**64.4**	2.6	0.9	0.2		12.9
Vermont	Mar. 5	58,113	10.6	**40.3**	16.7	15.6	---		16.8

presidential nomination bid (but become a Republican) removed one of the major roadblocks to Dole's victory.

2. The surge and decline of Steve Forbes. From nowhere—although with a personal treasure chest that was unfathomable—magazine publisher and self-styled outsider Steve Forbes began a meteoric rise in the national polls in January, pulling even or ahead of Bob Dole in the key early states of Iowa and New Hampshire. Suddenly, it was Steve Forbes's face behind his thick glasses that could be seen smiling at Americans from the covers of most of the national magazines. Significantly, in the major televised debate for the Iowa caucuses, Steve Forbes was treated by most of the other candidates as the frontrunner, with his flat tax plan coming under attack. After this increased scrutiny, Forbes's support began to soften, and an ill-tempered complaint that Dole was engaging in negative campaigning began to make Forbes look like an amateur who could not stand the heat. Suddenly his support began to decline, tumbling even more quickly than it had arisen. The remarkable aspect of Forbes's joyride in the polls and the media was that it all occurred before Forbes had actively contested for a single delegate. By the time Forbes won his first delegates and a primary (he finished first in both Delaware on February 24 and Arizona on February 27) he was on his way down.

3. The fall of Phil Gramm. Senator Phil Gramm, widely considered the most serious rival to Senator Dole, never even enjoyed the experience of a rise (unless it was winning a few straw polls in 1994 and 1995). Gramm began 1996 at his apogee, with a well-financed campaign and a second-place standing to Bob Dole in most polls. Gramm then went straight down. Following his embarrassing defeat in the Louisiana caucus to Pat Buchanan, Gramm's painstakingly built campaign in Iowa collapsed, and he finished fourth in that state. Facing his own Senate campaign in Texas, Gramm withdrew before the first primary in New Hampshire and shortly thereafter endorsed Bob Dole.

4. The rise and fall of Pat Buchanan. As Colin Powell had been the media event of the early fall of 1995, so Pat Buchanan was the big story of the late winter of 1996. A surprise winner against Gramm in Louisiana, Buchanan went on to finish a surprising second in Iowa and then, confounding all the experts, won the New Hampshire primary. During this period there was not a news magazine, political column, or talk show where the focus of discussion was anything other than

Pat Buchanan. But Buchanan's victory in New Hampshire proved to be the highpoint of his national campaign. Buchanan summoned his brigades from the deep in Arizona, but they stopped coming. In Arizona, he finished behind Steve Forbes and Bob Dole. By then it was becoming clear that much of the voting was turning into a choice against Pat Buchanan. Buchanan then lost decisively to Dole in South Carolina, a state in which his base support groups of social conservatives and economically disaffected workers were thought to be strongest. Buchanan never seriously challenged thereafter, losing most of the races to Dole by more than a 2–1 margin. Indeed, many of the votes he did receive reflected buyers' regret on Dole, rather than a pro-Buchanan sentiment.

5. The ascent and descent of Lamar Alexander. To speak of a rise for Alexander would be an overstatement, but he did enjoy a brief moment of ascent. A respectable kind of person, Alexander enjoyed a respectable kind of third-place finish in Iowa. He then when on to a near second-place finish in New Hampshire to Bob Dole, which he sought to interpret more or less as a victory over Dole, telling Dole it was time "to step aside." A mild flurry of publicity for Alexander followed the New Hampshire race, along with the infusion of some much needed cash. Then it all ended, not with a bang but a whimper. Just before Alexander was about to take Bob Dole to the woodshed in his home region in the South on Super Tuesday March 12, Alexander turned in dismal performances in South Carolina and Georgia. Without a Southern base—or any base at all—he pulled out and endorsed Dole.

6. The last man standing. After all these rises and falls, surges and declines, and ascents and descents, one man at the end of the day was left standing: Bob Dole. His victory seemed a feat more of survivability than inevitability. As Tom Pauken, Chairman of the Texas GOP, said, Dole won because he was "everybody's second choice."[3] By good fortune, Dole's weaker opponents in the early stages helped to knock out his stronger ones: Buchanan took out Gramm on his right, while Forbes weakened Alexander on his outside. Dole managed to avoid the truly fatal blow and stumbled back to his corner, hurt but victorious. His prize would be the right to face the heavyweight Bill Clinton.

Powell Mania

Treating the Powell phenomenon in a chapter on the Republican nomination race is more a matter of organizational convenience than an accurate account of the history of events in 1995. For Powell all along faced two distinct decisions—whether to run for the presidency at all and, if so, whether to run as an independent or as a Republican. All along pundits considered an independent candidacy as likely as a Powell contest for the Republican nomination. (Indeed, there were many who speculated that under other conditions, he would have offered himself as a Democrat.)

"Powell mania" was the name that the national media assigned to its own preoccupation in the summer and early fall of 1995 with the possibility of a Powell candidacy. The fact that the national press corps—and the nation—would wait patiently and respectfully for months trying to read every sign of Powell's behavior was unprecedented. To run or not to run, that was the question. For the national media to act so deferentially, there had to be a deeper "cultural" explanation. And there surely was. Colin Powell had a quality that is in short supply in modern American politics: stature. Everyone knew who General Powell was, and almost everyone professed respect for him. Here was a Black American who rose to the top of the military profession and who, during the Gulf War, offered the public a picture of steadiness, strength, and competence. Powell appeared to be not just outside of politics, but above it. When he stood next to the others, the President of the United States included, they looked smaller and less significant than he. Possessing this kind of stature gave Powell an aura of self-sufficiency rarely seen today. Powell did not need the presidency to complete himself, and evidently in the end did not want it. As he said himself, he was in a position in which he did not "have to appeal to, appease, or try to champion anyone's position or any party's position."

Inherent in modern democracy, yet promoted to excess by our presidential selection process, is a system in which candidates must ingratiate themselves before the public, playing the petty popular arts in order to win the public's favor. In this process, any semblance of distance for the candidates—let us not even speak of dignity—is difficult to find. The "requirement" that politicians demean themselves and run the media's gauntlet, yet everyone's clear sense that this has all gone too far, is the explanation of Powell mania.

Of course, if General Powell had entered the race his stature would certainly have come under attack, and by the time he withdrew articles were beginning to appear scrutinizing his position in the Gulf War and the Somalia mission. In addition, the majority of reporters in the national press were aware that the coverage they had given Powell to that point alternated somewhere between the laudatory and the gushing. Elementary fairness demanded that something would have to change. Either reporters would have to treat Powell a little bit more critically, or else they would have to treat the other candidates more respectfully. Perhaps the distaste of entering this fray played some small role in Powell's decision not to run, or perhaps he had a much keener sense than others at the time for Clinton's real strength in 1996. But there is no reason to doubt his own simple explanation: "It is a calling I do not yet hear."

Within the Republican party, a Powell candidacy had both enthusiasts and detractors. Powell offered the prospect of a candidate who many argued would be in the best position to defeat Bill Clinton. Some of Washington's most respected intellectual figures, among them William Bennett and William Kristol, were urging a close look at Powell. But many social conservatives in the party maintained that a Powell candidacy would mean that the party would be hijacked from its conservative base. In fact, Powell gave these people more than sufficient reason for concern, calling himself a "Rockefeller Republican" and announcing himself as pro-choice and in favor of affirmative action. Presumably, if Powell had really wanted the nomination, he would have offered the social conservatives something on one of these two issues.

Powell mania merits attention more for the possibility it posed of an independent candidacy than a race for the Republican nomination. Had Powell pursued an independent candidacy, it would have marked the second presidential election in a row with a strong campaign from outside of the parties. Polls, which admittedly must be lightly regarded when testing such a hypothetical, indicated that Powell would have fared well as an independent in a three-way race against the presumptive party nominees of the Republican Party (Senator Dole) and the Democratic Party (President Clinton). In addition, 62 percent of the American people expressed their willingness in principle to vote for a third party (or independent) candidate in 1996.

Although the viability of an independent Powell candidacy may be viewed as a unique response to his extraordinary personal stature, it may also be seen as filling the same slot as the Perot candidacy of 1992. This claim in no way seeks to liken the two men. Besides the one fact that they both have lived versions of the American dream—Perot rising from the middle class to become a billionaire, Powell coming from the outside in society to reach the highest levels of the government—it is hard to think of two men who are more different. Perot is little and jerky in his mannerisms, while Powell is large and deliberate. Perot is folksy and populist in his appeal, with more than a touch of paranoia to go with his megalomania. Powell is a picture of dignity, whose persona exudes self-control and whose rhetoric is lofty. Powell could and did pass up a chance to run for the presidency, while Perot, though always protesting disinterest, found it impossible to put such a chance aside. But for all of these differences, running as independent candidates from outside the charmed circle of ordinary politicians was something they almost shared. Perot all but introduced this idea in 1992, when he ran a campaign that was beyond and even against parties. His candidacy represented a substitution of personalism for party. An independent candidacy by General Powell would have filled in the same political "space," lending further legitimacy to personalism as an alternative path to the American presidency. The result could well have been an end to the monopoly of party nomination as the only recognized means of accession to the presidential office and the development of a system that combined personalism with partyism.

This did not occur. By declaring himself a Republican, Powell tied his political fate, temporarily at least, to a political party. So too, to a lesser extent, did Ross Perot, who ran in 1996 less as an independent than as the *party* candidate of the Reform Party. For the moment at least, the genie of personalism seems to have been put back into the bottle of partyism.

A Field of Dreams?

Never before have the Republicans had such a cornucopia of contenders. Opening day at the Louisiana caucus found nine Republican candidates still in competition, a record for any modern Republican nomination race. Along with Dole, Gramm, Forbes, Buchanan, and Alexander, there was Senator Richard Lugar of Indiana, Alan Keyes, Morry Taylor, and Congressman Robert Dornan of California. In addition, two other declared candidates, Governor Pete Wilson (Ca.) and Senator Arlen Specter (Pa.), had by then already dropped out. All in all this made eleven candidates for the 1996 Republican nomination.

Yet amidst this feast of candidates was a famine of expected "big names." David Frum, a leading analyst of the Republican Party, wrote in his book *Dead Right* in 1994, "If Kemp does blow up in the primaries or before, the likeliest Republican alternative to him will be . . . Richard Cheney."[4] Neither of these "likeliest" nominees ever made it into the race. Nor did some other prominent Republicans whom commentators named as potential contestants: Dan Quayle, Jim Baker, Bill Bennett, Newt Gingrich (who was seriously considering a run until late in 1995), and at least one of the new-breed governors (Tommy Thompson, John Engler, Christine Todd Whitman, or William Weld).

Surveying this field, two notable facts stand out. One is the low rate of "mentionables" who actually competed in the race. (A mentionable can be defined as someone who, if he chose not to run, would be expected to hold a news conference to explain his decision.) The other is the high rate of "nonmentionables" who did enter. (A nonmentionable is someone who, if he chose not to run, would have no reason to hold a news conference to explain his decision to anyone, including his wife).

By traditional standards, then, the Republican field seemed to be missing a number of candidates who should have run, while it was filled with a large number who should not have. The reluctance of so many prominent Republicans to compete in 1996 followed a similar occurrence on the Democratic side in 1992, when most of the "first-tier" Democrats—Gore, Gephardt, Bradley, Cuomo, and Nunn—decided not to run. But the immediate reason in the two cases appears to have been different. Democrats stayed out in 1992 not because they thought that winning the nomination would be impossible, but because they thought winning the general election would be impossible. (Democrats in 1992 were making their decision to run at a time when President Bush appeared invincible.) Republicans in 1996 stayed out not because they thought that winning the election would be impossible (they made their decision when President Clinton looked highly vulnerable), but because they concluded that it was too difficult to win the nomination.

The fact is, then, that the Republican field in 1996 contained two early and quite strong candidates—Phil Gramm and Bob Dole. Arguably it was their strengths that deterred others from entering. Phil Gramm was a logical candidate of the conservative Republicans. He was among the first in the Senate to oppose Clinton's health care plan, and he was the Senator most closely associated with the Spirit of '94 and the Contract With America. Gramm was also fully devoted to becoming President; he pursued the nomination early on with a remarkable single-mindedness, managing to lock up a good deal of the conservative money. Indeed, in his money-raising strategy Gramm appeared to be following Notre Dame's old practice of recruiting good football players just so they couldn't be used against them. Bob Dole, as noted, was by far the most plausible of the established Republicans. Finally, for those who wanted a reasonable long-shot type, who had many friends among Washington's intellectuals, and who could package himself mildly as an outsider, there was Lamar Alexander.

Modern politicians have been faulted by some for their lack of ambition, as if somehow the drive for high office is less among the current generation of politicians. But the reasoning of the candidates about whether to enter is also influenced by the institutional elements of the nomination system, and it is perhaps there that analysts should be searching for the problems. Compared to earlier systems, this one may serve to limit the entry of certain "expected" contestants. The reasons include not just the oft-noted ones of the need for a great deal of money up front, the amount of energy that the candidates must expend, or the amount of prying and scrutiny they must suffer, but also the simpler fact that the candidates in this system cannot be half in, allowing their names to be considered, without going all out. Candidates must either run or not run. If ambitious politicians think that they have only so many shots at the nomination for the presidency, and that a run now sometimes makes a later run more difficult, then they will be careful—perhaps too careful—about when they put their names on the line. No doubt, as everyone says, the system is fair in that it works the same for everyone. But what is fair to the prospective candidates—or logical from the viewpoint of their careers—does not necessarily equate with what is good for the American people, the interest of which is to have a nomination process that allows a great range of choice among the mentionable or plausible candidates.

The Republican decision in 1996 was thus structured by those who did not run as well as by those who did. Following the 1992 election, pundits came to a consensus on the leading candidates for the 1996 Republican presidential nomination that included HUD Secretary Jack Kemp as the clear favorite, followed by (in rough order) Senate Minority Leader Bob Dole, White House Chief of Staff James Baker, Vice President Dan Quayle, and Secretary of Defense Dick Cheney. Of these, James Baker was the most closely tied to George Bush, and Bush's defeat made a Baker candidacy highly unlikely. Only if foreign affairs had risen to the top of the American people's concerns might the former Secretary of State have entered the race. For different reasons, Dan Quayle's decision not to compete made sense. Although positioned well in the party, years of late-night mockery clearly had taken their toll and left Quayle without the kind of *gravitas* he would have needed as a candidate. Quayle thought long and hard about making the race, but in the end decided against it.

The two others on the list who did not run were perhaps more serious prospects: Jack Kemp and Dick Cheney. In the summer of 1992, Kemp's star shone brighter than any other in the Republican firmament. During his nine terms in the House he had helped father the New Right, authored the 1981 Reagan tax cuts, and mentored a number of bright young conservatives (most notably, Newt Gingrich). While his tenure at HUD lacked concrete accomplishments, it reestablished Jack Kemp as a legitimate pretender to Ronald Reagan's throne. He carried Reagan's mantle of optimism together with the supply-side credo and was especially popular among younger Republicans, who identified him with the future of the Republican Party. But a combination of events and personal characteristics—above all indecisiveness—began to hurt him. There were growing tensions with some of his conservative activists, who had been his strongest backers since the 1970s. When conservatives were focusing on cultural issues, Kemp talked about economics. (His speech at the 1993 Christian Coalition convention turned into yet another lecture on the merits of free trade, and he did not bother to attend the 1994 gathering.) When Republicans were emphasizing a "get-tough" approach to social problems, Kemp continued to stress "empowerment" and stirred controversy within conservative ranks by opposing limits on immigration and attacks on affirmative action. Plus Kemp refused to pursue the nomination with the obsessiveness of a Phil Gramm or a Lamar Alexander, often preferring to lecture and write op-eds. By the beginning of 1994 Kemp had lost his status as co-front runner with Dole and he was now being more and more discounted. When he announced on January 30, 1995, that he would not pursue the Republican presidential nomination, few were surprised. Kemp became so marginalized from his own party that in the summer of 1996 he seriously entertained entering the nomination contest of the Reform Party. When Dole chose Kemp as his running mate, Kemp admitted that he had been rescued from oblivion.

Then there was Dick Cheney, who was widely respected by both journalists and political activists. Cheney had an enviable reputation for intelligence and dependability and espoused a brand of conservatism that was both more rigorous than Dole's and less idiosyncratic than Kemp's. No one doubted that he had the ability and character necessary for the presidency. Every faction in the party, from Whitman-like moderates to the religious right, found him acceptable. Cheney had a real record of achievement. He had served as Gerald Ford's chief of staff at the age of 34. He had spent a decade in the House of Representatives, climaxing with a brief stint as Minority Whip. As George Bush's Secretary of Defense, Cheney had guided the nation through the end of the Cold War and to victory in the Persian Gulf War. But Cheney's support in national polls rarely rose above 10 percent, and he was squeezed from the conservative side by Gramm and never could equal the visibility or stature of Dole. While Cheney tried to raise his profile on domestic issues, he was still seen as a defense expert during a time when public interest in foreign affairs was nonexistent. Cheney announced on January 3, 1995, that he would not seek the Republican presidential nomination. If there was one candidate who did not run who should have been on the list, it was Dick Cheney.

The flip side of the coin was the high rate of nonmentionables competing in the 1996 contest. This fact draws on the opposite logic in the modern nomination in which anyone can run, and in which experience has now shown that anyone does. The modern system dramatically lowers the cost of entry for nonmentionables, while it offers some real incentives to running. Jesse Jackson in 1984 and Pat Robertson in 1988 show how much a nonmentionable can gain for his career or cause by making a run under the right conditions. Nor do they put a political career at risk, as they may not have one. Candidates can make a national reputation by running for the presidency, instead of having to build a national reputation in order to run for the presidency. This aspect is surely the most curious, or perverse, of the modern system, which operates at one and the same time as a competition among the most prominent names and a point of entry for amateurs. It is a competition for the Heismann trophy and a high school football tryout wrapped into one. The competitors run from Bob Dole to Morry Taylor.

The list of nonmentionables in 1996 included entrepreneur Morry Taylor, who spent $6.5 million of his own money and threw $100 bills into the crowds; Alan Keyes, a former undersecretary in the State Department in the Reagan administration and a brilliant orator; Robert Dornan, the colorful congressman who seemed to be in it for the fun (Dornan figured that his own congressional seat was safe, but ended up learning, as others have, that a truly embarrassing run for the presidency can endanger a political career); and Steve Forbes. Pat Buchanan might more properly be classified as a mentionable than a nonmentionable in 1996, but only by virtue of having run as a nonmentionable in 1992. Taking all of these candidates together, there was considerably more experience in talking about politics than in practicing it. Indeed, only Bob Dornan had been elected to anything, although he wound up receiving the fewest votes in the primaries.

The Elements of Nomination Choice

When all is said and done two basic factors weigh in the public's think-ing about the candidates and thus in how candidates try to present themselves to the voters: who you are and where you are. "Who you are" refers to a claim of being the most worthy *person* to serve as the party's standard-bearer. The focus here is on whether a candidate is really hewn from presidential "timber"—whether he has a record of meaningful service, a proven ability to win elections and to lead, and perhaps some measure of charisma. "Where you are" refers to a claim to being placed correctly in a space or position that should become the standard for the party and the nation. Placement may be either on an ideological spectrum or, as we hear more and more, on a spectrum of distance between being on the "outside" and the "inside."

Affirmations of "who you are" and "where you are" generally exist in a mix of some sort. Hardly anyone who claims to be somebody admits to being nowhere, and hardly anyone who claims to be some-where concedes he is nobody. But no matter how candidates try to present themselves, they cannot escape their past histories or their weaknesses as candidates. For the nonmentionables, generally the only claim they can make is one to where they are, because nothing in their record makes them stand out as presidential. They emphasize the im-portance of place over person. For the mentionables, while it is always initially thought that they have substance and direction to go along with their charisma or record of leadership, the campaigns can often indicate otherwise, showing a candidate who can express no compel-ling view of why he should be President. A prime example of this occurrence took place in Senator Ted Kennedy's challenge to President Carter in 1980. Asked in an inaugural national television interview with Roger Mudd why he was making the challenge, Kennedy had literally almost no answer. (The *Washington Post* called it "stuttering, vacuous, . . . that portrayed a man who had no clear reason for run-ning."[5]) Clearly, the charge of being nowhere was the one that was constantly being leveled against Bob Dole during the 1996 nomination contest.

The candidates who put forth a strong claim of "who they are" were Senators Richard Lugar and Bob Dole. Both emphasized their personal qualifications and their experience and record. "Trust" and "leader-ship" were terms they used frequently in their speeches. In his an-nouncement speech Lugar sounded this theme: "In a Lugar Administration, Americans will have confidence that their president is up to the job."[6] He touted his knowledge and experience in dealing with issues in foreign affairs ("I have the most experience and expertise in leading national security and foreign policy"[7]), but he also played up his domestic executive experience as a former mayor of Indianapolis, which was a bid to mix in a little bit of outsider appeal in contrast to Bob Dole.

Dole clearly preferred to have the dimension of "who you are" be controlling for the campaign. As he said in his announcement speech: "My friends, I have the experience, I have been tested and tested and tested in many ways. I am not afraid to lead, and I know the way!"[8] As the campaign got under way Dole contrasted his record to the inexperience of his major rivals (Buchanan and Forbes). To an audience in Waltham, Massachusetts, he observed: "You wouldn't hire a plumber to fix your faucet if he didn't have experience. Why would you elect a President who doesn't have one day of experience?"[9] Along with this leadership experience Dole had another element of his persona that distinguished him from the others: his war record and personal sacrifice for his country. Although Dole—like Coriolanus—had the dignity to feel uncomfortable showing his wounds in public, his campaign staff insisted he "must talk about it." And so he did: "I ended up being wounded, like a lot of men were, I spent 39 months in the hospital. It taught me a lot. . . . I'm not asking for pity; I want you to know who I am. I'm a real person, I wasn't born Senate majority leader."[10] This was also a way of answering some of the charges that Dole was a career politician entirely out of touch with the public: "I know that people sometimes have to be on welfare. I know that sometimes people are down and out."

The candidates with no notable elective experience could run only on the basis of where they were, emphasizing either ideology or outsiderism (or a combination of the two) as the dimension that ought to be the focus of the race. For those who stressed ideology, the claim was that the candidate's plan or program was more important than any considerations of who you are. Pat Buchanan's crusade fit this mold, although he also indicated that his previous campaign experience, when he showed courage against all odds, earned him some leadership stature. As he said in announcing his candidacy in New Hampshire, "The Buchanan Brigades are not leap-year conservatives. We have borne the day's heat. We have labored in these vineyards from the very first hour. And we stand here today to resume command of the revolution that we began here three years ago. . . ."[11] For those stressing the theme of distance from Washington, the campaigns celebrated the virtue of outsiderism. In the words of Steve Forbes: "I am running because I believe this nation needs someone . . . who can unlock the stranglehold that the political class has on American life. An outsider who knows firsthand, as I do, the promise of the new economy."[12] The claim of outsiderism makes a more direct assault on considerations of "who you are," because the idea here is that a demonstration of political experience on the inside is a *disqualification*. This argument could be made "with all due respect" (as Lamar Alexander did of Dole), or more aggressively, as Steve Forbes did.

There were two other candidates—Phil Gramm and Lamar Alexander—who made a dual claim. Phil Gramm offered himself in part on the basis of being a legislator with a significant record of achievement (who you are) and in part on his role as a strong voice of fiscal conservatism (where you are). His plan was to run against the other conservatives on the basis of who he was and then run against Bob Dole on the basis of where he was. Lamar Alexander based his early campaign on the other dimension of where you are ("an outsider who can make a difference"), but he also had a long record of previous public service, which he often brought up as an argument to try to prove his experience and establish his stature.

The logic of the nomination decision resides in the complex interplay between the voters' judgments about the importance and relative weight of these two factors and the candidates' efforts to appeal to and affect those judgments. Models of prediction are impossible respecting the relative importance of these two factors, as their weight is constantly being reassessed according to the qualities of the particular candidates and the situation. Candidates try to set the dimension on which they wish to run at the same time as they try to blunt the criticisms of their opponents. Not only this, but in a multi-candidate field the candidates run on different dimensions against different opponents. Inside any campaign there are only so many slots that in the end can compete for the nomination, so where there is more than one claimant to the same space there are a series of primaries within the primaries. This produces the various subplots, or contests within a contest, of a nomination campaign.

Ideology

Almost everyone who runs for the Republican nomination nowadays claims to be a conservative of one kind or another—and usually an heir of Ronald Reagan. (The only one who called himself a Rockefeller Republican was General Powell, and if he had decided to run this comment itself would have proven an obstacle to his success.) But if they are all in fact conservative relative to big government liberals, among themselves they differ greatly. When liberalism was the dominant public philosophy, these shades of difference hardly merited notice. But now that conservatism is far more in the mainstream, they are important. The 1996 Republican nomination contest became a national seminar in the meaning of different strands of conservative thought. Analysts began the election year by talking about three major slots in the Republican race from left to right, with the right containing differing shades of emphasis. But by the time the campaign was underway and people had the opportunity to observe Pat Buchanan, most analysts began to speak of a distinct fourth slot, a far right.

TABLE 3.2
The Position of Republican Contenders, 1996

	Outside	Inside Outside	Inside
"Left" or Moderate			Specter
		Wilson	
Center			Dole
			Lugar
	Alexander		
Right -supply side -fiscal -social	Forbes Taylor		
	Keyes		Gramm Dornan
Far Right	Buchanan		

The leftmost slot (often called "moderate" by media analysts) combined social liberalism, at least on the abortion issue, with economic conservatism. (This slot was, of course, not "left" in an absolute sense, but only within the range of Republican nomination politics.) Entrants in this slot were Senator Arlen Specter and Governor Pete Wilson. The contest produced one of those great rarities in political races: a perfect dead heat. Neither candidate got a single vote, as both pulled out before the race began. This space—or so both of these candidates concluded—proved too weak to sustain a viable candidacy. But this did not mean that the slot was unimportant in the Republican Party, and some of the candidates—notably, at different points, Dole, Lugar, Alexander, and Forbes—later sent signals that they were receptive to these concerns. Although adherents of this position are generally outvoted in GOP primaries, they remain a significant fraction of the party's membership and count among their ranks many elected officials. For example, five of the nine largest states have pro-choice Republican governors: California, New York, Pennsylvania, Illinois, and New Jersey. In addition, part of the difficulty was with the particular weaknesses of these two candidates, neither of whom exactly exuded warmth or charisma. Senator Specter never seemed like a plausible nominee, not only because he was pro-choice but because he seemed to make it the centerpiece of his campaign. Governor Wilson was of course different in this respect, and he added the hard-line socially conservative themes of opposition to illegal immigration and to affirmative action. But Wilson was breaking a promise he made to Californians not to seek the presidency, and some of his current positions were so at odds with his previous record that they seemed more the products of opportunism than genuine conversion.

The second slot was the center, made up of fiscal conservatism (but without a past record of purity) and a muted social conservatism (but without a record of crusading). In addition, those in this part of the party counted foreign policy as important and stressed adherence to a version of realistic internationalism, although foreign policy as an issue never resonated much with the voters in 1996. In this central group were Bob Dole and Richard Lugar, and—by reputation, if not always by the positions he espoused during the campaign—Lamar Alexander. (Alexander tended to take positions to the right of how many voters perceived his record.) For Dole and Lugar as well, there was the added element of a concern for the Republican Party itself as an institution. There was a Disraelian character to their conservatism that was somewhat suspicious of ideology and that was more concerned about preserving institutions than in following abstractions. Dole clearly had moved on many positions over his career and did so with the idea of accommodating the different developments inside the party. Thus it was not always easy to believe that this 35-year congressional veteran genuinely favored term limits or that he really wanted to take aim at federal programs in the fashion of some of the revolutionaries.

The race for the center is almost certainly less likely to carry ideology very far, if only because the center is somewhat less clearly defined and wants to be able to maintain a wide range of maneuvering. Relative to the races for the other slots, the substantive debate will ordinarily generate less heat and division, as all candidates who wish to maintain this position in the end cannot risk offending those on the wings. The campaigns of Lugar and of Alexander (to the extent it was a campaign of the Center) were based on being viable alternatives to Dole in this center slot in the event that Dole faltered or they could knock him out of the race. If Dole fell—like Ed Muskie did in 1972—this time there would be someone to occupy the space in the middle. As Senator Lugar explained after the race—and he was probably correct—"I retained a chance to win the nomination and the general election if Senator Dole left the field. . . . Other candidates, taken more seriously by apparently knowledgeable journalists . . . , had absolutely no chance of ever winning either the nomination or the general election."[13]

The race for the center slot was the race against the front-runner Bob Dole. It rested on the argument that whatever Dole's stature, he was somebody who was all but nowhere—perhaps instinctually in the center, but without any real vision. Others, of course, made this same argument against Dole, claiming that the closest he came to a vision was his "aboutism." He often would say that this campaign is "about young people," "about values," "about family" or "about jobs, "self-reliance" or—when he was being more philosophical—"about sending power back to the states." The Economist noted that this trait expressed "what is widely seen as the defining characteristic of the Dole vision: he has none."[14] After the New Hampshire primary, Alexander called himself the "candidate of fresh ideas; Buchanan the candidate of old ideas: Dole the candidate of no ideas." These were fairly strong words, but revealed well the core of this part of the campaign.

Third—and initially analysts would have said finally—there was the slot of what was called the right or the conservatives. In fact, there were four different issues or points of emphasis on the right, which many had once somehow thought could more or less fit together, but which in fact exploded into different pieces in 1996. The four strands were:

the supply-side tax cut, a market-oriented fiscal conservatism, social conservatism, and—what opened into a distinct slot on the far right—an anti-free trade nationalism.

The first strand was built around the issue of a supply-side tax cut, accompanied by a rhetoric based on the mantra of hope, growth, and opportunity. This particular position had been Jack Kemp's, and it was now assumed by Kemp's friend and benefactor Steve Forbes, who advocated the idea of the flat tax. This position was on the right because of its place inside the philosophy of Ronald Reagan, but as noted, it had an increasingly uneasy relationship to social conservatism. This position placed the emphasis on individual economic rights, not on themes of culture. Indeed, there was a reluctance to talk very much about social and cultural problems as distinct from economic ones, as the solutions to many of the cultural difficulties would come from reigniting America's greatness through economic opportunity and growth. Forbes was not a social conservative and indeed preferred not to speak about these issues. Asked once about his position on abortion, he answered he wanted the issue to "vanish."[15]

The second position was a market-oriented fiscal conservatism, which had become the major theme of the Republican revolution in Washington. Its champion within the field was Phil Gramm. It made balancing the national budget a top priority, with a large tax cut as part of the package. It was hence distinguishable from the supply-side strand not on the issue of tax cuts or a general theme of economic growth, but primarily by its equal emphasis on cutting the size of the national government. For fiscal conservatives, this was the responsible approach.

The third was social conservatism, the agenda most associated with the Christian Coalition. The central themes here were a package of strong family values and a pro-life position. Gramm spoke to these themes, but the candidates who emphasized them most were Alan Keyes and Patrick Buchanan.

Finally, there was the issue of protectionist nationalism championed by Patrick Buchanan. Buchanan offered a mix of hard-core cultural conservatism with his nationalism, which combined together offered what many regarded as a break from traditional American conservatism of any stripe. Indeed, these two elements of the Buchanan mix— social conservatism and blue-collar protectionism— while potentially coherent, appealed to substantially different constituencies; and the most salient and unique of the two positions (trade) was also the one that most firmly placed him outside the consensus of his own party.

Buchanan's populist-nationalist approach to economics borrowed from both the left and an older right. Patrick Buchanan occasionally portrayed himself as a neo-Reaganite devoted to smaller government, but his heart never seemed in it. He espoused a populism and ultra conservatism that put economic rights behind solidarity and that resembled Southern agrarianism (or Continental ultra conservatism) more than the orthodoxy of the *Wall Street Journal* editorial page. His populism went after both economic and cultural elites, attacking government and business alike for betraying working-class voters. Like traditionalists, Buchanan sought to promote an idea of community and thus distrusted capitalism —particularly its aspect of "creative destruction." (He often asked fellow conservatives what it was they wanted to conserve). He denounced corporate executives as mercenary and unpatriotic for laying off Americans while expanding operations overseas. Buchanan broke with 150 years of Whig-Republican orthodoxy by openly proclaiming the struggle between capital and labor, with labor now identified as embodying the true America that was being besieged by cosmopolitan capitalism. Capitalism disrupted traditional society, benefitted the wrong people, and eroded national loyalties.

Buchanan supported protectionism more for cultural than economic reasons. His "conservatism of the heart" seemed to abandon Enlightenment individualism in favor of more visceral notions of group solidarity. Buchanan, who once noted that "race and tribe" were the true motivators of human action, offered the reddest meat on immigration and affirmative action during the campaign. Such views led to frequent accusations that Buchanan was a fellow traveler for the extreme right of bigots and racists, and the campaign was put on the defensive when a top official, Larry Pratt, agreed to step down after charges were made that he attended white supremacist meetings. Buchanan disavowed all such connections, but he rekindled older suspicions of anti-Semitism after he denounced in an all too obvious reference Treasury Secretary Robert Rubin, Supreme Court Justice Ruth Bader Ginsburg, and the Wall Street firm of Goldman Sachs.

The race on the right was the most intense and interesting of the campaign. Gramm's plan was quickly to consolidate the whole right on a platform of fiscal and social conservatism. As the only person with genuine stature on the right, he would run largely on the basis of who he was, quickly eliminating his opponents without having to present views so strongly that they might alienate the center of the party, which Gramm would eventually have to lead. But this strategy foundered. Whatever stature Gramm had, he lacked the charm and personal appeal of some of the other candidates. More importantly, Steve Forbes and Pat Buchanan squeezed Gramm from different sides and transformed the race on the right into a contest of where you are. Forbes appealed viscerally to the economic growth conservatives and to those seeking an outsider, while Buchanan laid much more emphasis on social conservatism than Gramm and then opened the new dimension of nationalism and economic populism. In Louisiana, Buchanan proved that being a bleeding-heart conservative had the stronger appeal. In his withdrawal speech Gramm called Buchanan's views "a dagger aimed at the heart of everything we stand for . . . . There has always been a recessive gene in the American character that has found protectionism appealing. But we have always been wise enough to reject it."[16] Shortly after Gramm endorsed Bob Dole. For Gramm, as well as for many other conservatives, there was not only a major difference between the right and the far right, but also far more distance between the right and the far right than there was between the right and the center.

The final race on the right showed only a glimpse of what it might have been. It was the contest between Steve Forbes's philosophy of the primacy of individual rights (including economic and property rights) and Pat Buchanan's idea of community virtue (to which many elements of rights would be subordinated). The fuzziness of certain political categories has dictated that both of these two positions have been classified recently on the right, whereas in reality they are in some sense at the poles not only of the conservative movement but also of the entire spectrum of the Republican Party. The Forbes-Buchanan contest would only have opened up in full if the center of the party had collapsed, leaving Buchanan and Forbes as the alternatives. Such a debate did get underway in Iowa, when Buchanan forces attacked Forbes for his social libertarianism and devotion to economic rights and when Forbes made the mistake of lashing out against the Christian Coalition. It was a measure of these two men's inexperience or overconfidence that they began to set their sights on each other before pursuing a common tactical objective of eliminating Dole.

Insiderism-Outsiderism

The 1996 Republican race was not just about ideology, but also followed the politics of 1992 by invoking the new "inside-outside" dimension that came into full bloom in that year. Outsiderism is a peculiar standard in that it celebrates the absence rather than the presence of something. Its virtue, depending on who is speaking, consists of not being part of the prevailing consensus, or not being a politician from Washington, or not being a politician of any kind, or not having thought about politics. A frequent tag line of Steve Forbes's television ads summed it up nicely: "not Washington."

Those who have made use of outsiderism also have tried, when and where possible, to claim that it is somehow beyond ideology. Again, it was Perot who blazed this trail of ideological plasticity in 1992 by asserting that the challenge of American politics was "to just fix it," whatever "it" might be. All of the outsiders, whatever their ideological positions, were appealing to the same undifferentiated anger and cynicism—hence Jerry Brown, Bill Clinton, and Pat Buchanan all intimated that at some level they were soul mates of Ross Perot, tapping into the same wellspring of popular frustration. In the same way in 1996, Steve Forbes, commenting on Buchanan's victory over Gramm in Louisiana, saw it as proof that "the people want someone from the outside and not from the political establishment," of which he (Forbes) could rightfully assert he was the truest model.

Because outsiderism seeks to negate many of the traditional claims to the nomination by virtue of who you are, it was a natural instrument of many candidates in the Republican field in 1996. Pat Buchanan, while locating himself primarily by ideology, also invoked the outsider theme and gave it one of its classic statements after his victory in New Hampshire: "You watch the establishment, all the knights and barons will be riding to the castle, pulling up the drawbridge in a minute. Because they are coming, all the peasants are coming with pitchforks after them." Morry Taylor can perhaps be credited for pioneering outsiderism in 1996 in its pure form. But clearly the candidates contesting most assiduously for the outsider slot were Lamar Alexander and Steve Forbes—a Morry Taylor with more smarts and much deeper pockets.

The race for the outside dimension was reminiscent of the race on the right. Lamar Alexander was squeezed from the far outside wing by Steve Forbes, somewhat like Phil Gramm was squeezed from the far right wing by Pat Buchanan. Alexander's initial claim to the mantle of the outsider—which came complete with an outsider uniform of red flannel shirts—was met with some skepticism. A competent, well-respected professional politician, Alexander presented himself as "Lamar!" the ultimate outsider who pledged to cut Congress's pay and "send them home" for half the year. This plan did not jibe with his career as an establishment Republican: clerk to pro-civil-rights Judge John Minor Wisdom, aide to Howard Baker and Richard Nixon, activist governor of Tennessee, and an able Secretary of Education. But Alexander had a ready answer; he had been in Washington "long enough to be vaccinated, but not infected." He explained: "I have worked for short terms for two Presidents, but unlike the other candidates—I came home. I have spent about half the last 25 years in public service and half in the private sector. I live in Nashville, not Washington, D.C. Where I come from has everything to do with where I stand."[17]

Alexander's outside bid was easily topped in January by Steve Forbes. Forbes was an outsider with a twist—in fact, every successful outsider has had some new item to differentiate him from the others. Forbes's was a flat tax plan that he invoked as a kind of talisman and universal panacea. While the logic and rhetoric of this plan had supply-side roots, and while Forbes could discuss it with great knowledge and acumen, its initial appeal was less ideological than symbolic. It represented an outside nostrum developed from a thinking beyond the beltway. Whatever the merits of the plan, no one ever conceived of becoming the nominee of a major party, let alone a President, on the strength of a single plan. Forbes's entry into the race had been welcomed by many who believed that, with his evident intelligence and gift of straightforwardness, he could add to the discussion. (Using the nomination campaign for this purpose is only one of many signs of its evolving function in American politics.) But after investing some twenty million dollars in December and January, mostly on television ads, Forbes suddenly found himself a contender rather than merely a discussant, and what makes for virtue in a discussant is not the same as what makes for virtue in a statesman. Forbes turned to the most obvious weapon of choice in seeking to win: a strident outsiderism. His ads made use of all the small popular techniques intrinsic to this genre, from a disparagement of the political art, to attacks on his competitors' compromises without regard to the context, and ultimately to disparagement of persons who have served their country and party for the very act of serving.

The Alexander-Forbes contest for the outside brought to American politics the embarrassing spectacle of two men in the prime of their careers squabbling like children over who was more truly an outsider. Forbes charged Alexander with insider political deals while governor of Tennessee, attacking Alexander's integrity. Alexander tried to use Forbes's total political inexperience against him, although this tactic only undercut his own argument. Alexander and others then turned to the expedient of labeling Forbes an insider of a different sort—a "Wall Street insider." By playing too long with the fire of outsiderism, both candidates in the end got burned by it. Perhaps, too, this campaign exhausted this genre of symbolic politics. A new century may require a new kind of trick.

The Races

Once the subplots of the races within these various slots had been resolved, the final races among the different slots were almost anticlimactic. Dole had the good fortune that the extremes had won the two contests for where you are, making the final races easier for him. In those races the insider beat far outsiderism, and the centrist beat the far right. In the race on the insider-outsider dimension, Dole ended by confronting Steve Forbes as the outsider rather than Lamar Alexander. Although Forbes initially looked like a greater challenge, Alexander was in fact a plausible alternative, while Forbes was not. Outsiderism has been a useful instrument in recent American politics for getting a candidate started, but pure outsiderism has never triumphed in a presidential campaign. The moment Forbes showed his inexperience in Iowa and Republicans saw the real face of amateurism, his campaign collapsed. Alexander's subsequent challenge to Dole was in fact far more muted on the dimension of outsiderism and played on his ABC theme (Alexander Beats Clinton) and his other promises for fresh ideas.

In the ideological race, Dole ended by confronting Buchanan rather than Gramm. Although Buchanan's campaign seemed threatening, this race worked greatly in Dole's favor, at least for winning the nomination. Gramm was a plausible alternative, Buchanan was not. Dole recognized this fact, and his supporters were known to have aided Buchanan in the Louisiana caucuses in hopes of hurting Gramm. As the occupant of the outer wing of the party, Buchanan's hope might be compared to that of George McGovern in 1972, when the wing proved strong enough to collapse the center and capture the party. But the Republican Party in 1996, judging from its success in the 1994 election, was not in a state of disarray of that magnitude. Notwithstanding all the sound and fury of January and February, the party was strong by ordinary standards, and was not about to turn itself over to its outer wing. By the time of the South Carolina primary, even majorities of self-identified members of the "religious right" were voting for Dole over Buchanan. Buchanan's victory over Gramm helped Dole in another way. A fear of the far right seemed to put pressure on politicians and voters to wrap up the race as quickly as possible, putting an end to any kind of deliberate consideration of alternatives.

The Republican Divisions and the Effect of Buchananism on the General Election

An analysis of a nomination contest must consider not only who won, but also how the race affected the party's image and chances of victory in the general election. Contests can harm a party's chances in two ways. The first is to bruise the victorious candidate and expose some of his weaknesses. Of course if there is to be a nomination contest at all, some collateral damage to the eventual nominee is both unavoidable and "fair." Primary campaigns involve the candidates' attacking one another, with the pack normally ganging up on the front-runner; and there is no way that a candidate in a serious competition can stay above the fray and avoid showing himself to the public. Bob Dole in 1996 certainly received his fair share of attack, and—with the money Steve Forbes had available—then some. And some of Dole's weaknesses as a candidate began to become strikingly manifest. It is no coincidence that negative appraisals of Dole in national polls surpassed positive appraisals for the first time in March 1996. Because damage to the nominee tends to occur in both parties, this result does not systematically damage one party more than the other. Only when one candidate avoids a nomination contest, as President Clinton was able to do in 1996, is a relative advantage gained.

The other way to harm a party's chances is to present an image of the party that displays serious rifts and associations with extremism. This kind of harm may be difficult if not impossible for the candidate to repair in full. Every primary contest reveals cracks and fissures in a coalition, so it is important to distinguish between cleavages that are bridgeable and those that are unbridgeable or that tend to drive away other voters in the party or electorate. Although there was much talk in February and March that the Republican Party was hopelessly fractured, in fact Dole did succeed quite well in uniting the bulk of the party for the fall contest. No wing of the party was openly in revolt or anywhere near it.

A major question of the 1996 nomination contests was whether the candidacy of Pat Buchanan, with all the attendant discussions of "extremism," did not damage the party and harm Dole's prospects. (Recall that the word "extremism" was used not only by Democrats and many observers, but also by many Republicans). Answering this question requires one first to determine whether the Republican Party was indeed associated with Buchanan, and then whether that association proved to be harmful. Both points are in dispute. In one sense, of course, Pat Buchanan was rejected definitively by the party. Among the party's elites Dole (as well as almost all the other candidates) made it abundantly clear that they had differences with Buchanan that went far beyond the ordinary range of candidate differences—differences that went to the "heart and soul" of the party. A number of prominent Republicans threatened to abandon the party altogether if he were nominated. Dole also made himself look more moderate by rejecting Buchanan. But setting aside all the statements and the mathematics, there was one major political story of 1996 and that was Pat Buchanan. Brief as his moment of national exposure was, its intensity was extraordinary. And rejected or not, he remained willy-nilly associated with the Republican Party.

Did this association harm the Republicans? Buchanan and his supporters argued that this was not the case—indeed, at least some argued that if Dole had embraced some of Buchanan's cases and positions more firmly, he would have done much better. The reason Dole and Kemp lost, wrote the columnist and Buchanan supporter Samuel Francis, "is that they deliberately chose to ignore and shut out the ideas, the proposals and the personalities that have emerged on the Populist Right during the last four years."[18] Of course, other conservatives such as Charles Krauthammer also argued that Dole failed to do enough to firm up his conservative base during the campaign, but by conservatism here Krauthammer did not mean to include Buchanan's positions from the far right.

The contrary interpretation is that the Buchanan candidacy saddled the Republicans with a huge image problem that was never overcome and that hurt Republicans with immigrants, especially Hispanics, with women, and with moderates across the board. Dole lost too many among the moderate Republicans and independents—those from these groups who are naturally part of the Republican vote share—to win the race. (This is a different proposition than the one that held, after the fashion of Jack Kemp's thinking, that Dole had to make huge *new* inroads among liberals in these groups in order to win.) In fact, Dole did lose a large part of the natural share of voters in these groups to Clinton.

Certainly from the side of the Clinton campaign, there was an artful effort to depict the Republican Party as extremist and to drive away votes from the middle. This not-so-subtle campaign that Democrats conducted during the first half of 1996 may not have been entirely "logical," in the sense that Dole and other leaders in the party explicitly sought to distance themselves from Buchanan, but this did not prevent the strategy from being effective. The essence of this effort was to create a slippery slope of extremism that ran from Buchanan to Gingrich and from Gingrich to Dole. Mixed in this cocktail was Oklahoma City, tied to a kind of zealous tribal nationalism, and then—to keep the connection going—the church burnings. The chords that played on this association were kept alive throughout the spring and summer and were the soft background music to the louder blare of the so-called "Mediscare" campaign.

Factors of Power

Students of nomination politics always pose the question of what factor of power counts the most: money, organization, or message. All in some measure are helpful, and they are not completely commensurable resources. The race of 1996 nevertheless provides some indication of the importance of each. As for money, Dole clearly raised the most, but Forbes had more money on hand to spend. As Forbes did not accept public funds, he was able to spend without limits in the early states where the other candidates faced spending limits. Forbes believed it was possible to launch a modern campaign based on message and money, with money paying for an intense media campaign to disseminate the message. The Forbes campaign certainly proves the importance of money—without it his campaign might not have gotten as far as Morry Taylor's—but it also shows that money alone is not enough. Forbes ended up paying millions for a handful of delegates.

There is also the resource of organization, which may be built or borrowed. All of the major candidates—with the exception of Steve Forbes—spent a good deal of time and effort trying to recruit a personal organization in Iowa and New Hampshire. No candidate tried to build a major personal organization past the first few states, and the task today would seem almost impossible with the large number of primaries being held on the same day. Pat Buchanan tried, with some success, to borrow elements of the Christian Coalition in Iowa and New Hampshire. Oddly, however, the most effective organization may have been the one borrowed from the regular party. In New Hampshire, Dole relied on Governor Steve Merrill and parts of the state organization. Although Dole lost the primary, it is a safe bet that without the help of Merrill Dole would have finished below Alexander. In South Carolina, which became the decisive primary where Dole defeated both Alexander and Buchanan, it was once again remnants of the official party under Governor David Beasley that spelled the difference. It is no exaggeration to say that the party man, Bob Dole, was saved in the end by the party organization.

Finally, the message is important. A strong message lifted Pat Buchanan to prominence without a large amount of money. And in the end Dole too won mostly because of his message. Republicans decided they did not want a candidate from the far right, and when the choice came between Buchanan and Dole, it was Dole's message—faintly articulated though it was—that proved decisive.

Notes

1. For a careful analysis of the invisible primary, which neither overstates nor understates its significance, see Emmet H. Buell, Jr., "The Invisible Primary," in William G. Mayer, ed., *In Pursuit of the White House* (Chatham, N.J.: Chatham House Publisher, 1996).

2. Actually, Hawaii and Alaska have held rounds of their caucuses even earlier, and this year Hawaii started on January 25 and Alaska held its first round from January 27–29. Alaska conducted a straw poll of the candidate preferences of the participants that received some national coverage and that reflected some of the national sentiments of the time. Buchanan won with 33 percent, Forbes had 31 percent, and Dole trailed far behind in third place with 17 percent.

3. Kevin Sack, "Why Dixie Was Buchanan's Waterloo," *New York Times*, March 14, 1996, B10.

4. David Frum, *Dead Right* (New York: Basic Books, 1994), 183.

5. T. R. Reid, "Ill-Starred, Stumbling, Ever Gutsy," *Washington Post*, June 4, 1980, A1.

6. Declaration speech, April 19, 1995 (Indianapolis). Lugar Web home page.

7. Declaration speech, April 19, 1995 (Indianapolis). Lugar Web home page.

8. Dole presidential announcement speech (Topeka), April 10, 1995. Dole Home Page.

9. David Talbot and Joe Sciacca, "Dole Hits N.E. Trail as Foes Battle in the South," *Boston Herald*, March 2, 1996, 1.

10. *Boston Globe*, Monday, March 4, 1996.

11. Buchanan announcement speech, March 1995. N. H. Buchanan web site.

12. Steve Forbes presidential announcement speech, September 22, 1995. Steve Forbes Home Page.

13. Richard Lugar, "Why I Ran for President," *Washington Post*, July 10, 1996, A17.

14. "Bob Dole. What Does He Stand For?" *The Economist*, March 16, 1996, 23.

15. Robert Marshall Wells, "Measuring Forbes' Impact," *Congressional Quarterly*, March 16, 1996, 716.

16. Peter G. Gosselin, "Gramm Exits with Blasts after Dual Dismal Showings," *Boston Globe*, February 15, 1996, 21.

17. Lamar Alexander presidential announcement speech (Maryville, Tennessee), February 28, 1995.

18. Samuel Francis, "Dole lost because he ignored Middle America," *Conservative Chronicle*, 11:47, November 20, 1996, 5.

Chapter 4

In the Doledrums: The Interregnum from March to September

By mid-March 1996, Bob Dole had effectively captured the Republican nomination. Yet the Republican convention was not scheduled to begin until mid-August. Because of a combination of primary front-loading, which ended the nominating race earlier than usual, and the Summer Olympics, which pushed the GOP convention back by a month, Dole and the Republicans faced an unprecedented five-month interregnum. Never before had a presumptive nominee had so much time to build up his strength—or lose momentum and sink out of the limelight. At this point Clinton held a significant but not overwhelming lead of eight to ten points. Throughout the five months, the Dole campaign seemed to be running in place. Bill Clinton, on the other hand, made excellent use of the time to consolidate and lengthen his lead.

This period was crucial, as the spring has traditionally been a time when incumbent Presidents either slip into trouble or consolidate their position in preparation for the fall campaign. Of postwar Presidents prior to 1996, all four who had built approval ratings over 50 percent in April before the election wound up winning; three of the four who had lower approval ratings lost (the exception was Harry S Truman).[1] The institutional context after 1994 was the most decisive factor leading to Clinton's resurgence, but his performance during the interregnum was also important. Indeed, the profile the President built at this time—compared to the floundering of Bob Dole—counted for more toward Clinton's victory than anything he did in the post-Labor Day campaign.

The five months can be roughly divided into an equal number of stages. At first, Clinton steadily widened his lead as Dole became bogged down in the Senate and as Democratic ads continued to take their toll. Dole's resignation from the Senate marked the beginning of a second stage, a stage with no clear winner, in which he and Clinton sparred in a political no man's land with no defining events and little public attention, except that which was focused on the miscues of each. In the third stage, Clinton capitalized on a flurry of legislative activity, capped by welfare reform. Fourth, Dole seemed to be poised for a comeback effort with the announcement in early August of his economic plan, the selection of Jack Kemp as his running mate, and a successful national convention. Finally, the Democrats counterattacked with presidential proposals and their own successful convention.

Except for the fourth stage, President Clinton remained in tactical control of the message and refused to allow Dole use of potentially damaging defining issues. Clinton maintained a huge financial advantage owing to his early campaign start and lack of serious primary opposition; Dole had been forced to come very close to his spending limit just to survive the nominating season. The President also embarked on a campaign of "micro-issues," announcing his support for school uniforms, curfews for teenagers, a national registry of sex offenders, an expansion of family leave legislation, and a nationwide 911-type number reserved for domestic violence cases, as well as his opposition to deadbeat dads, truancy, teenage smoking, and teen sex.[2] If anything held the mini-proposals together, it was an emphasis on the tie between traditional cultural values and activist government. As journalist E. J. Dionne said, "Clinton uses his most conservative rhetoric to revive support for the very government whose era is supposed to be over."[3] (As one cartoonist inveighed, the President was opposed to big government but supported lots and lots of little government.) If it could be said that the structure of the presidency in the post-Cold War era was at least partially miniaturized, Bill Clinton was not merely a hapless occupant of that structure but an architect.

Stage Number One: Neither a Talker Nor a Doer

Starting in mid-March, with the nomination wrapped up but almost out of money, the Dole campaign focused on the question of what to do for the next five months. The decision was to use Dole's position as Senate Majority Leader as a platform for his ideas and a showcase for his political skills. Thematically, the goal was to show Americans that Dole was "a doer, not a talker." He may not have the silvery-tongued eloquence of a Bill Clinton, but he could get things done. He could also be guaranteed consistent "free media," an important consideration for a campaign nearly out of money.

While the strategy had a certain degree of plausibility—Dole had in fact benefitted in January from his willingness to end the government shutdown—it overlooked one crucial fact. Bob Dole was no longer Senate Majority Leader; he was the Republican nominee for the presidency who also happened to be the Senate Majority Leader. The rules of the Senate make it possible for a determined minority to prevent action, and Senate Democrats proved willing and able to use those rules to the fullest extent to embarrass Dole and deprive him of significant accomplishment. It was unrealistic to expect that the Senate minority would willingly participate in a strategem aimed at the downfall of their President.

Some significant measures were passed, like the Freedom to Farm Act, which ended the New Deal agricultural regime, a telecommunications reform act, and an experimental line-item veto. Some other measures, like health insurance reform, were put back on a legislative fast track after languishing for months. But for the most part, rather than prove he was a "doer," Dole was tied down for two months in legislative minutiae and bickering.

No overarching budget deal was reached; no deal on welfare, Medicaid, or Medicare. Dole was badly embarrassed in April when he lost a Senate vote on medical savings accounts, and was put on the defensive by Senate Democrats who brought amendments attaching a minimum wage increase to numerous pieces of legislation. Only once was Dole able to seize the initiative, when Republicans proposed a rollback of Bill Clinton's 1993 gasoline tax increase, but even this idea became entangled with the minimum wage battle.

Consequently, Bob Dole was seen daily as an insider, and an ineffective one at that. He also was trapped in Washington, unable to campaign or formulate a consistent campaign message. Columnist Mary McGrory observed, "Everything the voting public is learning about Dole these days comes from the Senate floor."[4] By May, he had little legislation to show for this strategy and nothing but worsening poll numbers.

Dole's problems in this regard were mostly not of his own making. They were, rather, inherent in his position. Pundits during this period liked to point out that never before had a Senate Majority Leader faced an incumbent President in a presidential election. And indeed, only five other members of the top House or Senate majority leadership have ever actively sought the presidency, and none before Dole actually won their party's nomination. Among sitting House Speakers, Henry Clay lost in the electoral college in 1824, before the era of party nominations (he also lost in 1832 and 1844 when he was not Speaker). Of those seeking party nomination, Thomas B. Reed failed miserably in 1896, Champ Clark failed in 1912, and John Nance Garner lost out to Franklin Roosevelt in 1932 (only to become Roosevelt's running mate); Senate Majority Leader Lyndon Johnson failed in 1960 (also settling for the vice presidency).[5] While each failure was surrounded by its own particular circumstances, the pattern also reveals underlying structural difficulties in simultaneously attempting to govern Congress and run for President. In yet another example of the benefits derived by Bill Clinton from the Republican victory of 1994, Bob Dole's elevation from Senate Minority Leader to Senate Majority Leader forced Dole to share in the responsibility of governing, vastly complicated his strategy, pulled him down during a critical phase of the campaign, and ultimately drove him from the Senate entirely. Clinton's strategy of running as a check on Congress found a perfect foil in Dole.

Bill Clinton's lead steadily grew throughout this period to about twenty points. His actual numbers increased only slightly; most of the expanded gap between the candidates reflected Dole's plummeting standing. It gradually became clear that Dole's legislative strategy of emphasizing performance was not working and was not likely to work. Instead, it was dragging him down and making it impossible for him to run to the outside of Bill Clinton.

This realization led to a radical shift of direction. At first, some suggested Dole might keep his post as Senate Majority Leader but hand over day-to-day duties to Whip Trent Lott; then some thought he might resign his leadership post altogether. In the end, in a closely guarded decision, Dole chose the boldest (or, depending on one's point of view, most desperate) course. On May 15, he announced to stunned colleagues that he would be leaving the Senate. Aided by speechwriter/novelist Mark Helprin, the laconic Dole turned eloquent: He would fight for the presidency, he said, "with nothing to fall back on and nowhere to go but the White House or home."

On the downside, the decision accentuated Dole's failure to make a positive mark legislatively. And by leaving the Senate Dole surrendered a platform from which to gain substantial free media and opened the campaign to charges of desperation. The White House accused

Dole of being a "quitter" who cared more about his political ambitions than about serving his constituents as he had been elected to do. A Democratic ad to that effect was televised briefly, advising voters, "He [Dole] told us he would lead. Then he told us he was quitting, giving up, leaving behind the gridlock he helped create."

Dole's resignation, effective June 11, accomplished several things. Most importantly, it freed Dole from both the time commitment and political bog of the Senate. It allowed him greater tactical flexibility and made it easier for him to take the strategic offensive. It promised to release him from captivity as an "insider." And it temporarily energized Republicans by reassuring them that Dole had the "fire in the belly" necessary to make a full-fledged commitment to the presidential race. Conservative intellectuals, many of whom had nearly written off Dole, almost universally acclaimed his departure from the Senate.[6] Like Cortez, who burned his ships upon arrival in the New World, Dole had no option but to press forward with all his energy.

Stage Number Two: Rollercoaster to Nowhere

Dole immediately tried to sculpt a new image by campaigning tie-less in Chicago. Thus opened the second stage of the gray period of the interregnum, a stage lasting from mid-May until mid-July. This interval was devoid of any decisive events but was characterized by a rollercoaster series of miscues and misfortunes suffered by both campaigns. In the end, Dole had gained nothing.

First, the White House, which had performed nearly flawlessly for several months, began to experience difficulties reminiscent of the bad days of 1993–1994. In late May, doubts about Clinton's presidential stature were revived when he made salacious comments regarding a 500-year-old (or 14-year-old, depending on one's perspective) Inca mummy on loan from Peru. "If I were a single man," Clinton said at a Connecticut fundraiser, "I might ask that mummy out. That's a good-looking mummy." In an amazing example of poor timing, the President's lawyer, Robert Bennett, stirred a firestorm of criticism when he argued near Memorial Day that the President was exempt from lawsuits while in office because he was protected by the Soldiers and Sailors Relief Act of 1940. As commander-in-chief, Bennett said, Clinton was on "active duty." Outraged veterans groups forced Bennett to withdraw the brief within a matter of days.

On May 27, the Whitewater investigation gained new momentum

and credibility when Independent Counsel Kenneth Starr obtained convictions of Arkansas Governor Jim Guy Tucker and close Clinton associates James and Susan MacDougal. Media predictions of the demise of Whitewater as an issue were quickly retracted, and attention turned to a new set of trials, this time involving White House aide Bruce Lindsey as an unindicted co-conspirator.

The White House was soon engulfed in another major imbroglio when it was discovered in the course of the "Travelgate" investigation that Hillary Clinton had likely made misleading statements about her role in the 1993 firings, and that the White House security staff under the direction of Craig Livingstone had acquired hundreds of confidential FBI files, many of them on prominent Republicans. The latter revelation ballooned into a scandal of its own, "Filegate," as the number of files involved steadily escalated and concerns mounted of a White House "enemies list." Secret Service testimony flatly contradicted the accounts emanating from the White House, and no one seemed to be able to remember who hired Livingstone, though several indications pointed to the First Lady. Indeed, no one seemed even to remember who Livingstone was or what he did. White House aide George Stephanopoulos had told the *Pittsburgh Post-Gazette* in 1994 that Livingstone "does a terrific job. All I know is that anything that has to do with security or logistics—Craig's going to take care of it. . . . And he knows how to cut through the bureaucracy and get things done." When Filegate erupted, Stephanopoulos said of Livingstone, "I don't know him that well. He's a guy that was around."[7]

Meanwhile, a new spate of revelatory books came out, all potentially damaging. Reporter Bob Woodward's book on the early stages of the 1996 campaign revealed that Hillary Clinton had used a new age psychic to have "conversations" with Eleanor Roosevelt and Mahatma Gandhi. Former FBI agent Gary Aldrich published a book, *Unlimited Access*, claiming that President Clinton had repeatedly snuck out of the White House for illicit romantic liaisons at the Washington Marriott, though it turned out that the story had reached Aldrich thirdhand and had not been verified independently. From the left side of the spectrum came an investigative tome by Roger Morris, *Partners in Power*, which essentially confirmed the general outline of the "character" case against Bill and Hillary Clinton, but the book received little media attention. By mid-1996 revelations about Bill Clinton had become news on the order of "dog bites man," boring to reporters and voters alike. Other presidencies might have collapsed under the weight of these and other scandals and accusations, but a large proportion of the public "discounted" them, conceding their probable validity but choosing not to care.

Dole failed to take full advantage of Clinton's difficulties. His campaign, caught off-guard by his resignation, was not prepared for an intensified campaign schedule. For at least a month, much of his new-found time was wasted.[8] Dole pinpointed a few issues like missile defense and welfare reform and attacked the administration for Filegate. Some consideration was also given to the idea of announcing a "shadow cabinet" in an attempt to make the election more programmatic and less personal, though the idea was quietly dropped. Because Dole's campaign was broke, the Republican National Committee also reluctantly took up the task of countering widespread Democratic advertising, though there had already been a dangerous delay in responding to the Democratic attacks that had saturated the airwaves since the previous fall. Nevertheless, the accumulation of White House difficulties did have some effect and the gap between Clinton and Dole seemed to be shrinking. One CNN poll even showed Dole behind by only six points, though the poll was taken immediately after Dole's moving exit from the Senate on June 11 and thus reflected an unnatural bounce. Other polls showed a gap in the low teens.

Whatever gains Dole may have made at Clinton's expense were promptly negated as a result of his own mistakes. As Dole faltered, Clinton was able to minister to the national wounds following the explosion of TWA flight 800 and bask in the ceremonial glory of the Atlanta Olympics.

Dole stumbled badly four times. First, seeking a way out of the Republicans' abortion dilemma, Dole proposed adding general language to the platform preamble emphasizing that people of all views were welcome in the Republican Party. No sooner was it apparent that this compromise was essentially satisfactory to most factions than Dole changed course and insisted on inserting the tolerance language in the abortion plank itself. This proposal enraged social conservatives, who asked why abortion should be singled out, while it encouraged pro-choice advocates to hope that if they exerted enough pressure Dole could be forced into further concessions. The modified tolerance proposal thus stirred up a hornet's nest with little for Dole to gain and much to lose. By highlighting Republican disunity on abortion, the renewed controversy also served to obscure the Democratic disunity caused by Clinton's veto of the partial birth abortion ban. That ban of particularly gruesome late-term abortions had received the votes of 72 Democrats in the House and a dozen in the Senate, including Richard

Gephardt and Daniel Patrick Moynihan, and Clinton's veto had earned him the wrath of the nation's Catholic bishops. Just at the moment the Republicans had found a way to paint the administration as extremist on abortion, their own platform flap intervened. That dispute was not resolved until the eve of the convention, and then in a way that embarrassed Dole by stripping most of the tolerance language from the platform.

Second, in response to White House attacks that he was indebted to tobacco interests, Dole argued that tobacco was not always addictive. Put on the defensive and haunted by "Butt Man" at campaign stops, Dole lashed out at Katie Couric on NBC's Today Show, accusing her of doing the bidding of the Democratic National Committee by pestering him about tobacco. The old, "mean" Bob Dole broke through, irritating the nation, frightening small children, and delighting the White House.

Third, in another ham-handed attempt to move toward the center, Dole announced that a repeal of the 1994 assault weapon ban would no longer be a priority for him. Then, compounding his difficulties, he said days later that he might actually veto a repeal if it reached his desk. Forced to explain and backtrack, Dole convinced virtually no one that he had really changed his mind but did manage to infuriate the National Rifle Association, which threatened on July 16 to withhold its endorsement from Dole for his apostasy. (It later made good on that threat.)

Finally, Dole appeared rigid and defensive when he rejected an invitation to speak to the National Association for the Advancement of Colored People. Pointing to the liberal record of NAACP chairman (and former Democratic Congressman) Kweisi Mfume, Dole claimed the invitation was a "setup." He thus appeared to many Americans as a candidate who would only deign to speak to groups already favorable to him, hardly the sort of behavior one would desire from someone seeking to be the President of all Americans (curiously, President Clinton paid no similar price for turning down an invitation to speak to the Christian Coalition in August).

Arguably, the content of Dole's second stage missteps was much less important than the cumulative image they conveyed. In all, Dole presented the picture of an unfocused candidate with no clear message, distracted by peripheral questions, alternatingly rigid and vacillating, and unable to satisfy either his friends or his enemies. At the end of the second stage Dole was in no stronger position than he had been at the beginning of June.

Stage Number Three: Presidential Action and the Symbiotic Politics of Repulsion

In the third stage of the interregnum, Bill Clinton moved—with the help of the Republican Congress—to establish a stronger legislative record on which to run in November. Clinton and congressional Republicans thus formed a symbiotic relationship in which both rose together at the expense of their copartisans, Bob Dole and the congressional Democrats. Clinton's insistence on the minimum wage hike finally paid off, as Republican resistance collapsed and Congress passed the measure in late July. Congress also passed a health insurance reform measure improving portability and restricting the denial of insurance on the basis of preexisting conditions. Finally, and most importantly, Congress passed and the President signed a major overhaul of the federal welfare system.

Republican House leaders had long hoped to pass (for the third time) a welfare reform-Medicaid reform package that would force Clinton into a highly visible third veto. The change of strategy on welfare was indicative of the broader strategic dilemmas faced by Republicans in Congress, many of whom felt they had to decide whether to take a gamble to help Dole or to take steps to secure their own future as the congressional majority. By early July, Republican backbenchers, fearing for their seats and beginning to despair of Dole, began pressuring the leadership to allow a stand-alone welfare bill with the aim of passing a reform the President might sign.[9] If he did not, the issue would be alive for Dole to exploit; if he did, the reasoning went, he would do so at the cost of alienating his base. Dole, understanding the danger to his own position, sought to maintain the welfare-Medicaid linkage by applying pressure on Congress through the nation's Republican governors, but to no avail.[10]

Once the stand-alone welfare bill passed Congress, there was, predictably, furious debate in the White House over whether to cast another welfare reform veto. Anonymous presidential aides reported, "War is going on in the White House,"[11] and initial indications were that Clinton might indeed veto. Campaigning in California, the President seemed to ridicule the legislation, saying, "You can put wings on a pig, but you don't make him an eagle."[12] To the surprise of many Republicans and the consternation of liberal Democrats, the President decided to sign. Willingness to sign welfare reform was perhaps the crown jewel in Clinton's election-year move to the right, an act the President's advisers hoped would provide unassailable innoculation against Republican attacks. Indeed, adviser Dick Morris had warned the President that a third welfare reform veto could be "politically catastrophic."[13] In the end, Congress got a major legislative accomplishment, Bill Clinton finally fulfilled his 1992 promise to "end welfare as we know it," and Bob Dole lost a powerful campaign issue.[14]

The longer-term political implications of the welfare bill were more difficult to assess. If the bill did not fatally alienate Bill Clinton's base in 1996, as Republicans hoped, it held the very real prospect of rending the Democratic Party in the future. Half of the House and Senate Democrats voted no, and two-thirds of the House Democrats who voted yes shifted their position only after Clinton announced he would sign the bill. The party's liberals were infuriated, though often privately, and the most influential liberal media organs bitterly decried the President's decision. The normally supportive *Washington Post* exclaimed that "only the terminally gullible could think after this much unashamed waffling and gyrating on Bill Clinton's part that his decision to sign the bill has anything to do with principle or substance. . . . This decision was about political expediency and opportunism—both very old and nothing to brag about. . . . The president's disingenuous defense of the decision made the matter worse. It added to the squalor that it sought to cover up."[15] As David S. Broder remarked, "Already, it is clear that [Clinton] has driven a wedge down the center of his party and caused a split that is likely to echo in the primaries of the year 2000—and beyond. . . . More than anything he has done until now, Clinton's welfare decision puts his party's future at risk."[16] For the time being, at least, the damage seemed containable; Clinton was protected by the specter of unified Republican control of government.

The welfare reform bill underscored three crucial points. First, unless his standing began to improve dramatically, Dole would be on his own. Republicans in Congress, under pressure themselves, had served notice that it was every man for himself; and indeed the third stage was only a prelude to presidential-congressional cooperation in the fall on issues like immigration. By the end of the year, Clinton's legislative success score had risen from 36 percent in 1995 to 55 percent in 1996, the largest one-year gain recorded since *Congressional Quarterly* began calculating scores in the 1950s.[17] Congress thus deviated from the successful strategy of obstruction and confrontation used by previous midterm congresses to discredit and defeat opposition Presidents (as after 1894 and 1930).[18] Second, Clinton's reversal on welfare underscored the degree to which the campaign and American politics in general was being fought out on a conservative playing field. Democrats took pains to argue that action on the minimum wage and health care meant they had regained the initative, and in some respects they were right. Yet if one took 1994 as a baseline, the argument rang hollow. In the central debate of 1994, Democrats argued that health care was in crisis and required fundamental transformation while welfare needed incremental tinkering; Republicans argued the reverse, that circumstances called for incremental health reform and a fundamental transformation of welfare. What happened in July 1996 was incremental health reform joined to fundamental welfare reform. If the 1996 version of Bill Clinton could call that outcome a victory, it was only because he and his party had been forced to move so far to starboard since the day in January 1994 when he vowed to veto any health reform providing less than universal coverage. Finally, enactment of welfare reform was but one event at the time that indicated just how difficult Bob Dole's task was going to be, regardless of any rightward tide that might be flowing in American politics.

In the same week that Bob Dole lost welfare reform as a major campaign issue, economic figures for the second quarter of 1996 showed growth of 4.2 percent, one of the best quarters of the Clinton presidency and far better than the modest two percent growth rates the economy had averaged since 1993. The stock market, which had taken a sharp downward turn earlier in July, recovered nicely. And an Arkansas jury handed down acquittals on the most important charges in the latest Whitewater trial. Everything, it seemed, was going the President's way. By the beginning of August, polls showed Clinton's lead growing again to the twenty percent range while his approval ratings remained over 50 percent. No President with approval ratings over 50 percent that late in the year had ever lost reelection. Furthermore, several state polls showed Dole's standing actually worsening after visits to Michigan, California, Pennsylvania, and Texas.[19] Other polls showed Republicans generally in trouble; for the first time since Clinton's inauguration, the Democratic Party was viewed more favorably than the Republican Party, and Republicans had higher negative than positive ratings.[20]

Consequently, the buzzards began circling Dole. Republican governors and other Republican leaders started grumbling in mid-July. As the weeks passed, numerous observers declared the race essentially over. Some conservative columnists like George Will and Cal Thomas suggested that Dole should do the honorable thing and step down as the party's nominee, while a few even advocated that the convention ditch him in favor of a more electable candidate. Such proposals were implausible in the extreme; as long as Dole wanted the nomination it was his, and there was no indication that he no longer wanted it. The talk did, however, add to a sense of gloom in Republican circles.

Yet there remained glimmers of hope for Dole. While leading handily in head-to-head polls, Clinton did not fare nearly as well in polls on the abstract question of whether he deserved reelection, where he held a bare plurality. In a *New York Times* poll, 52 percent said that they did not know enough about where the President stood to say what he might do if he won reelection.[21] According to a detailed analysis by Everett Carll Ladd of the Roper Center, polls showed very little shift from early 1995 in public opinion about issues; furthermore, the Republican/ conservative position was favored on two-thirds to three-fourths of issues.[22] Finally, in perhaps the best indication that Clinton's huge lead was not written in stone, one poll indicated that Clinton would actually lose a head-to-head matchup with former President George Bush by 49–43.[23]

However, potential softness in Clinton's lead did not mean the race was predestined to narrow. He was, after all, running against Bob Dole, not George Bush or (at least explicitly) himself. And the lead would not melt of its own accord; Dole would have to show considerably more boldness, discipline, and fire than he had yet demonstrated; he would have to find a way to turn the conservative disposition of the electorate into a voting reality. For the first three stages of the interregnum, Dole had done little more than run in place, while Clinton bolstered and solidified his lead.

Stage Number Four: A Moment of Revival

The fourth stage of the interregnum began when Dole unveiled his long-awaited economic program on August 5. The program was one leg of a tripod aimed at bringing Dole back to within striking distance by Labor Day; the other two legs would be his vice-presidential selection and the Republican National Convention in San Diego. By mid-August, all three had been executed with considerable success. Though the benefits were short-lived, they established at least a credible campaign.

Economic plan

For the second time, Dole surprised friends and critics alike by taking the boldest possible step with his economic plan: a 15 percent across-the-board tax cut coupled with a $500 per child tax credit, a one-half reduction in the capital gains tax rate, and a variety of other tax cuts. The total static revenue loss was estimated at $548 billion over six years, or about five percent of federal revenue. Dole called his tax plan a first step toward a complete overhaul of the tax system, and promised to "end the IRS as we know it." He also proposed that tax increases require a 60 percent vote in Congress rather than a simple majority, codifying an internal rule already adopted by the House in January 1995. Dole's economic plan was aimed at achieving an economic growth rate of 3.5 percent.

The tax cut plan was the product of nearly three months of serious consideration and debate in the Dole camp. Yet its origins could be traced to Ronald Reagan, who first proved the enduring political appeal of an across-the-board tax cut. Christine Todd Whitman played the formula to perfection when she ousted tax-raising New Jersey Governor Jim Florio in 1993 on the basis of a pledge to cut income taxes 30 percent; Whitman's example played an important role in the Dole deliberations.[24] The Republican budget of 1995 and the Steve Forbes primary campaign also had an impact on the Dole plan.[25] Finally, as the day of decision approached for Dole, an ad hoc conference of Republican leaders, organized by Jack Kemp, urged Dole on July 23 to adopt a major tax cut.

The plan Dole ultimately chose carried with it risks that became more apparent as the campaign progressed. Most notably, the economy might continue to improve, thus negating the salience of the economic issue. Indeed, one set of Dole strategists (who were ousted in early September) held that the tax cut plan would not work in a relatively strong economy; they argued for moral and social issues to take a central place, both as a theme in itself and as a "backdoor" to the "character issue."[26] They believed also the plan was out of character for Dole, the inveterate deficit hawk (and frequent tax raiser). Critics could (and did) argue that the plan made a mockery of Dole's attempt to contrast his genuine and straightforward qualities with Clinton's willingness to say and do anything to get elected. The *New York Times* accused Dole of pandering, saying "Mr. Dole is a historic deficit hawk, with a longstanding contempt for politicians who call for tax cuts without explaining where they will cut the budget to make up the lost revenue. Last week Mr. Dole became what he has always disdained."[27]

Given the performance of George Bush and Bill Clinton on taxes, Dole would inevitably face a considerable amount of public skepticism over a tax cutting promise. Without specified spending cuts to cover the revenue loss, the plan would threaten to balloon the deficit; with spending cuts attached, the plan would invite redistributionist assaults.[28] Emphasis on the need to change economic policy would also rob congressional Republicans of the opportunity to claim a share of the credit for the expansion. And an emphasis on tax cuts, while in theory not contrary to the goal of a balanced budget, nevertheless made it difficult to point out the little-noted but vitally important Congressional Budget Office projections released in August showing the deficit rising dramatically after 1996 to over $400 billion by 2006 without further action.

Economists were naturally divided over the merits of the proposal. It was not the substantive debate that was central, however, but the political implications. In that realm, the plan seemed to the Dole campaign to offer benefits in excess of the risks.

First, by offering a bold economic plan and making it the centerpiece of his campaign, Dole refused to give Bill Clinton a free ride on the economy. Despite encouraging signs, the state of the economy remained somewhat ambiguous, and much would depend on the ability of the parties to define in the public mind whether the glass was half full or half empty. That this calculation was reasonable—that there was room for Dole to make headway on the economic issue—was indicated the same week the economic plan came out. At that time a *New York Times* poll indicated that a 46-38 plurality believed Republicans to be better equipped to handle the economy than Democrats, despite the ongoing recovery.[29] For the economic strategy to have a chance of succeeding, however, the case had to be pressed vigorously and consistently.

Second, the tax plan held the potential of establishing a clear defining issue that the Dole campaign hoped Bill Clinton could not coopt or fudge. From welfare to cultural values, Clinton had been able to steadily appropriate Republican themes, depriving Dole of a defining issue. Taxes, however, are the very lifeblood of government, and a tax cut of the magnitude proposed by Dole struck directly at the heart of welfare liberalism. Clinton could not copy the Dole plan except weakly. In the battle to define Bill Clinton as a big government liberal, the tax issue was one of the few issues in Bob Dole's arsenal that stood a serious chance of succeeding. According to Dole's pollster, "From a purely political perspective, we want to draw a very bright line for the voters and give them a clear choice between someone who's committed to reducing taxes and balancing the budget, and someone who is committed to raising taxes and never balancing the budget."[30] The tax cut plan invited a single potentially devastating question: If the era of big government was really over, why should Americans still have to pay big government taxes? (It was, however, a question Dole never asked.)

Third, the Dole tax plan held out the prospect of unifying and energizing all factions of the Republican Party. Those concerned primarily with economic growth were attracted to the income tax rate cuts and the capital gains cut. Those concerned primarily with questions of political liberty were attracted to the message of returning power from government back to the people. And "pro-family" conservatives applauded the $500-per- child tax credit and the overall lessening of the tax burden on families.

Fourth, the tax cut revived the message of growth and optimism that had been one of Ronald Reagan's greatest legacies to the Republican Party, a message that had been largely obscured during the great budget cataclysm of 1995–96. "At this moment," Dole said, "Bill Clinton and his party are the defenders of the status quo and we are the party of change." The tax cut sought to set a trap for the Clinton administration, the same trap it fell into in 1994. That year, Clinton's response to the Contract with America was to attack it as a reversion to Reaganism, forgetting that Reagan remained much more popular than he was. Dole's economic plan invited the same kind of response, and initially received it. It was never clear why Clinton preferred to run against Reagan rather than against Dole, and eventually he stopped. Almost a decade after he left office, Ronald Reagan was still being underestimated at Georgetown cocktail parties, even as the guests scrambled to coopt his themes.

The White House's immediate and vehement reaction to the Dole economic plan—Clinton said with uncharacteristic firmness that he was "unalterably opposed"—betrayed a sense that, for the first time in months, Dole might pose a threat worth taking seriously. Almost immediately, Democrats started airing ads criticizing the Dole plan in 25 swing states, attacks that the Dole campaign lacked the resources to counter.[31]

Vice-presidential selection

The second leg of Dole's comeback strategy was the vice-presidential selection, announced on August 10 in Russell, Kansas. In a third surprise in as many months, he named Jack Kemp as his running mate. Kemp had been George Bush's Secretary of Housing and Urban Development, a successful American Football League quarterback, and member of the House of Representatives, where he co-authored the Kemp-Roth tax cut at the heart of Ronald Reagan's economic policy. The enthusiasm with which the choice of Kemp was announced, however, belied the long and tortuous process leading to his selection.

Because of Dole's age and lack of charisma, campaign officials and outside observers agreed that the vice-presidential pick would probably be more important in 1996 than usual. Dole expressed three basic goals: to find someone who had the unquestioned stature and qualifications to become President, someone with whom Dole felt personally comfortable, and someone who would help the ticket. In short, Dole hoped for a "10." In addition, the vice-presidential choice had to unify the party, neither driving away moderates nor alienating the party's conservative base. Finally, the campaign had to decide whether to seek a running mate who would add special regional strength in swing states or who would provide some national boost.

Speculation on the "veepstakes" began as soon as Super Tuesday ended, leaving an unusually long period for consideration by Dole and jockeying by prospective candidates. Attention centered almost immediately on Colin Powell, and remained there until shortly before the convention. If he would not run for President, many Republicans hoped he would accept the vice-presidential nod, which would entail no fundraising and much less risk. Such a selection might irritate social conservatives, but Powell would mollify moderates. And none could question his ability to assume the presidency. Furthermore, polls showed Powell adding a healthy national punch to the ticket. A survey that showed Dole by himself behind by 17 points narrowed to a four point deficit with Powell added to the ticket.[32] The one insuperable obstacle to this "dream ticket" was that Colin Powell, despite consistent speculation and entreaties, did not want to run.

Until early August, more realistic speculation swirled around two other sets of figures: governors and senators. The governors offered regional strength and promised to highlight the party's commitment to problem-solving at the state and local level. The senators also offered some regional strength and were more likely to meet Dole's comfort test. The governors came first, with attention initially focused on the four Republican governors of the upper Midwest, an area assumed to be a crucial battleground: John Engler of Michigan, Tommy Thompson of Wisconsin, George Voinivich of Ohio, and Jim Edgar of Illinois. Other governors or former governors were also mentioned, including Christine Todd Whitman of New Jersey, former Governor Carroll Campbell of South Carolina, and Tom Ridge of Pennsylvania, yet all ran afoul of some disqualifying problem— lack of stature, inability to materially aid the ticket, and/or unacceptability to one of the party's factions.

As the gubernatorial pool began to thin, the senators came to the fore. John McCain of Arizona was on the list the longest, as a man of evident stature who would reinforce Dole's war record (McCain was a Vietnam POW). He was joined much later by Sen. Don Nickles (Oklahoma) and Sen. Connie Mack (Florida); Kay Bailey Hutchison of Texas was a long shot. Nickles was a close Dole associate in the Senate and was well liked by both economic and social conservatives, while Mack offered strength in pivotal Florida. A week before the decision, Jack Kemp predicted Mack would be the one.

Other names, some prominent and others not, were floated. House Budget Committee Chairman John Kasich of Ohio and California Attorney General Dan Lungren were said to bring youthful vibrance and inroads into important regions, but lacked national visibility. Dick Cheney, Donald Rumsfeld, and James Baker met the national prominence and comfort tests, but had little constituency outside the beltway. Even retiring Democratic Sen. Sam Nunn of Georgia was floated briefly, to his own consternation. Seldom had a vice-presidential net been so widely cast.[33] But Dole was not satisfied with his choices and ordered the search broadened. This brought him in contact with Bill Bennett, who was approached by the Dole camp in early August. Expressing no interest, Bennett relayed the story of his meeting to Kemp. Kemp told his friend, "I'd have said yes."[34] About a week later Kemp got his chance.

The Kemp choice was unexpected, not even showing up on the proverbial radar screen until two days before it was announced. It was a surprise, above all, because Kemp almost certainly flunked the comfort test that was reportedly so important to Dole. In the 1980s, Dole and Kemp had frequently clashed, mostly over the priority of tax cuts versus deficit reduction. At times the conflict had grown quite personal, and it had continued into the 1988 campaign for the Republican presidential nomination. The tension between the two men was as much stylistic as substantive: Dole, the stolid Midwesterner, and Kemp, the sunny Californian, never fully understood each other.

When Republicans regained control of Congress in the 1994 elections, some reconciliation seemed possible. Dole even appointed Kemp to head a congressional commission on tax reform in 1995. Kemp squandered whatever goodwill might have been accrued when he belatedly endorsed Steve Forbes prior to the 1996 New York primary, after Forbes had savaged Dole but at the very moment Dole seemed poised to clinch the nomination. On these grounds, the conservative *National Review* wrote off the possibility of a Kemp selection, pointing out that Kemp had "trampled all over Dole's cherished virtue of loyalty with his Keystone Kops endorsement of Steve Forbes."[35] Aside from the past friction, Kemp presented the additional risk of straying dangerously from the party line on issues like immigration and affirmative action; even after he moved closer to Dole's position, his past views made it difficult for him to help Dole take the offensive on those issues. Furthermore, he lacked a solid geographical base that he could be guaranteed to deliver.

Dole was ultimately drawn to Kemp despite these drawbacks. Several considerations were crucial. Kemp was thought to possess a national stature and potential to help the ticket across the board that was matched by few if any of the other contenders. Yet, while he possessed national appeal, Kemp was believed—as it turned out, incorrectly—to put into play both California (where he grew up) and New York (where he played football and served in Congress). Furthermore, his selection was capable of unifying and energizing the party. He was strongly pro-life but was also liked and respected by the moderates. He promised to bring a dynamism to the campaign that it had largely lacked. The day before the choice was announced, a senior Dole aide said that Kemp was an attractive possibility because "he, simultaneously, is the most popular Republican among Republicans and the most popular Republican among Democrats."[36] And he was one of the few people in the Republican Party who could address both of the questions that were likely to plague the party through the election: do the Republicans care about people and do they really mean they will cut taxes? The first question, whether fairly or unfairly, had permeated the budget debate, and was arguably central to the wide "gender gap" in polling. The second question was driven by public cynicism about tax cuts that had been fueled by Bush's and Clinton's violation of tax promises. In this sense, Kemp was probably the best available choice, exuding compassion and perfectly complementing the thrust of the Dole economic plan. Despite past friction between Dole and Kemp, the alliance was not as farfetched as it seemed. Dole had already moved significantly in the direction of the Kemp agenda. During the internal debate over the tax cut proposal, analysts noted that "to a degree that many Republican strategists said amazes them, Dole appears to have already undergone a conversion, on both intellectual and political levels, to the need for tax-cutting, 'pro-growth' policies that he once held in such disdain."[37] Indeed, Dole had apparently expressed a vague interest in Kemp as a running mate in early 1995.[38] For his part, Kemp had many friends on the Dole campaign, including Dole's campaign manager Scott Reed, communications director John Buckley, and domestic advisers Vin Weber and Donald Rumsfeld.[39] Throughout his campaign Dole relied heavily for ideas on Empower America, the think tank cofounded by Kemp.[40]

Republicans and Democratic strategists alike were nevertheless stunned by the choice of Kemp. President Clinton, vacationing in Wyoming, expressed "shock." The White House quickly tried to paint Kemp as an "extremist," the White House epithet of choice, and almost as quickly backed off. Behind the scenes, Democrats expressed concern that Kemp could change the dynamics of the race, while former New York Governor Mario Cuomo openly declared a Dole-Kemp ticket to be "formidable."

The convention

The third and final leg of the Dole comeback strategy rested on the national convention, held in San Diego. Republicans, stung by criticism of their 1992 convention and their first year and a half of congressional control, made a concerted effort to present a smiling and "inclusive" face to the nation. "The first order of business," predicted journalist R. W. Apple, Jr., "is to make San Diego the non-Houston."[41] Pat Buchanan, whose 1992 prime-time convention speech roused the faithful but appeared harsh to the media and to many voters, was not even allowed to speak. Instead, the first night featured Gerald Ford, George Bush, Nancy Reagan, and, in a highly awaited address, Colin Powell. Powell declared himself to be a Republican because "I believe the policies of our party will lead to greater economic growth. . . . I truly believe the Federal Government has become too large and intrusive in our lives." Powell also implicitly attacked Clinton's integrity, and he mentioned his disagreements with the party position on abortion and affirmative action only in passing, as evidence of the diversity of the party. The keynote address was given the following night by Rep. Susan Molinari (N.Y.), who emphasized the struggles of working families and the ways Bob Dole's tax plan would benefit them. The convention ended with the acceptance speeches of Kemp and Dole.

With a generally forceful delivery, Dole outlined his program and his vision. Directly confronting the age issue, he offered himself as a bridge back to an America of better days and stronger values. He used his tax plan not just as an economic statement but as a statement of political and moral values, a defense of common people against big government. In doing so he turned the "trust" issue in a new direction: the real test, Dole proclaimed, was not only whether the people trust the President but whether the President trusts the people.

Journalists complained that the convention was highly scripted, and indeed it was. Most speakers were limited to ten- minute speeches, and the Republicans made heavy use of "infomercial" videos. ABC anchor Ted Koppel even left early, telling his viewers that there was "no more news here." Most networks carried only five hours of coverage, leaving convention managers little choice but to carefully script events. Democrats complained the convention represented a transparent attempt to "makeover" a fundamentally meanspirited Republican Party; conservatives complained that it was dominated by feel-good mush, devoid of the ideological edge that attracts Reagan Democrats and other swing groups.

The convention nevertheless attained many of its short-term goals. Republican unity remained intact and the Dole-Kemp ticket appeared to have positioned itself for a serious challenge. A CNN poll showed a significant plurality had a better impression of the Republican Party as a result of the convention, in contrast to the results of a similarly phrased poll four years earlier. A CNN focus group composed of undecided Ohio voters also gave an enthusiastic thumbs-up to the Dole speech.[42] Other polls taken shortly after the convention showed that Dole had changed important conceptions of himself: the proportion of voters saying they thought they knew what Dole would do if President jumped from 24 percent to 54 percent, while the proportion calling him an "insider" fell.[43] It is, of course, difficult to sort out the effects of the tax plan, the Kemp selection, and the convention, coming as they did in an almost continuous burst of activity, but the gap between Clinton-Gore and Dole-Kemp had shrunk considerably. A *Newsweek* poll said the margin was two points, an ABC poll said four, while a variety of other polls showed a margin of 3–5 points.[44]

Stage Number Five: Democratic Counterattack

The substantial Republican convention bounce was cut short by two factors. The first was a rapid counterattack in which Bill Clinton continued utilizing the benefits of incumbency to seize the headlines. The "micro-issues" strategy was resumed, with presidential announcements of anti-tobacco initiatives and talk of a ban on hollow-point (so-called "cop-killer") bullets. Clinton also announced a much smaller targeted tax cut initiative in hopes of deflating the Dole economic plan. The second factor was the Democratic convention itself, which showcased Clinton and Gore with a minimum of public bickering over welfare. Associated with the convention was a cross-country train trip by Clinton to Chicago. Democrats clearly benefitted from the fact that their convention followed the end of the Republican convention by less than two weeks, in contrast to the normal month-long gap between conventions.

The Democratic convention, like the Republican, was highly scripted and designed to emphasize several themes, most notably "family values" (which seemed to be as appropriate a topic in Chicago in 1996 as it was inappropriate in Houston in 1992). Additionally, the convention was in large measure a platform for Al Gore, who arrived on Monday, and spoke on Wednesday and again on Thursday. Clearly, the 1996 Democratic convention was the first step in the race for the Democratic nomination for the year 2000.

The early days of the convention featured emotional speeches by paralyzed actor Christopher Reeve and Sarah and Jim Brady. Stalwart liberals like Mario Cuomo and Jesse Jackson were kept out of prime time, prompting some commentators to accuse Clinton of having "erased the party's past, principles, and personality" in exchange for a Clinton "cult of personality."[45] When the President delivered his acceptance speech, it was typically articulate and confident, if also typically over-long. If there was a theme, it was built around a clever reversal of Bob Dole's pledge to serve as a bridge to the past. "With all respect," Clinton said, "we do not need a bridge to the past. We need a bridge to the future." This sentence served as the overarching theme of the Clinton-Gore campaign for the remainder of the race, and was particularly powerful for several reasons. It evoked the natural optimism of Americans and was a not-too-subtle reminder of Dole's age. It also served to obscure one uncomfortable fact: that on the most important issues—from tax cuts to budget balancing to tort reform to education—it was Clinton, not Dole, who was the candidate of the status quo.

Substantively, the speech was the very embodiment of the "micro-proposals" strategy; Clinton rattled off a laundry list of small, new initiatives. While the proposals created a sense of furious action, the strategy also ran the risk of reducing Bill Clinton's "vision for America" to 48-hour hospital stays for new mothers. As happened so often in the Clinton administration, the cloud of scandal also hung over the coronation. Earlier that day, top Clinton adviser Dick Morris—the man who championed the "triangulation" idea and masterminded Clinton's political revival—was forced to resign amid published charges that he had engaged in an affair with a prostitute.

The convention was clearly a success in the sense that no disasters occurred and Dole's momentum was blunted. Some polls showed the President reopening his 20-point lead of early August, while others showed a much smaller bounce. Intermingled with Clinton's convention bounce was a rally effect in public opinion during a mini-crisis with Iraq soon after the convention. In short order the margin was at least back in the 10-point range where it had stood in mid-March, at the beginning of the interregnum.

The Reform Party and Ross Perot

While the main battle between Clinton and Dole proceeded, the interregnum also saw an important sideshow. One of the crucial imponderables of the 1996 race was whether there would be a third party campaign, and if so what form it would take and what effect it would have on the election. The question of whether and how Ross Perot and his Reform Party would interject themselves into the 1996 campaign was settled in August 1996. Perot moved to institutionalize his party, but was unwilling to surrender personal control of its structure or its image. Indeed, the underlying tension throughout this process was between Perot's contradictory (and perhaps even mutually exclusive) desires for legitimacy and control.

Perot had flitted in and out of view since 1992: he was deflated in the NAFTA debate in 1993, reemerged in time to urge his supporters to vote Republican in 1994, brought a string of Republican presidential hopefuls to parade nervously before a United We Stand America conference in Dallas in 1995, and dropped out of view again just as the budget battle heated up. On September 25, 1995, Perot announced on Larry King Live (where else?) that he would fund efforts by his supporters in California to form a new political party, claiming (what else?) that he was only responding to the entreaties of the people. His intention was to make it into a nationwide party, and he predicted that the new party would ultimately replace either the Democrats or the Republicans. Perot claimed that it would run a presidential candidate in 1996 but that he himself would not run, and he declared that he expected the party to become financially self-sufficient after receiving some help from him to "get it started." At roughly the same time, a group of socially liberal but fiscally conservative figures spanning both major parties had separately begun secretive discussions about the possibility of running an independent "centrist" candidate in 1996. This so-called "Gang of Seven" (later expanded to eight) included Senator Bill Bradley (D-N.J.), Governor Angus King (independent of Maine), former Senator and 1992 Democratic presidential candidate Paul Tsongas, former Senator Gary Hart and former Governor Richard Lamm (both Colorado Democrats), former Republican Congressman and 1980 independent presidential candidate John Anderson, former Congressman Tim Penny (D-Minn.), and Lowell Weicker, a former Republican Senator and then independent Governor from Connecticut.[46]

With some difficulty, the Perot forces succeeded in passing their first tests getting on the ballot in California, Ohio, and Maine. They would ultimately gain ballot position in every state, as in 1992. By summer 1996, it became clear that no really big-name candidate (like Colin Powell or Bill Bradley, whom Perot had touted) was going to run for the Reform Party nomination. Finally, Richard Lamm indicated that he was interested in doing so. Lamm, the former Democratic governor of Colorado, was a maverick who had infuriated both liberals and conservatives with blunt talk about everything from entitlement reform to immigration to population control to health care rationing. Finding the socially conservative cast of the Republican Party disagreeable but increasingly uncomfortable with the spending proclivities of the Democrats, Lamm had been one of the "gang of seven." Now he was prepared to cast his lot with a new party of the "radical center."

Lamm initially indicated he would not seek the nomination if Perot did, but when Perot remain noncommittal, Lamm finally decided in early July to run without knowing Perot's intentions. Lamm calculated that many Reform Party members truly wanted an independent movement and would support him even if Perot ran.[47] Within days, Perot announced his own candidacy, and it appeared to many observers that he had been baiting Lamm to enter the race so his own nomination would gain legitimacy. Analyst William Schneider postulated that this minuet was all part of Perot's "master plan," which included the following six parts: first, "Be vague and elusive;" second, "Lay the groundwork;" third, "Keep control of the operation;" fourth, "Make it look competitive;" fifth, "Wait until the last minute;" and sixth, "Insist there is no master plan."[48]

The Reform Party nominating process contained four steps: a nationwide vote of its members to select finalists, a convention in Long Beach, California, on August 11 to allow the finalists to give speeches, a second nationwide balloting process, and a second convention in Valley Forge, Pennsylvania, to announce the winner. The final outcome was hardly surprising: Perot won handily. Great dissension accompanied the nominating process, however, which was the central issue in the debate between Lamm and Perot. The Lamm campaign had difficulty obtaining a list of the 1.3 million Reform Party members (defined as those who had signed Reform Party petitions). The voting process also raised the ire of Lamm supporters. Each Reform Party member was to receive a ballot and a personal identification number by mail, after which they could vote by phone, mail, or electronic mail. Yet many Reform Party members, including Lamm and his daughter, never received a ballot (they were only allowed to vote after personal intercession by Ross Perot), and some enterprising journalists were able to vote multiple times by phone. Ballots never reached most New York party members, and one Lamm supporter in Manhattan had to call party headquarters four times to receive a ballot. He was then sent four ballots.[49] Ultimately, less than 5 percent of Reform Party "members" voted. The whole voting process was supervised by the accounting firm Ernst & Young, which Perot had handpicked. Advertisements for the Long Beach convention featured a picture of Perot but did not even mention Lamm.[50] In the end, Lamm realized that the Reform Party was not so much about reform as it was about Perot. "I don't think it has been a fair playing field or party-building endeavor as I was promised," Lamm said.[51] While endorsing the party's message, he refused to endorse Perot's candidacy and pledged to continue working to turn the party into a truly independent organization.

Perot had maintained control, but had only achieved a small portion of the legitimacy he desired. His party was institutionalized, with its own formal nominating system and a claim to $30 million in federal campaign funds. But it was still *his* party and few believed that his nomination was the result of an evenhanded process. Indeed, in many ways the August balloting and convention had only served to accentuate his control and to deepen the split between those who were primarily Perot supporters and those who wanted to depersonalize the party. The low voting turnout also served to highlight how difficult it might be to form a permanent party out of voters who were largely attracted to Perot because they distrusted the very idea of party.

Whatever the long-term effect of the events in the Reform Party during the interregnum, the short-term effect was to virtually guarantee that the third-party effort would be marginalized in 1996. Perot went on to play little role in the fall elections, remaining largely invisible and garnering only half his 1992 level of support. He did influence the end of the campaign, and his showing was still the fourth-best vote total for a non-major party candidate in the twentieth century. A Lamm candidacy (or a candidacy by Bradley or some other major figure) might have shaken up the race with unpredictable consequences; a Perot reprise had no such potential.

The Interregnum: Summary and Critique

The interregnum was, above all, a very long time as time in politics is measured. The five months between Super Tuesday and the Republican convention in San Diego were twice as long as the time between San Diego and Election Day. Much could happen, and in some respects, much did, including a dramatic resignation, an assortment of scandals and gaffes, various cross-party deals, and the conventions of not two but three parties. Yet not nearly as much happened as one might have expected. The third-party option was largely rendered impotent by the Perot nomination and in only one stage of the five did Dole clearly seize the initiative. For most of the period the Dole effort was lackluster, caught first in the briar patch of the Senate and then in the self-made thicket of an unfocused message. The message that ultimately emerged—a bold tax cut plan—may have been the wrong message for a relatively prosperous time, and in any event the campaign failed to use the months at its disposal to lay the necessary groundwork for the plan in the public mind.

Meanwhile, the Republican Congress, still shell-shocked from the budget wars, failed to serve the supporting role it might have. Only once did it score a hit against Clinton, when it forced him into a veto of the partial birth abortion ban. Clinton dodged another bullet by promising to sign the Defense of Marriage Act aimed at freeing states from the obligation of recognizing gay marriages promulgated in another state. And congressional Republicans did use investigative hearings to some advantage on questions, including Whitewater, Travelgate, Filegate, and the junketing of Energy Secretary Hazel O'Leary. Otherwise, Congress threw its bullets away, from its decision to pass stand-alone welfare reform to pulling back bills on missile defense, affirmative action, and school prayer, to refusing to repass its 1995 tax cut separately. Burned once by confrontation gone awry, congressional Republicans during the summer of 1996 gave Bill Clinton a free ride on a large handful of issues that could have played havoc with presidential self-assurance. In the end, they heaved Dole overboard.

On the other hand, Clinton took skilled advantage of the respite. In retrospect, the interregnum (and especially the period immediately preceding it) was more crucial for Clinton than the fall campaign. The first and third stages were particularly important. It was in the first stage that Clinton built a double-digit lead as Dole flailed in the Senate; the crucial season of spring belonged to the President. And in the third stage, Clinton broke the logjam with Congress, capped his rightward move with welfare reform, and received news that neither the economy nor Whitewater trials would stand in the way of his reelection. The President adeptly shifted with the tides and undertook a strategy of announcing literally dozens of small initiatives, forming a picture of continuous motion.

Throughout the interregnum, Dole was badly hurt by the imbalance in advertising. The Republican National Committee had to carry on the advertising wars alone, facing a combination of the Clinton campaign (with $24 million to spend), the Democratic Party committees, and organized labor, which launched its own multi-million dollar campaign. The Democrats had already hit the airwaves earlier and much more aggressively than customary, shucking the traditional nostrum that incumbent Presidents in good political shape do not pay heed to their opponents. This campaign only intensified in the interregnum. Rare was the Democratic ad that did not attack Dole by name—often linking him to Newt Gingrich—and Republicans in general. Much of this "invisible" advertising campaign occurred outside the mega-markets, and thus away from scrutiny by the Washington- and New York-based elite media. The *Denver Post* reported in early September, for example, that pro-Clinton ads had run on four local television stations "virtually every day—often several times a day—for the last 11 months. The Democratic National Committee and the Clinton/Gore '96 Committee have paid a combined total of $1.65 million for 1,941 30-second television ads" in the Denver media market in that time period.[52] The aggressiveness of the Democratic campaign in this interval likely established a precedent for the future, a textbook example for incumbents to copy and a warning to challengers that they must try to match their opponents step for step. The "permanent campaign" became more permanent than ever before, raising important questions about whether governing will be damaged by the elimination of any breathing space between elections and by the unremitting application of public campaign technqiues.

Dole's lack of focus and the omissions of Congress were not inevitable, but the imbalance of campaign resources was largely unavoidable (except to the extent that Republicans could have shortened the interregnum by scheduling their national convention at the regular time in July). Other challengers engaged in tough primary campaigns have also been stretched to the limit, but they were so vulnerably exposed for much shorter periods of time. Dole's problems in this regard introduce important questions, though ones which are not answerable on the basis of one case: Does the frontloaded primary system with its intense spending requirements and early conclusion provide an inherent advantage for unopposed incumbents? Will all challengers find themselves with a pyhrric victory at the end of the primary season, with no money and facing four or five months of largely unanswered pummelling? If it was possible to win by losing, as first congressional Republicans and then President Clinton showed, it was also possible to lose by winning, as Bob Dole discovered in the summer of 1996. For future prospective nominees, Dole's predicament during the interregnum will be carefully studied.

An interregnum period such as we had in 1996 may not be repeated. Before the primary season was over, calls were heard within and outside the parties for a reexamination of the frontloaded system. Republicans tackled the problem more seriously, as they were most affected by it. Yet the traditional decentralization of Republican rules and the philosophical tendencies of the party mitigated against any top-down, centralized solution. An added complication was the need for coordination with the Democrats in many states. A subcommittee of the RNC was formed to make a recommendation to the convention. After considering a variety of options, the subcommittee decided on a voluntary system of bonuses that would add 5 to 10 percent more delegates to the allocation of states that choose to hold their primaries later in the schedule. It remains to be seen whether the incentive will work; even 10 percent more delegates will bring little additional influence if the race is already decided by primary day. If this incentive fails to bring major changes, the interregnum may become a lasting feature of presidential election politics and a constant challenge to candidates and their advisers.

Notes

1. See Rhodes Cook, "Hill Issues Rise to Dominate 1996 Race for White House," *Congressional Quarterly Weekly Report*, April 27, 1996, 1099–1101.

2. Todd S. Purdum, "Clinton's Use of Incumbency Puts Little Things to Big Use," *New York Times*, July 24, 1996, A1.

3. E. J. Dionne, "Clinton Swipes the GOP's Lyrics," *Washington Post*, July 21, 1996, C4.

4. Mary McGrory, "Democrats' Democrat," *Washington Post*, April 30, 1996, A2.

5. Four other House Speakers—Samuel Randall in 1880, John G. Carlisle in 1884, Joseph Cannon in 1908, and Joseph Martin in 1948—received a few delegates at national conventions, but did not run serious campaigns. In addition, two former House Speakers—James Polk and James G. Blaine—received their parties' nominations, but had held an intermediary office. Only Polk won.

6. See *The Weekly Standard*, May 27, 1996.

7. Cited in "For the Record," *National Review*, July 15, 1996, 8.

8. See *Washington Post*, June 28, 1996, A1.

9. Rich Lowry, "Jumping Ship," *National Review*, August 12, 1996, 25–26.

10. James A. Barnes, "Too Little, Too Late?" *National Journal*, November 2, 1996, 2337.

11. Robert Pear, "Republicans Finish Writing Welfare Measure: Clinton May Announce Position Today," *New York Times*, July 31, 1996, A9.

12. *Memphis Commercial Appeal*, July 24, 1996, 1A.

13. John F. Harris and John E. Yang, "Clinton to Sign Bill Overhauling Welfare," *Washington Post*, August 1, 1996, A1.

14. See Richard L. Berke, "Master Move in Campaign," *New York Times*, August 1, 1996, A1.

15. "The Welfare Decision," *Washington Post National Weekly Edition*, August 12–18, 1996, 25.

16. David S. Broder, "Clinton's Big Gamble," *Washington Post National Weekly Edition*, August 12–18, 1996, 4.

17. See Carroll J. Doherty, "Clinton's Big Comeback Shown in Vote Score," *Congressional Quarterly Weekly Report*, December 21, 1996, 3427.

18. Andrew E. Busch, "Midterm Elections, Congress, and Realignment: Three Cases," paper delivered at the annual meeting of the Western Political Science Association, San Francisco, California, March 14–16, 1996.

19. Richard L. Berke, "Dole Seeks a Lift As Campaign Tilts to the Convention," *New York Times*, August 4, 1996, A1.

20. Richard L. Berke, "Democrats Top G.O.P. in Poll, Clinton Backed," *New York Times*, August 8, 1996, A1.

21. Alison Mitchell, "Despite Reversals, Clinton Stays Centered," *New York Times*, July 28, 1996, A11.

22. Everett Carll Ladd, "Survey Says? Little New," *The Weekly Standard*, June 17, 1996, 15–16.

23. Kate O'Beirne, "Bread & Circuses," *National Review*, August 12, 1996, 28.

24. See Richard W. Stevenson, "On Tax Cuts, a Dole Model Is New Jersey," *New York Times*, August 22, 1996, A12.

25. Berke, "Dole Seeks a Lift," A12.

26. Barnes, "Too Little, Too Late?" 2338.

27. "Mr. Dole's Newest Beginning," *New York Times*, August 11, 1996, A12.

28. Dole specified spending cuts enough to cover about 60 percent, claimed that economic growth would recover about a quarter of the static loss, and left the remainder unspecified, arguing that a president serving with a Republican Congress and armed with the newly passed line-item veto could make up the difference: "Cutting taxes and balancing the budget are just a matter of presidential will. If you have it, you can do it. I have it. I will do it." While widely ridiculed, the estimate of a 27 percent recovery from economic growth was well within the range of historical experience. Econometric analysis has indicated, for example, that the Reagan tax cuts recovered about 50 percent of the static revenue loss. The *New York Times* reported on July 27 that the 40 percent recovery estimate then ascendant in the Dole campaign would have been "in the middle of the range of what most current research suggests." Richard W. Stevenson, "Dole Appears Moving Toward Tax-Cut Stand," *New York Times*, July 27, 1996, A8. Overall, the cuts identified by the Dole campaign to compensate for the revenue losses, while lacking some specificity, were at least as plausible as the numbers contained in the Clinton balanced budget plan, which foresaw over 90 percent of the spending cuts taking place after the end of his second term.

29. Berke, "Democrats Top G.O.P. in Poll, Clinton Backed," A1.

30. Adam Nagourney, "In His Images and His Ideas, Dole Courts the Middle Class," *New York Times*, August 6, 1996, A1.

31. See Richard L. Berke, "With a Studied Calm, Democrats Feverishly Attack the Dole Plan," *New York Times*, August 6, 1996, A1; Katharine Q. Seelye, "Vows Deficit Cut," *New York Times*, August 6, 1996, A1, A7.

32. Ladd, "Survey Says? Little New," 16.

33. For a discussion of the search and prospects it produced, see Fred Barnes "Veepstakes: A Dirty, Bloody Battle," *The Weekly Standard*, May 6, 1996, 20–23; Rich Lowry, "See How They Run," *National Review*, July 29, 1996, 21–24.

34. Michael Barone, "A conservatism of the head," *U.S. News & World Report*, August 26, 1996, 29.

35. Lowry, "See How They Run," 21.

36. Richard L. Berke, "A Final Round in Dole's Dance to Pick a No. 2," *New York Times*, August 9, 1996, A10.

37. Stevenson, "Dole Appears Moving Toward Tax-Cut Stand," A8.

38. Robert D. Novak, "Amazing Choice," *Washington Post*, August 12, 1996, A13.

39. Adam Nagourney, "Kemp Will Find Familiar Faces as He Joins Dole Campaign," *New York Times*, August 11, 1996, A12.

40. See Barone, "A Conservatism of the Head," 29.

41. R. W. Apple, Jr., "Running from the Past," *New York Times*, August 13, 1996, A1. See also Dan Balz, "San Diego Message: This Isn't Houston," *Washington Post*, August 13, 1996, A1.

42. Live CNN Republican National Convention coverage, Thursday, August 15, 1996.

43. Richard L. Berke, "Poll Shows Dole Slicing Away Lead Clinton Had Held," *New York Times*, August 20, 1996, A1.

44. "It's All In the Timing," *New York Times*, August 20, 1996, A8.

45. Maureen Dowd, "Liberties; Le Parti, C'est Moi," *New York Times*, August 29, 1996, A25.

46. See Chi Chi Sileo, "Movement in the Middle: Centrists Lurk in Shadows," *Washington Times*, January 1, 1996, 19.

47. See Jack W. Germond and Jules Witcover, "Lamm: Instant Hero or Campaign Joke?" *National Journal*, July 13, 1996, 1546.

48. William Schneider, "Perot's 'Master Plan' for November," *National Journal*, July 20, 1996, 1610.

49. See James Toedtman, "A Third Convention: Perot, Lamm Vying for Reform Party's Approval," *Newsday*, August 9, 1996, A6.

50. See Ernest Tollerson, "Perot Aide Now Says Party List Was Never Filed in Colorado," *New York Times*, July 25, 1996, A20; B. Drummond Ayres Jr., "Reform Party's Split Widens With Its Convention At Hand," *New York Times*, August 10, 1996, A1; Donald P. Baker, "Perot Gets Reform Party Nod," *Washington Post*, August 18, 1996, A1.

51. Rhodes Cook, Juliana Gruenwald, and Alan Greenblatt, "Reform Party's Convention is Dominated by Perot," *Congressional Quarterly Weekly Report*, August 17, 1996, 2304–2305.

52. Thomas Frank, "Political ads raise concerns," *Denver Post*, September 9, 1996, A1.

Chapter 5

The Congressional Elections

Much more was at stake in the elections for the House and Senate in 1996 than in any recent congressional contest. A Democratic victory, even in one house, would have been taken as a repudiation of the Republican victory of 1994, while a Republican victory would allow Republicans to claim equal status with the Democrats and keep alive the idea of a national Republican majority. Capturing Congress also appeared to be a more valuable prize than at any time in the past half century. The end of the Cold War lowered the presidency's standing, while the vigorous role Congress assumed in policy initiation following the 1994 election heightened Americans' awareness of its importance. Congress in 1996 was seen as being an equal partner in national policy making, and the choice of the congressional majority was presented during the campaign as no less important than that of selection of the President. Finally, the congressional elections of 1996 were filled with far more suspense than the presidential election, where the outcome never appeared in doubt.

There is always some interplay between presidential and congressional elections, but what differentiated 1996 from all campaigns since 1948 was the extent to which the record and control of Congress were central to the presidential campaign. The presidential race was about the Congress as much as the congressional race was about the presidency. The anticipation of this connection led Clinton-Gore deputy campaign manager Ann Lewis to proclaim in the spring that "1996 is almost like a parliamentary election," meaning that the election would focus on the performance of each of the two parties judged as a cross-institutional team.[1] By the fall this "parliamentary" or team logic had faded. But the link between the presidential and congressional elections remained, only expressed in a distinctly non-parliamentary fashion. To win the presidency you had to lose Congress, and to win Congress you had to lose the presidency. This was the politics of "opposites attract," or the shotgun marriage of Bill Clinton and Newt Gingrich.

There are in theory three possible ways in which a party's presidential candidates and congressional candidates can interrelate with one another in a general election. Think of each institution as a magnet capable of exerting a possible effect on the election campaign of the other. In the first case, which we have called "attraction," the magnets are oriented so that one attracts the other. The normal manifestation of this attraction is for the successful presidential candidate to exercise a positive pull upward on his congressional copartisans. For this attraction to operate to its fullest, the party's presidential candidate and its congressional candidates will need to be running in large measure on a national party idea or common agenda. Attraction has been the traditional way of conceiving of general elections and is the source of the logic of the "coattail effect." Its operation is most evident in elections like 1980, when Ronald Reagan and congressional Republicans rose together, and 1964, when Lyndon Johnson carried numerous Democrats into Congress.

The second possibility, which we have called "separation," occurs when the races for the two institutions have no significant influence on each other. The magnets are far enough apart that each exercises only the slightest effect on the other's field. The two campaigns are delinked, in many cases with congressional elections becoming localized events without clear connection to either the presidential candidate or a national party campaign. Separation has recently become far more evident in describing the results of American elections, and it has been adopted as a conscious strategy by both members of Congress and presidents. It has almost always included an attempt by the congressional candidates of the weaker presidential candidate's party to delink themselves from him, as Democratic congressional candidates did in 1988 and 1984, and as Republicans did in 1992. Sometimes it has been the incumbent President who has not wished to tie himself too closely to his congressional party, especially if it is the minority, as Richard Nixon showed in his personal landslide of 1972.

The third possibility, which we have called "repulsion," occurs when the presidential and congressional campaigns have a relationship in which one reacts against or opposite the other. The magnets are close enough to exert force on each other, but in ways that repel rather than attract. As the candidate of the party for one institution systematically rises, the candidate for the other institution systematically falls. The success of one positively hurts the other. Of the three possibilities, repulsion has been used least often in the past to explain general elections.

These three models are distinct, but they can exist side by side with one another. Each can surface at different times in the same election campaign and then wax and wane in its relative importance. And each model can operate at a different level: the level of campaign strategy and the level of voter decision making. In both parties' campaigns in 1996 there were efforts at different points to forge strategies of attraction and strategies of separation. But the distinguishing feature of the campaign was the unusual degree to which repulsion guided the thinking of major actors and made its way into the decision-making process of a critical, although perhaps small, segment of voters. Repulsion may have been a subtle or underlying theme in some past elections (like 1984), but it came of age in 1996.

The National Context

The Republicans swept into control of Congress in 1994 by gaining 52 House seats and 8 Senate seats. Within 100 days the House had passed all but one item of the "Contract with America." But by the end of 1995 the Republican congressional momentum had slowed. Many Contract items were stalled in the Senate, and several others were vetoed by President Clinton. Attention then turned from the Contract to what became the true centerpiece of the Republican agenda, the seven-year balanced budget plan that offered tax cuts and a significant slowing of the rate of growth of federal spending. President Clinton, preferring higher levels of taxation and spending, vetoed the giant budget reconciliation bill and several smaller appropriations bills. In a test of wills Congress and the President allowed two partial government shutdowns rather than retreat on the budget. Finally, with budget negotiations exhausted, the two sides agreed to make substantial cuts in discretionary domestic spending but to leave the larger questions of tax cuts and the entitlements to the November elections.

Throughout spring and summer 1996, both Clinton and congressional Republicans weighed a strategy of continued confrontation against one of accommodation on critical issues like welfare, health insurance reform, and immigration. In the end both chose accommodation in hopes of establishing a positive record for the election. As the

Republicans undercut Bob Dole with their willingness to compromise, so Clinton undercut congressional Democrats whose campaign attacking Republican "extremists" seemed less plausible once Clinton started making deals with them.

A crucial question throughout the 1996 election season was whether the interplay between the congressional and presidential elections would be characterized by party attraction, separation, or repulsion. Early in the year, numerous factors pointed to the increasing importance of partisanship and therefore to an election that would follow the model of attraction. Partisanship in Congress had increased considerably in 1995–96, reaching a 40-year high. Two out of every three roll calls in both the House and the Senate resulted in "partisan" votes pitting more than half of one party voting against more than half of the other party. Furthermore, the twentieth-century trend toward "ticket-splitting" by the electorate has recently been reversed. In 1984, 45 percent of congressional districts voted for a presidential candidate of one party while electing a congressman of the other party. In 1988, that figure was only one-third and by 1992 it had fallen to less than one-fourth.[2]

There were also common national themes that linked the presidential and congressional elections in 1996, especially on the Democratic side. Two reasons made such a connection almost inevitable. First, with the legislative branch after 1994 publicly taking on the role of policy initiation, the record of the 104th Congress necessarily became a focal point of political debate in both the congressional and the presidential contests. Second, Bob Dole became the first Senate Majority Leader in American history to gain his party's presidential nomination, which made the Republican congressional record even more important to the campaign.

Democratic Party television ads in 1995 attacking the Republican budget laid the groundwork for a common Democratic front, and throughout 1996 there was a large degree of congruence between Clinton's themes and the themes adopted by Democratic congressional candidates. This linkage provided the "agenda convergence" that is an essential component of any campaign of attraction. The convergence for the Democrats in 1996 expressed itself first and foremost in terms of what the Democrats were against. Hardly a campaign in America failed to depict the Democratic candidate attacking Newt Gingrich and the Republican plan to "gut Medicare, Medicaid, education, and the environment." Indeed, by one account, Gingrich was personally targeted in approximately 75,000 Democratic attack ads across America by the end of the campaign.[3] Democrats also offered a positive program to rival the Republicans' 1994 "Contract with America." Known as the "Families First" agenda, this program was unveiled with great fanfare by congressional Democrats in Washington on June 23, 1996. "Families First" contained no new initiatives, but promised to promote several Clinton administration proposals and followed nicely Clinton's "micro-issues" strategy. House Minority Leader Richard Gephardt took pains to emphasize that the plan was "modest, moderate, and achievable. It is not about big government handouts."[4] Once the fall campaign got into full swing, Gephardt declared, "We are all New Democrats now."[5] In striking contrast to 1994, Democratic congressional campaigns consciously modeled themselves after Clinton's now-successful political formula. Despite a strong undercurrent of resentment in the party's liberal wing, Clinton had succeeded, at least in the short term, in transforming the Democratic Party—a success made possible only by the disaster of 1994.

For their part Republicans as late as mid-1996 expressed hopes that Bob Dole's evident weaknesses as a candidate might be overcome in a campaign of attraction based on "reverse coattails." A unified Republican congressional campaign focusing on the accomplishments of the 104th Congress might pull Dole up in a reversal of roles of the classic coattail scenario. (This strategy was talked up most when Republicans were still most confident of the popularity of the "Revolution.") Hopes were expressed that the nation's 30 Republican governors would provide a boost for Dole, and it was even suggested that Dole should name a "shadow cabinet" of respected Republican figures who could help him campaign. This approach was clearly a weak substitute for a strong candidate at the top of the ticket. But many considered it at least a viable strategy.

There were also a few signs that the congressional parties were acting more cohesively and that individual members were less inclined to ignore the fate of the party as a whole. The House Democratic leadership asked approximately 100 safe Democrats to raise at least $20,000 each for Democratic challengers. As one party official said, "We'd been in the majority so long, most members hadn't thought beyond their own districts. We reminded them that even if every single member gets reelected, we'd still be in the minority."[6] The House Republican leadership likewise called on safe Republicans to help fund a $10 million NRCC ad campaign that started in late July 1996 and ran through the summer. Speaker Newt Gingrich, Majority Leader Dick Armey, and Majority Whip Tom DeLay each gave $250,000 from their own campaign war chests as a positive example.

Despite these early indications that attraction might predominate and that a genuine party election might be in the offing, other signs pointed to a separation of the presidential and congressional campaigns and even to a novel strategy of repulsion. Ultimately, of the four sets of actors involved—Clinton, Dole, congressional Republicans, and congressional Democrats—all but the congressional Democrats seemed more interested in a campaign effort involving elements of separation and repulsion than in a coordinated party effort.

Bill Clinton well understood that he was a much more popular President with a Republican Congress than he had been with a Democratic one, and in the polls he consistently ran well ahead of congressional Democrats as a whole. Some distancing and even a dose of repulsion therefore seemed like good personal politics. Clinton justified this move on the grounds of the dealigned character of the modern electorate. In a January 1996 interview he argued that it would be "self-defeating" to seek a Democratic Congress too vigorously: "The American people don't think it's the president's business to tell them what ought to happen in the congressional elections."[7] Despite Clinton's subsequent assurances to nervous congressional Democrats that he was not abandoning them, many had their doubts. Ultimately, the restoration of Democratic control of Congress was not a major Clinton campaign theme, and the connections between the Clinton campaign and the Democratic campaign for Congress tended to be indirect and thematic rather than explicit. Nothing illustrates this point better than Bill Clinton's convention acceptance speech, which went on at great length but made only one passing mention of a Democratic Congress.

Bob Dole's relation to his congressional candidates was more ambivalent than President Clinton's. Dole followed a mix of strategies of separation and attraction. Although Dole's retirement from the Senate in June was primarily an attempt to escape being bogged down in what was then an unproductive congressional session, it was also at least partially motivated by Dole's growing recognition of the disadvantage of being associated too closely with his co-partisans in the 104th Congress. Newt Gingrich's negative ratings had soared, and by July a plurality of Americans expressed disapproval of the Republican congressional agenda. Dole aides publicly blamed the unpopular Speaker for dragging down the Republican ticket.[8] Attacked in Democratic ads as the head of a "Dole-Gingrich" team, Dole felt compelled to distance himself from House Republicans and to proclaim that "it's got to be my agenda, not Newt's or anybody else's."[9] Speaker Gingrich was notably absent from most of the proceedings of the Republican

National Convention, which downplayed the 104th Congress and devoted much time to calming popular concerns about Republican "harshness." At the same time Dole hoped that Congress would coordinate its legislative activities with the needs of his campaign, and he was clearly disappointed when it did not. He maintained hope for a strategy of subtle attraction long after congressional Republicans had given it up.

For their part congressional Republicans were reluctant to tie themselves to Dole or even to run a common congressional campaign as in 1994. Shaken by criticism of their budget, Republicans de-emphasized the 1994 Contract, and moderate Republicans and many Republicans from marginal districts positively asserted their independence from it. Democrats largely succeeded in demonizing the Contract as "extremist" and "out of the mainstream." (This attack was in sharp contrast to their initial criticism in 1994 that the Contract catered too obsequiously to public opinion.) Any hope for a unified party strategy for Republicans was destroyed by mid-summer, when congressional Republicans decided to cut loose from Dole and to fend for themselves. The Republicans' decision to pass a welfare reform bill acceptable to the President, thus giving Congress an important accomplishment but depriving Dole of an important campaign issue, was the watershed event in this strategy. Congressional Republicans also failed to unify around the Dole tax cut plan. Although most supported it, few made it an important part of their campaign. Despite Dole's concerns about being dragged down by the 104th Congress, congressional Republicans were running ahead of Dole in most polls and feared being pulled down in a presidential landslide. As freshman Indiana Congressman Mark E. Souder remarked, "We were already looking to be cloned into Newties. And now we've got Dole on top of that. One recourse is to go independent." Oregon freshman Jim Bunn said, "Bob Dole's running his race. I'm running mine."[10]

Of the four sets of actors only congressional Democrats had reason to think they would benefit from a wholehearted campaign of attraction. With nothing to lose and Clinton riding high, they hoped to be carried back into the majority on the strength of his coattails—hence the "Families First" agenda, which dovetailed so closely with Clinton's themes. But the attraction to Clinton, especially among the incumbents, clearly was born more of convenience than affection, as many congressional Democrats remembered all too well the price they had paid two years before for too much loyalty. Such are the cruel ironies of politics that congressional Republicans, who genuinely liked and admired Bob Dole, ended generally by distancing themselves from him, while many congressional Democrats, who deeply mistrusted President Clinton, moved much closer to him.

Along with these campaign plans based on the idea of separation, many began to mix in or substitute strategies drawing on the logic of repulsion. Indeed, the 1996 campaign represented the first time the strategy of repulsion was openly pursued by both parties—or, to speak more precisely, by one part of each party. Bill Clinton ran for most of 1996 on the argument that his reelection was necessary in order to check the Republican Congress, which was an argument that assumed the continuation of a Republican majority. (This was a striking reversal of Clinton's call in 1992 to end "gridlock.") During the spring and summer Clinton was not only reconciled to but also might even have preferred governing with a Republican majority. Yet in the last few weeks of the campaign, with his own victory seemingly assured and with all the possible benefit already wrung from the logic of repulsion, Clinton began more actively to seek congressional control for the Democratic Party, although even then his efforts were not very direct. A Democratic victory in either house of Congress would at this point have been perceived in large measure as his victory, with a significant part of the new Democratic majority beholden to him and more likely to accommodate his wishes. And a Democratic majority would also discontinue hostile investigations and facilitate an offensive against the Independent Counsel.

At the moment when repulsion ceased being a major theme for Clinton, it became more explicitly the strategy of congressional Republicans. As Bob Dole's chance for victory seemed increasingly remote, Republicans began openly to argue that Americans should retain a Republican Congress in order to provide a check on Clinton. Republican National Committee chairman Haley Barbour reminded Americans that "if Clinton is re-elected, heaven forbid, the last thing the American people want is for him to have a blank check in the form of a liberal Democratic Congress."[11] Republicans ran television advertisements based on this theme. Repulsion represented the essence of losing to win in the immediate context of 1996. As Dole went down, the Republican Congress went up.

The rationale behind this strategic approach lay in the growing belief that a critical segment of the electorate was opposed to entrusting both of the elected branches of the government to the same party. This preference for divided government was based less on any kind of abstract commitment to the principle of divided party rule than to an ambivalence about the role of government.[12] Neither party's unchecked view of domestic policy was acceptable to a clear majority of the American public. Thus, a vote for divided government would be a vote to install two negative coalitions simultaneously: one to block President Clinton (and the Democratic "big government" majority of 1992) and the other to block the Republican "revolution" of 1994. In the end, this calculation by both parties was borne out.

Structural Factors and the Congressional Elections

In addition to general effects of the interplay between the presidential and congressional races, the outcome of congressional contests is also strongly influenced by a number of other structural factors such as the level of fundraising, the quality of the candidates recruited, the effects (where applicable) of redistricting changes, the number of congressional retirements in selected states, and the number of marginal districts. These factors tend to play out in part prior to the national themes of the fall campaign and they often function on a local or district basis. The candidates or parties that have the advantage in regard to those factors have an incentive to localize and "separate" congressional elections from the presidential election.

The level of fundraising

In their long years in the wilderness before 1994 House Republicans operated at a substantial fundraising disadvantage. Incumbency attracts money, and Republicans had fewer incumbents. Majority party status, especially for leaders and committee chairs, also attracts money, and Republicans seemed permanently stuck in the minority. Thus prior to 1994 even business-oriented political action committees (PACs) often favored Democrats as a matter of political expediency. When Republicans gained control of the House, this changed. Freed from the dissonance between principle and expediency, business groups poured funds into Republican coffers throughout 1995. Individual Republicans raised money at a much higher rate than Democrats, as did the fundraising arm of the House Republicans (the National Republican Congressional Committee) as compared to that of the Democrats (the Democratic Congressional Campaign Committee). Similar patterns held for the Senate. Things evened out a bit in 1996, as the popularity of the Republican Congress began to decline and many PACs hedged their bets. But in the end the Republican congressional candidates held an enormous fundraising advantage over the Democrats. Some estimates had Republican congressional candidates outspending Democrats by a margin of 2-1 (or about $280 million to $140 million).[13]

Two factors helped Democrats to mitigate this Republican advantage. First, the AFL-CIO launched an independent campaign of unprecedented magnitude aimed primarily against 75 potentially vulnerable Republican House members. Funded by a special assessment on union members, the AFL-CIO spent at least $35 million (many claimed it was much more) to restore a Democratic Congress. By February 1996 the AFL-CIO was already running advertisements attacking the Republican Medicare proposal. The spending continued throughout the campaign, and a large AFL-CIO campaign was also credited for forcing a reluctant Congress to accept a minimum wage increase in the summer of 1996. The AFL-CIO effort, identified by one observer as a "campaign against irrelevance" for the union movement, represented a major renewal of union activity as a partisan force.[14]

Second, in many Senate races Democrats offset the Republican fundraising advantage by fielding independently wealthy candidates without extensive political resumes who had the resources to create instantly credible campaigns. This group included Tom Bruggere in Oregon, James Sears Bryant in Oklahoma, Elliot Close in South Carolina, Walt Minnick in Idaho, John Rauh in New Hampshire, Charlie Sanders in North Carolina, Tom Strickland in Colorado, and Mark Warner in Virginia.[15] Bryant, Rauh, and Sanders lost their bids for the party nomination, but the rest went on to wage fairly competitive campaigns, although none actually won. Many of these mini-Perots had been personally recruited by Democratic Senatorial Campaign Committee chairman Sen. Robert Kerrey (Neb.), who not only appreciated their financial resources but also thought that business careers might help to change the image of the Democratic Party from one that was too closely tied to career politicians and big government. Republicans also fielded wealthy candidates in the open seats in Georgia (Guy Millner, who lost) and Oregon (Gordon Smith, who won), although Smith had also served as president of the state senate. Relying on independently wealthy candidates is, of course, nothing new, but the practice was very much in evidence in 1996.

The entire campaign finance picture was framed by an important Supreme Court ruling decided in June of 1996. In *Colorado Republican Federal Campaign Committee v. Federal Election Commission*, the Court ruled unconstitutional a federal election law that restricted independent expenditures by political parties on behalf of candidates for federal office. Based on the landmark decision of *Buckley v. Valeo* (1976), which struck down limits on how much candidates could spend of their own money, the majority in the *Colorado* case argued, "We do not see how a Constitution that grants to individuals, candidates and ordinary political committees the right to make unlimited independent expenditures could deny the same right to political parties."[16] The effect of this decision over the long term may be to help the institutions of the political parties, as previous finance rules gave a relative advantage to individual contributors and PACs against parties. For 1996 there were candidates from both parties who benefitted from this decision, but it clearly helped Republicans more than Democrats because Republican Party committees raised so much more money. The Republican National Senatorial Committee, for example, poured $5.5 million into independent expenditures for Republican Senate campaigns in the campaign's final days, whereas its Democratic counterpart could manage only $1.2 million.[17]

Candidate quality

One of the most important factors underlying election outcomes is the relative quality of the group of candidates that each party fields.[18] Quality is an elusive concept, but one important indication is prior political experience. Congressional candidates who have won other elective office tend to make stronger candidates. They have an electoral base, name recognition, contacts in the geographic community, a tested campaign organization and fundraising capacity, and experience in running and winning. This is why state legislators and mayors often make good House candidates and why state governors are exceptionally strong Senate candidates.

Good candidate recruitment was one of the keys to Republican success in 1994.[19] In 1996 Republicans again seemed to have the stronger crop of House candidates, and Democrats by most accounts had only a mediocre year in candidate recruiting.[20] After the disaster of 1994 many potentially strong Democratic hopefuls decided that 1996 was not the year to risk their careers. By the time it became clear that the party's fortunes might revive, it was too late for many to enter the race. In contrast, Republicans proved very aggressive in candidate recruitment efforts, coaxing and cajoling potentially strong candidates into running. The National Republican Congressional Committee under chairman Bill Paxon began recruitment as early as 1994, which included efforts to coax some conservative Democrats to switch parties and run as Republicans. In Paxon's words, "We play offense, offense, offense, never defense. Our first priority is out there finding candidates."[21] Finally, it is impossible for a party to win a seat without offering a candidate. On Election Day, twelve Republicans as against eight Democrats ran in districts with no major-party opposition.

Redistricting

Congressional districts are normally redrawn only once every ten years, so that the new districts are ready for the second year of each decade. The 1996 elections were a partial exception because of a series of Supreme Court rulings related to race-based redistricting that forced a redrawing of some lines in five states. The redistricting that took place for 1992, which had to conform to the Voting Rights Act Amendments of 1982, followed the rule that wherever possible House districts should be created containing a majority of racial minorities. In many states this led to Democratic-leaning minority groups being packed into some districts, thereby giving Republicans an advantage in the surrounding districts. After 1992 federal courts began to call into question the redistricting regime built on this interpretation of the Voting Rights Act Amendments. In *Shaw v. Reno* (1993) the U.S. Supreme Court scrutinized and remanded for further judicial consideration a bizarrely shaped congressional district in North Carolina, essentially declaring "racial gerrymandering" suspect. Writing for the 5-4 majority, Justice Sandra Day O'Connor said that a district plan "that includes in one district individuals who belong to the same race, but who are otherwise widely separated by geographical and political boundaries, and who may have little in common with one another but the color of their skin, bears an uncomfortable resemblance to political apartheid."[22] On the basis of this decision federal district courts ordered revisions in Florida, Louisiana, Georgia, and Texas.[23] If Republicans were thought to benefit from the 1992 redistricting process, it was believed that Democrats might derive a slight advantage from the readjustments of the last two years.

In all, six African-American House members were affected by these redistricting plans. Their fate was closely watched—as were the possible partisan implications of the changes. In the end, the redrawing of districts had virtually no immediate effect on black Representatives, as all five of those who ran for reelection from these areas (one retired) won despite the dilution of black voting strength. In addition, only one of the Republicans in adjoining districts was defeated. Steve Stockman of Texas, who was considered one of the most vulnerable of the House Republican freshmen, lost in his runoff. Some commentators argued that these results proved that racial gerrymandering was not necessary to achieve black representation, while others insisted that the five incumbents who won in 1996 might never have held office in the first place without race-based districting.[24]

Congressional retirements

Because it is much easier for the opposing party to win an open seat than to defeat an incumbent, the pattern of congressional retirements is always a crucial piece in the election puzzle. Indeed, Republican success in open seats in 1994 was a key to their takeover of Congress. Republicans won all nine of the open seats in the Senate, including six held formerly by Democrats, and in the House they won 39 of the 52 open seats. In 1996 the retirement picture again favored the Republicans in both houses.[25] In the Senate, 14 of the 34 seats up for election were "open seats" (resulting from a record 13 retirements and one primary defeat). Of those fourteen open seats eight had been held by Democrats and only six by Republicans. Furthermore, four of the eight open Democratic Senate seats were in the South (Alabama, Arkansas, Georgia, and Louisiana), where Republicans were gaining strength. In the House, the Democrats also had to defend more open seats than did the Republicans (30 to 23), and two-thirds of the open Democratic seats were in the South.

Marginal districts

A notable change over the last decade in House elections has been the increase in the number of competitive districts. Because the Democrats held the majority in the last decade, this increase came for the most part by putting once safe Democratic seats into play. The Democrats' declining share of the national vote for the House illustrates the broad contours of the change. The Democrats' share of the congressional vote steadily declined in every election from 1982 through 1994, except 1988 when they enjoyed a slight increase. In 1982 Democrats won 55 percent of the national House vote, and 1994 only 45 percent (these figures include votes for third parties). This broad secular change in favor of the Republicans continued in some measure into

1996. Republican strategists believed that close to two dozen seats in the South (where Republicans had experienced their largest gains over the decade) might be in play in 1996, as well as up to 30 Democratic-held House seats from outside the South.[26]

The Republicans' sudden surge in 1994 changed the general equation for marginal districts. As a result of their gains in 1994, Republicans were now often the ones in an exposed situation in many districts. The first place to look was in the districts held by the 74 House Republican freshmen, 43 of whom had won in 1994 with 55 percent of the vote or less.[27] The large number of new Republicans who owed their victories to narrow margins raised hopes among Democrats, who believed in the spring of 1996 that they might have a reasonable shot at defeating 30 and an outside chance at 20 more.[28] Democrats saw possible Republican over-exposure in another fact. Looking beyond the freshmen to the House as a whole, only 21 Democrats served in districts won by George Bush in 1992 while 78 Republicans served in districts where Bill Clinton had prevailed in 1992.[29]

All eyes in the election focused on the House Republican freshmen. But in the end, only 12 of the 71 Republican freshmen running for reelection (17 percent) were defeated, and many of these had been weak all along, pulled into office in 1994 only by a fortuitous tide. Many other 1994 freshmen, it is true, survived in close calls in 1996, with 23 winning reelection with under 53 percent of the vote. But the big story was that Republican freshmen were advanced to sophomore status at a rate that compared favorably to other classes—worse than that achieved by the legendary Democratic class of 1974, which lost only two of its members to electoral defeat, but considerably better than that of the Republican class of 1980 (the so-called "Reagan robots"), which lost 13 of 50 freshmen in 1982 (or 26 percent). Overall, the trend of more competitive districts in the 1990s continued: 84 winners in 1996 won with a margin of 10 percent or less (49 Republicans and 35 Democrats).

Term Limits and Congress

One of the most notable popular movements in American politics in this decade—the proposal to impose limits on the number of terms that could be served by members of Congress—has been directly affected by the recent outcomes of congressional elections. The movement for term limits was born of a deep frustration with Congress, perhaps with the feeling that, in the House, incumbents—and hence the existing majority—had a permanent lock on the system. The first term limits initiative was approved by state voters in 1990, and in 1992 14 more states approved such initiatives, most by large margins. Those ballot initiatives sought to impose through state law a limit on how many terms could be served by that state's members of Congress. But this route to term limitations was invalidated by the U.S. Supreme Court in May 1995 in *U.S. Term Limits v. Thornton,* when a 5-4 majority decided that states could not add to the qualifications for federal office stipulated by the federal Constitution. The decision struck down limits in 23 states.

Another possible method of attaining term limits is through constitutional amendment. A term limits amendment was part of the House Republican Contract with America in 1994, but it failed to receive the requisite two-thirds vote when it came to the House floor in March 1995. As there is no indication that support for this amendment gained adherents in the 1996 congressional elections, this route seems blocked as well. Recognizing that a constitutional amendment is the only means to success and that Congress will not discharge such an amendment, some supporters of term limits in 1996 began looking to the alternative amendment process, in which state legislatures call for a convention for the purpose of amending the Constitution. Several state initiatives seeking to prod state legislatures in this direction were introduced in 1996. But unlike 1992, the results in 1996 were more mixed, and for the first time the term limits movement suffered widespread defeats. Five of the fourteen term limits initiatives lost, and the winners won with a smaller percentage of the vote than the initiatives received four years earlier.

This relative loss of momentum has two sources. First, although the electorate is still in favor of term limits in the abstract, anti-incumbent and anti-government feeling declined. This may well have been a result of the ballot-box revolution of 1994, which responded at least in part to many of the frustrations about the impossibility of changing Congress. Second, the new term-limits strategy of seeking an amendment by a constitutional convention has moved beyond what many previous supporters were willing to accept. A significant split has now emerged, with organized opposition arising out of fears of a "runaway convention" that might rewrite the entire Constitution. The steam seems to be going out of the term limits movement, at least for the moment.

Congressional Election Results

Following their 1994 victory, Republican leaders were predicting gains of 15–30 seats in the House in 1996 and perhaps a six-seat gain in the Senate, enough to give the GOP a filibuster-proof majority. But as the election year began, these estimates were continually revised downward, and as the fall campaign approached everything had turned around. Democrats began predicting major gains, perhaps enough to win control of one or both houses. The evidence of the polls and the views of most experts confirmed the Democrats' view.

When the votes were finally tallied both parties had reasons for disappointment and satisfaction. Republicans did not make major gains, but they succeeded in holding on to control of both houses of Congress, the first time since 1928 that an existing Republican majority was returned. Democrats saw their hopes for a return to majority status dashed, but they suffered none of the devastation they earlier feared. In addition the vote was close, and a number of races were decided by the narrowest of margins. Minority Leader Richard Gephardt pointed out that if 14,000 voters in key congressional races had voted for the Democratic candidate instead of the Republican candidate, he would have been Speaker.

There was in the end remarkably little change in Congress, especially given the vituperative campaign and the Clinton victory. Republicans lost a net of only nine seats in the House while gaining a net of two seats in the Senate, where they won 20 of 34 contests and expanded their majority to 55-45. Compared to their Election Day performance of 1994—that is, forgetting all the party switchers and special elections—Republicans in 1996 were three seats behind in the House and three seats ahead in the Senate.

The rumbles of voter dissatisfaction that had produced so much change in 1992 and 1994 were largely missing, and incumbent reelection rates moved back up to levels not seen since 1990. In the Senate only one incumbent (Republican Larry Pressler of South Dakota) was defeated, producing a reelection rate among incumbents of 95 percent, compared to 92 percent in 1994 and 85 percent in 1992. In the House only 21 incumbents were defeated (18 Republicans and three Democrats), yielding a reelection rate of 95 percent, compared to 89 percent in 1994 and 93 percent in 1992. (One of the incumbents defeated was the irrepressible "B-1 Bob" Dornan, Republican of California, whose quixotic 1996 campaign for the GOP presidential nomination diverted his attention from a district that was shifting demographically beneath his feet.) Indeed, going back a step further to the primaries, only two House incumbents lost renomination contests—one Democrat with ethics problems (Barbara-Rose Collins of Michigan) and one Republican who was a recent party-switcher (Greg Laughlin of Texas). Except for 1988 and 1990, when only one incumbent lost a primary, 1996 had the fewest House primary defeats in half a century. In the Senate, Republican Senator Sheila Frahm of Kansas was defeated in her primary by Rep. Sam Brownback, but Frahm had only been appointed a few months before to fill the seat vacated by Bob Dole. No other Senator lost a primary in 1996.

Another indication that voter alienation had subsided in 1996 was the continued decline in third-party activity in congressional elections. In 1992, 73 House districts had a third-party vote of five percent or greater. This decreased to 54 districts in 1994 and 44 in 1996.[30]

After several sessions of significant change, the 1996 elections guaranteed that the 105th Congress would be characterized primarily by continuity. In the demographic composition of Congress, the number of women remained unchanged at nine in the Senate and grew from 49 to 51 in the House. Hispanic membership in the House also grew by two (to 19), while black membership lost one seat from 38 to 37. The Senate freshman class of 15 is larger than any since 1980, but the number of incoming House freshmen (75) is smaller than in any year since 1990.

The Republicans' share of the total national vote for the House fell from 53 percent in 1994 to around 50 percent in 1996. The decline occurred more or less across the board, though greater losses among some groups were recouped by gains in others.[31] There were two particularly important facts that accounted demographically for the ability of the Republicans to hold on to Congress while losing the presidency: the "gender gap" did not hurt congressional Republicans as it hurt Bob Dole, and congressional Republicans won among the group of "independent" voters Dole lost. The much-noted gender gap did exist— Democrats had a 55-45 edge among women, the GOP had a 54-46 advantage among men—but obviously in this case it was no more damaging to Republicans that it was to Democrats. During the course of the campaign itself, there were indications that women's perceptions of Congress improved dramatically from March to November, holding down Republican losses among women.[32] Furthermore, Republicans were able to do what Dole could not do (and did not really try to do), which was to open up a compensating advantage among men. And while the Republican share fell among Independents from 1994 to 1996, Republican House candidates still held a slight lead among this group. The Perot voters, a smaller contingent than in 1992 but nevertheless a crucial swing group, gave both Republican House and Senate candidates a seven-point margin over their Democratic opponents.[33]

Some evidence was to be found of a countermobilization of the left in response to the 1994 Republican takeover of Congress. Although the Republican share of the vote among union households only fell slightly from 1994 (from 40 percent to 37), union turnout rose considerably. Union households represented 23 percent of the 1996 House electorate, up from 14 percent in 1994. Likewise, the turnout of self-described Democrats and liberals both rose as a proportion of overall turnout. On the other hand, this upsurge from the left was largely mitigated by other factors. The Republican share of self-described white members of the "religious right" increased by ten percentage points. White Protestants and white members of the "religious right" also both showed modest increases as a proportion of national turnout, and the South—the Republicans' best region—was the only region to increase its share of the turnout in 1996. As in the presidential race, the East was the worst Republican region and the South the best.

While the Republican vote share among Hispanics declined by 12 percentage points, the GOP gained by 11 points among Asian-American voters and, in a little-heralded but potentially important shift, by 10 points among black voters. Surprisingly, given the Democratic drumbeat on Medicare, the Republican share among voters 60 years of age and older did not change, remaining in 1996 at its 51 percent level of 1994. Rather, the Republican dropoff was greater the younger the age cohort. The "extremism" attack also had its limits: self-described moderates voted for Republican House candidates in unchanged proportions since 1994 (43 percent). In all, Democrats won four demographic groups in 1996 that they had lost in 1994—18–29 year-olds, high school graduates, Catholics, and suburban women—and two regions (the West and the Midwest).

Attraction, Separation, and Repulsion

Did Bill Clinton have coattails in the congressional elections? This is one important test of whether there was an effective campaign of attraction in 1996. By an absolute standard President Clinton came into his second term casually clad without any coattails. Republicans remained in control of Congress, and the Democratic gain of nine House seats and loss of two Senate seats was at the lower end of the range shown by incumbent Presidents running for reelection in the postwar era. The House gain was smaller than that of all Presidents except Eisenhower, and the Senate loss was tied for worst. In comparison to Truman, whose comeback Clinton hoped to repeat and whose popular vote total Clinton essentially matched, Clinton fell 66 House seats and 11 Senate seats short. In perhaps the greatest indignity, Clinton's coattails proved insufficient to prevent the election of Republican Tim Hutchinson to an open Senate seat in the President's own state of Arkansas. Overall, the Clinton years have not been kind to Democrats, who since 1992 have lost 61 House seats and 12 Senate seats, as well as eleven governorships and almost 600 state legislative seats.

TABLE 5.1
Coattails in the Postwar Era For Reelected Presidents

President	Year	% Pop. Vote	House	Senate
Truman	1948	49.5%	+75	+9
Eisenhower	1956	57.4%	−2	−1
Johnson	1964	61.1%	+37	+1
Nixon	1972	60.7%	+12	−2
Reagan	1984	58.8%	+14	−2
Clinton	1996	49.2%	+9	−2

Yet by comparison to recent Presidents, Clinton's performance in 1996 cannot be judged too severely, bearing in mind of course that most of the major damage had already been done in 1994. Coattails in absolute terms have been quite short for a good time now, both for first- and second-term Presidents. A more meaningful but difficult kind of analysis of coattails must take into account a comparison of actual performance with what performance would have been without the effects of the presidential race. Obviously a potential result is impossible to quantify, but political judgments on this count are critical to the strategies of candidates during campaigns.

The greater part of impressionistic evidence suggests that Democratic congressional candidates believed they were helped by Bill Clinton—at least up until the campaign finance imbroglio of the last two weeks. It was President Clinton who clearly set the tone for the campaign in a manner that made the "excesses" and supposed extremism of the Republican Congress a central issue, putting the Republicans on the tactical defensive in congressional races around the country. While Republicans gained two seats in the Senate, they could conceivably have won several more had national tides been moving in their direction. In four states—Iowa, Louisiana, Massachusetts, and Minnesota— Democratic Senate candidates won tough races with fewer votes than Clinton received, and they may have been pulled first over the finish line by his relative strength. In the House, the Republicans lost five seats (out of a net national loss of nine) in the Northeast states of Connecticut (1), Maine (1), Massachusetts (2), and New York (1), where Clinton won by huge margins. Republicans lost another five seats on the West Coast, where Clinton handily won the states involved— Washington by 15 percentage points (GOP loss of 1), Oregon by 10 (GOP loss of 1), and California by 13 (GOP loss of 3). Given the advantages Republicans held on many structural factors, the Democrats performed remarkably well.

Another rough indication of the existence of a direct link between the presidential and congressional elections can also be found in what occurred in the last two weeks of the campaign. Attraction in this one instance worked to the disadvantage of Clinton and the Democrats. When the financial contribution scandal hit, there was a parallel fall in Clinton's support and support for Democratic congressional candidates, and a parallel rise of Republican congressional candidates and of Bob Dole (and even more of Ross Perot). As Clinton lost much of his lead, Democratic hopes for retaking Congress also visibly faded.[34] Clinton had helped to bring congressional Democrats within sight of the promised land, but only he would be allowed to enter. Conversely, Dole's late foray into California and his 96-hour marathon were aimed as much at holding Congress as at winning the presidency.

The Republicans were able to maintain control of Congress because a combination of the effects of separation and of repulsion overcame the effects of attraction. Attraction failed to achieve the Democrats' greatest objective—and Republican strategies of separation and repulsion succeeded—not least because Americans clearly liked Bill Clinton better with a Republican Congress than with a Democratic one, and Democrats did not offer a compelling positive reason for a change. As Republicans discovered in 1984 with a much more popular standard-bearer than Bill Clinton, Presidents running status quo reelection campaigns place a ceiling on the gains that can be made by their congressional copartisans. The micro-issues agenda was sufficient for Clinton in a year when the economy was acceptably solid and no crises had erupted overseas, but it was not enough to persuade Americans to dislodge the majority party from Congress. Democratic reliance on "Mediscare" and on the endlessly repeated mantra of "extremism" was a good strategy to avoid further losses by putting Republicans on the defensive, but it was less well adapted to making major gains. Ultimately, despite extensive effort, Democrats never convinced most Americans that a new Democratic Congress would be different than the old Democratic Congress.

Aside from the underlying weaknesses of attraction for the Democrats, separation and repulsion had their own strengths for the Republicans. The effects of separation could be seen in the operation of some of the structural district-level factors, which favored Republicans. The House Republicans' loss of 18 incumbents was partly offset by winning 10 of the 33 formerly Democratic open seats, including seven in the South. The fundraising advantage of Republican candidates and the Republican Party committees also helped, especially in the last few weeks. If Haley Barbour was criticized for not spending enough money early in the campaign to counter the Democratic attack ads against Dole, he was praised for saving a reserve to spend at the end. Republicans also needed all the help they could wring from the strong group of candidates they fielded.

Endangered Republicans also were often successful at doing what majority Democrats had done for years—deliberately separating themselves from a seemingly doomed top of the ticket and sometimes even from Congress as an institution. Following the old rule of practicing district-level politics, many Republicans discovered the benefits of constituency service as a means of riding out unfavorable national tides. But the Republican version of separation was based less on a politics of pure localism than the variant Democrats had practiced. Separation Republican-style tended to emphasize the representatives' own voting records on national issues. The separation sought was thus not from issues or ideologies but from direct connection to the presidential race or prevailing national party images. Some of the national issues like Medicare that worked particularly well for Democrats in Florida and Arizona did not resonate with the same force everywhere. By midsummer John Heubusch, executive director of the National Republican Senatorial Committee, could say with some degree of relief, "I've seen very few national issues emerging. It's a state by state battleground."[35] In addition, Republican national issues of a balanced budget, smaller government, welfare reform, and crime had not lost their appeal since

1994, and Republicans still held an advantage on these and other issues.[36] A variety of polls showed virtually no change in the majority's distaste for big government from 1994 to 1996. In 1994, 63 percent of Americans supported the view that government was doing too many things better left to individuals and businesses, and 62 percent in 1996.[37] And the massive Democratic attempt to tie all Republicans to Newt Gingrich was also not a clear winner.[38] Gingrich himself, ruminating on the Democratic campaign in an Election Day interview, observed that the "average person began figuring out three weeks ago that their local candidate was not named Newt."[39]

The strategy of separation pursued by Republicans was also bolstered by a much overlooked fact: notwithstanding Gingrich's high personal disapproval rating, the Republican Congress as a whole was by Election Day actually receiving relatively high marks from Americans. Congress's approval rating stood at 35 percent, not an impressive number on its face but double that received by the Democratic Congress before the 1994 election (19 percent) and only slightly lower than that received in the heady early days of the 104th Congress in February 1995 (38 percent). In addition, a plurality of Americans considered the 104th Congress a success rather than a failure (44-39) and believed it had achieved more than the average Congress (43-36).[40] Thus by the end of the campaign, Republican efforts to emphasize the accomplishments of the 104th Congress seem to have paid off, confirming the political wisdom of the strategic decision in mid-1996 to seek an accommodation with the President and to achieve a positive legislative record. How much this record came at the expense of Bob Dole, who would have preferred a more confrontational congressional strategy, will never be known.

The behavior of House Republican freshmen illustrates the importance of a strategy of separation Republican-style for holding control of Congress. Although the Republican freshmen entered with great enthusiasm for a party-based or ideological strategy, by the summer of 1996 the prospect of being washed out provoked a reassessment. The freshmen went to great lengths to assert their independence from Gingrich and the congressional party. House GOP freshmen disproportionately voted for the minimum wage increase in the summer of 1996, and eleven of them (most in tough races) began voting "no" on the technical question of approval of the minutes, possibly (though they would not confirm it) to deflate the percentage of votes they cast with the House leadership.[41] Many began emphasizing constituent service. While asserting their independence, they also took the offensive, promoting the record of Congress and reiterating past campaign themes of a balanced budget, decentralization, and political reform. And it was freshmen and others with lower seniority who were the driving force behind the decision of the House leadership to make a welfare deal with Clinton. Finally, the freshmen overall benefitted from some of the structural advantages, particularly in fundraising.[42]

Although Republicans gained from the effects of separation, it was the novel force of repulsion that provided their final margin of victory. The importance of this effect is suggested by the sharp increase between 1992 and 1996 in the number of Americans who actually preferred divided party government. In 1992 those who wanted unified government rather than divided government held a margin of 34 percentage points (62-28), while in 1996 that margin had been cut in half to 17 points (55-38).[43] Put into the context of 1996, voters expressed approval of divided government in preference to either unified Republican or unified Democratic government. A *New York Times*/ NBC News poll in late October indicated that, by a 48-41 margin, Americans wanted a Republican Congress if Bill Clinton was to be reelected.[44] Election Day exit polls also showed that 50 percent feared a Democratic Congress would be too liberal, where only 42 percent feared a Republican Congress to be too conservative.[45] While split-ticket voting declined slightly compared to 1992, the overall drop masked an increase in split-ticket voting among Clinton voters (from 11 percent in 1992 to 15 percent in 1996). Indeed, Clinton voters in 1996 were twice as likely to split their tickets in House races than were Dole voters, and in this gap is found one of the keys to the continued Republican control of Congress.[46] In a national poll taken days after the election, 65 percent said they were happy that Republicans had maintained control of Congress, including a remarkable 4 in 10 Clinton voters.[47]

Repulsion played a complex role in the 1996 elections. At both the level of campaign strategy and the level of voter decision making, it was continually in play. How it operated depended on the moment of the campaign one is considering. Bill Clinton initially gained and solidified his lead by offering himself as a check on Republican congressional "extremism." But when his own victory seemed secure Republicans were able to turn the tables and use the same argument to help save control of Congress. The Republican campaign in the last two weeks, which implicitly conceded Dole's loss and concentrated on a "no blank check" argument, was based on the logic of repulsion and the popular fear of excessive one-party power. That fear was likely exacerbated by the Democratic fundraising scandal. Thus, the scandal not only hurt congressional Democrats through reducing the power of attraction by reducing Clinton's margin and coattails, but also hurt them by buttressing the Republican argument for a check on Clinton even among voters who did not desert the President. Even if only a small proportion of voters were swayed, their movement at a critical point proved decisive in congressional elections that often turned on tiny percentages.

The Future of Congress

Two important questions loom in the future: How long will the Republican majority last, and what will Congress do? After the election, Democrats noted that the Republican House majority had been cut in half—from 38 to 20—and that there were a large number of marginal Republican victories. (Twenty-nine Republican members won with 51 percent of the vote or less, as compared to eleven on the Democratic side.) Buoyed by such calculations, Democrats have set to work immediately preparing for the 1998 elections. House Minority Leader Richard Gephardt has sought to dissuade Democrats from retiring and, if that fails, to make their retirement decisions early enough to recruit high quality candidates. But if historical precedent has a say, it will speak in favor of the Republicans. It is the opposition party from the President which normally picks up support in the House. Not since 1934 has the President's party gained House seats in a midterm election, and William Jefferson Clinton, whatever else might be said about him, is not Franklin Delano Roosevelt. In the Senate, 18 of 34 seats up for election are currently held by Democrats.[48]

Some analysts are already building a case for extended Republican control of Congress. As political scientist Martin Wattenberg remarked, "It's hard to see how the Democrats could make up that [congressional] deficit if they couldn't do it this time."[49] This hopeful scenario for Republicans rests on expectations that Republicans will continue to enjoy a substantial fundraising advantage, that there may be more Democratic retirements when (or if) Democrats conclude that majority status may be too far off to wait for it, and that Republicans will be in a much stronger position in the states after 2000 than they were after 1990 to influence redistricting plans. If Republicans hold their gains at the state level, they may also assure themselves of a steady stream of well-qualified congressional candidates from a strong "farm team." Of course, unforeseeable events may intervene. Whatever historical precedents may indicate, the narrowness of the Republican majority in the House and the large number of competitive seats make any prediction hazardous. Continued erosion of Republican strength in the Northeast and Midwest could prove fatal over time; a crisis badly handled by Congress could lead to an across-the-board Democratic resurgence; campaign finance reform might negate at least some of the fundraising advantage. But Congress will probably be the Republicans' to lose for the next several election cycles.

What Republicans will do with their majorities remains to be seen, as well as how extended minority status will affect the Democrats. Republicans are likely to be less confrontational than in 1995, having been chastened by a close call. Newt Gingrich and other Republican leaders sounded a conciliatory note immediately after the election, and there were numerous signs of a shifting Republican strategy. Senate Majority Leader Trent Lott "graciously" offered to allow President Clinton to lead the way on Medicare reform, Republicans indicated that they would pursue a more incremental regulatory reform strategy, and the Republican leadership promised members a less hectic schedule in order to allow them to pay more attention to their districts. Overall, as Rep. Ernest Istook (R-Okla.) said, "I think some people are going to have to accept the idea of incremental change."[50]

Yet if Republicans are altering strategy, they are not abandoning the goals of 1994. In fact, having survived their close call, they are likely to be somewhat less accommodating than in the last days of the 1996 session. Confident in the durability of their majority, Republicans can afford to be both more patient than they were before the budget battle of 1995 and more assertive than they were after. Trent Lott, who is more ideological than his predecessor Bob Dole, will almost certainly assume the status of primary Republican spokesman.

On the surface the general philosophical orientation of the 105th Congress looks unchanged. By numbers alone the House will almost certainly be less conservative. But one of the most important hidden stories of the 1996 congressional elections is that Lott will be presiding over a Senate considerably more conservative than the Senate in the 104th Congress. One conservative (but pro-choice) Republican Senator was defeated by a moderately liberal (but pro-life) Democrat in South Dakota, but three other retiring moderate Democrats were replaced by conservative Republicans in Alabama, Arkansas, and Nebraska. In at least five races where there was no change of party control, retiring Republicans were replaced by Republicans of varying degrees to their right—one each in Colorado, Oregon, and Wyoming, and two in Kansas. In some cases this resulted from nomination contests inside the Republican Party between conservatives and moderates that conservatives tended to dominate.[51] The changed composition of the Senate might mean that whatever enthusiasm for conservative reform was tempered in the House will be reenergized in the Senate; indeed, to some extent that transfusion was rather direct, as four of the six Republicans who left the House to run for the Senate won. On a range of crucial issues, from welfare to Medicare to tax cuts to federal spending to investigations of the White House, congressional Republicans are unlikely to make life easy for Bill Clinton. They will, in any event, continue forcing him to the right as he searches for legislative accomplishments to secure his place in the history books.

The behavior of Democrats in Congress is more difficult to predict. Possessing little independent power of their own and impressed with Clinton's reelection, they may come even more under the sway of the President and his approach. The weakness of congressional Democrats has created a vacuum that Bill Clinton has already moved to fill in shaping his party; he may move more aggressively to that end now that he is freed of the complications of campaigning. There was some movement in that direction when House Democrats, shortly after Election Day, chose centrist Rep. John M. Spratt Jr. (S.C.) over liberal Rep. Louise M. Slaughter (N.Y.) for the position of ranking minority member on the House Budget Committee. On the other hand, if Democrats should continue losing ground to Republicans, they may be tempted to radicalize, a temptation that would surely grow if Clinton is significantly weakened by scandal or recession. Having failed to regain Congress through the "moderation" strategy, they may increasingly give vent to their unvarnished liberal impulses.

A key question—perhaps *the* key question—of 1996 was whether the dramatic Republican takeover of Congress in 1994 was an aberration or the beginning of a more durable era in American politics. Tied together with this issue was the question of whether Bill Clinton's move to the right marked the beginning of a durable strategy for the President and, ultimately, his party. The congressional election results of 1996 did not provide definitive answers to these questions, but they offered some important indications. They showed that the elections of 1994 were not the fluke that some Democrats had hoped. Democrats largely convinced themselves that the expressed uneasiness of many Americans with the 104th Congress was a rejection of the direction charted by the Republicans. But that uneasiness was much more likely a result of concern over the speed of change combined with an ingrained distrust of the Congress as an institution. If an ambivalent but essentially center-right public wished to modulate the pace of change rather than to completely reverse direction, the final results—Clinton reelected and Republicans returned to Congress—were perfectly logical and consistent with that desire.

The congressional elections of 1996 also continued the pattern of "losing to win." Republicans won Congress in 1994 by losing the presidency in 1992; Clinton won the presidency in 1996 by losing Congress in 1994; Republicans retained control of Congress in 1996 largely by losing the presidency again; and Clinton continued to win in his struggle to transform the Democratic Party because an alternative party power source in Congress was defeated both in 1994 and 1996. The negative coalition of 1994 survived, yet its very existence provoked the formation of the negative coalition of 1996. It is these two coalitions, wedded to each other by their mutual antagonisms, that are fated now to govern together.

Notes

1. Rhodes Cook, "Hill Issues Rise to Dominate 1996 Race for White House," *Congressional Quarterly Weekly Report*, April 27, 1996, 1099.

2. Cook, "Hill Issues Rise to Dominate," 1099–1100.

3. Francis X. Clines, "Dismissing Image in Attack Ads as 'Fantasy,' Gingrich Stresses Need for Diplomacy," *New York Times*, November 6, 1996, A11.

4. See Jackie Koszczuk, "Democrats Aiming Moderation At Revolution-Weary Voters," *Congressional Quarterly Weekly Report*, June 29, 1996, 1859.

5. Dan Balz, "Party Has Learned Its Lessons," *Washington Post*, September 16, 1996, A1.

6. John E. Yang, "Democrats Espousing One for All and All for One in Drive to Reclaim House," *Washington Post*, July 28, 1996, A10.

7. See Cook, "Hill Issues Rise to Dominate," 1101.

8. "Bridge to 2000: The Last Lap," *Newsweek*, November 18, 1996, 120.

9. Laurie Kellman, "As Dole Shifts Gears, He Backs Slowing Down," *Washington Times*, June 11, 1996, A1.

10. Richard L. Berke, "Unease Over Dole Leads to Separate Campaigns," *New York Times*, August 4, 1996, A18; see also Adam Clymer, "Republicans on New Tack," *New York Times*, August 4, 1996, A1; Jonathan D. Salant, "House Republicans Stray From 'Contract' Terms," *Congressional Quarterly Weekly Report*, July 6, 1996, 1929–1933.

11. Adam Clymer, "G.O.P. Pushes Congress Strategy That Shuns Dole," *New York Times*, October 23, 1996, A1.

12. See Morris P. Fiorina, "The Causes and Consequences of Divided Government: Lessons of 1992–1994," in *Divided Government*, ed. by Peter F. Galderisi (Lanham, Md.: Rowman & Littlefield, 1996), 35–59; Morris Fiorina, *Divided Government* (New York: Macmillan, 1992).

13. Donna Cassata, "GOP Positions Itself To Expand Margin of Control in Two Years," *Congressional Quarterly Weekly Report*, December 7, 1996, 3333.

14. See Robin Toner, "G.O.P. Leaders Proclaim Victory Over Labor," *New York Times*, November 7, 1996, B3.

15. Robert Marshall Wells and Jonathan D. Salant, "Wealthy Democrats Are Tapped To Challenge GOP Senators," *Congressional Quarterly Weekly Report*, February 24, 1996, 443–447.

16. Jonathan D. Salant, "Ruling Loosens Reins on Parties," *Congressional Quarterly Weekly Report*, June 29, 1996, 1857.

17. See Tim Curran, "Let the Hand-Wringing Begin Now That Both Parties Spent Big on Senate Contests," *Roll Call*, November 21, 1996, 11; James A. Barnes, "Forecast: Cloudy," *National Journal*, November 23, 1996, 2568.

18. See Gary C. Jacobson, *The Politics of Congressional Elections* 3rd ed. (New York: HarperCollins, 1992).

19. Gary C. Jacobson, "The 1994 House Elections in Perspective," in *Midterm: The Elections of 1994 in Context*, Philip A. Klinkner, ed. (Boulder: Westview, 1996), 11–12.

20. Julianna Gruenwald and Deborah Kalb, "Poll Results Boost Hopes of House Democrats," *Congressional Quarterly Weekly Report*, April 27, 1996, 1109.

21. Michael Weisskopf, "Replenishing the Troops for a Revolution," *Washington Post*, April 30, 1996, A1.

22. *Shaw v. Reno*, 113 S. Ct. 2827 (1993).

23. In Texas, the court redrew thirteen districts in August 1996 after the primaries had already been held and ordered a December 10 runoff election in those districts where no candidate received a majority on November 5.

24. For a good review of this debate, see Michael A. Fletcher, "Is the South Becoming Color-Blind?" *Washington Post National Weekly Edition*, December 2–8, 1996, 13.

25. Julianna Gruenwald and Jonathan D. Salant, "Open Seats Create Opportunity and Peril for Both Parties," *Congressional Quarterly Weekly Report*, May 11, 1996, 1319.

26. Academic analysts placed the number of such seats outside the South at closer to a half-dozen, and Republican hopes steadily declined throughout the election year. See Deborah Kalb, "GOP Plans to Extend Its Romp, Focusing on Vulnerable Foes," *Congressional Quarterly Weekly Report*, May 18, 1996, 1405–1407.

27. Traditionally freshmen were thought to be the most vulnerable of the incumbents, although recent analysis has questioned this contention. Freshmen members of Congress may no longer be as vulnerable as they once were, a point illustrated by the huge and highly successful class of 1974, only two of

whom lost reelection in 1976. Indeed, scholars have postulated a "sophomore surge" of several percentage points in the average House member's first reelection effort. Nevertheless, it was not clear whether the "sophomore surge," like so many other aspects of Congress, was a feature of the modern House or only of the Democratic House, oriented as it was toward pork and highly-localized constituency service. See John Alford and David W. Brady, "Partisan and Incumbent Advantage in U.S. House Elections," in *Congress Reconsidered* 4th ed., ed. Lawrence C. Dodd and Bruce I. Oppenheimer (Washington, D.C.: Congressional Quarterly Press, 1989), 158–162.

28. Guy Gugliotta, "GOP Freshmen Top House Democrats' Hit List," *Washington Post*, April 1, 1996, A1.

29. Rhodes Cook, "In White House and Hill Races, Democrats Keep Advantage," *Congressional Quarterly Weekly Report*, June 29, 1996, 1804.

30. The 1996 figure excludes the vote for Vermont's incumbent socialist congressman Bernie Sanders and for Missouri's Jo Ann Emerson, who won her deceased husband's seat as an independent because of a technicality that prevented her from appearing on the ballot as a Republican.

31. For full exit poll data, see "Who Voted for Whom in the House," *New York Times*, November 7, B3.

32. See Juliet Eilperin, "Democratic Women Hit a Glass Ceiling," *Roll Call*, November 25, 1996.

33. CNN/TIME AllPolitics Vote '96, November 6, 1996.

34. See R. W. Apple Jr., "After Victory, Clinton Doesn't Wallow in Win," *Rocky Mountain News*, November 10, 1996, 3A, 78A.

35. Helen Dewar, "Democrats' Senate Prospects Grow Brighter," *Washington Post*, July 15, 1996, A1.

36. Everett Carll Ladd, "Survey Says? Little New," *The Weekly Standard*, June 17, 1996, 15–16.

37. "Views on Role of Government: No Change, 1994 to 1996," *The Public Perspective*, October/November 1996, 25.

38. One-third of voters considered Gingrich and his policies very important to their votes, and these split their votes evenly between Republicans and Democrats. Adam Clymer, "Voters Dividing Almost Evenly in House Races, Survey Finds," *New York Times*, November 6, 1996, A15.

39. Clines, "Dismissing Image in Attack Ads," A11.

40. Clymer, "G.O.P. Pushes Congress Strategy," A1. In addition, election day exit surveys even showed a 50-50 split on approval of Congress. See James Bennet, "Voter Interviews Suggest Clinton Was Persuasive on Path of U.S.," *New York Times*, November 6, 1996, A11.

41. Guy Gugliotta, "GOP Freshmen With No Time for the Minutes," *Washington Post*, July 6, 1996, A12.

42. As of June 30, 1996, the average Republican House freshman had $276,726 in the bank, compared with only $90,942 for the typical Democratic challenger. Only 17 freshmen faced challengers who had at least $150,000 on

hand by June 30. Adam Clymer, "G.O.P.'s Freshmen Out on the Stump," *New York Times*, August 7, 1996, A1. See also Gugliotta, "GOP Freshmen," A1.

43. See CNN/TIME AllPolitics Vote '96, November 6, 1996; "A Loud Vote for Change," *The National Journal*, November 7, 1992, 2542.

44. See Clymer, "G.O.P. Pushes Congress Strategy," A1.

45. Clymer, "Voters Dividing Almost Evenly," A15.

46. See "EXIT POLL: Clinton Enjoys Broad Appeal in Victory," *USA Today*, November 4, 1992, 6A; CNN/Time AllPolitics Vote '96, November 6, 1996.

47. See William Schneider, "Will Clinton Sing Second-Term Blues?" *National Journal*, November 23, 1996, p. 2574.

48. Close students of electoral patterns will know that in 1998 Bill Clinton will be facing the "six-year itch," the notable (and for presidents deadly) phenomenon of the presidential party doing particularly poorly in the sixth-year midterm elections. The last six-year itch in 1986 saw Ronald Reagan's Republicans lose eight Senate seats and their Senate majority.

49. Thomas B. Edsall, "The Age of the Republican U.S. House," *Washington Post*, November 17, 1996, A8.

50. Marcia Gelbart and Jennifer Senior, "House GOP plans lightweight schedule for opening of 105th," *The Hill*, November 20, 1996, 12.

51. In several crucial Senate primaries—Colorado, Kansas, Illinois, Michigan, and Georgia—the conservatives won. These primaries were an indication of the dominance of conservatives in general, and the increasing importance of social conservatives in particular, at the grassroots level of the Republican Party.

Chapter 6

The Presidential Election and the New Era of Coalitional Partnership

Bill Clinton won the presidential election in 1996 with 49 percent of the popular vote, against 41 percent for Bob Dole and 9 percent for Ross Perot. He won in 1992 with 43 percent of the popular vote, against 37 for George Bush and 19 for Ross Perot. Removing Ross Perot from the picture, Clinton's share of the two-party vote in both elections was identical: 54 percent.

According to most observers, the basic explanation for both outcomes was the same: it was the economy, stupid. The economy was bad (or, to be more precise, perceived to be bad) in 1992, whereas it was good (or perceived to be good) in 1996. This explanation has been favored in part because it "works"—never mind that any number of other factors might have been the real cause. It is also a mode of explanation with deep roots in a school of academic interpretations of elections, which argues that presidential elections are determined by major structural factors, of which the condition of the economy is the most important. And the economy worked decisively in Bill Clinton's favor in 1996. If one wants to broaden this school a bit beyond the merely economic to take into account a more general structural factor—how people feel things are going—the same conclusion follows. People did not like where things were heading in 1992 and, despite signs of lingering anxiety, they did like where things were heading in 1996.[1] Borrowing a cue from Ronald Reagan, President Clinton during the campaign asked Americans if they were better off in 1996 than they were four years ago. And—student of the polls that he is—it is a sure bet he knew the answer. For the first time in years more Americans in 1996 believed the country was headed in the right direction than not. The application

149

of this theory is clear. Barring the most gross kind of tactical blunders on his part, or the explosion of some huge scandal, Bill Clinton was the inevitable winner. Dole (or any other conceivable Republican nominee) was doomed from the start, not because of any particular shortcomings of his campaign, but because of the trends working against him.

According to some other observers, no such structural feature determined anything in 1996. The basic outlines of the economy (as opposed to public perceptions of the economy) were not terribly different than in 1994, a big Republican year; and Clinton's potential vulnerability was underscored by polls as late as March 1996 showing that nearly half of Democrats nationwide wanted another candidate in the race.[2] Instead, the election result turned on political factors. It depended on the campaign, and unfortunately for the Republicans Bob Dole forgot to run one. Speaking from a Republican or conservative point of view—and it was mostly Republicans and conservatives who have made this argument—the election was in principle "winnable" for a Republican. As Charles Krauthammer wrote, "The reason for the Republican defeat is to be found not in the economy, not in the opponent, not in the stars, but in the candidate."[3] In this view, it was not Clinton who won, but Dole who lost. Not only did Dole run an awful campaign, but it mattered. If a hypothetical Republican candidate had played his cards correctly—not going back and forth on whether to make important questions issues in the campaign (and then refer to them as "wedge" issues), not taking character off the table early on only to raise it incessantly at the end—he might have defeated Bill Clinton. Dole campaign consultant Tony Fabrizio acknowledged the problem in mid-October: "We never did one thing well." But even this was spin control, because in fact they had done everything poorly.

Both of these interpretations fall short of the mark. The first denies any importance to political factors in the election process, while the second argues that if the cause of elections is political then a good campaign could have salvaged all. What we have argued is something different. We have said that the political situation was in fact a key to understanding the 1996 election results but that to ascribe causality to political factors does not mean that a campaign is always winnable. There was a strategic political context in which Clinton and Dole acted in 1996 which set important limits for the influence of this campaign. This political context—a political context that antedated the campaign—worked to Clinton's advantage and Dole's disadvantage. Above all, the Republican congressional victory of 1994—together with the fact that the Republicans assumed the role of running the government in 1995—created a situation that would have made it very difficult for any Republican presidential candidate to prevail in 1996. We do not say that Clinton was unbeatable even by Dole—such claims are best left to metaphysicians—but by the spring Bill Clinton entered the campaign with a huge built-in advantage, fashioned in part by some of his own political decisions. At the same time Clinton was forced to the right, Dole was forced to play the role of incumbent for an "administration" (the Republican Congress) whose central governing act was perceived to be a shutdown that was widely discredited. Any Republican nominee would have been thrown off course by this unusual political predicament. But Dole was especially vulnerable. Among all possible Republican candidates, with the possible exception of Phil Gramm, Dole, as Senate Majority Leader, was the most inescapably linked to the 104th Congress. If Clinton was able to conduct (partly) the campaign of a challenger, Dole was forced to run, with Newt Gingrich as his running mate, as a sort of "co-incumbent," responsible for a "government" that Americans had come to believe—with Bill Clinton's assistance—was too extreme.

It may be objected that the Republican Congress was not so terribly unpopular, as shown by the fact that Republicans won both houses and—by standards of judging Congress—had received fairly good marks. Yet this was not exactly the same Congress as it was in the spring, but a more repentant one. And any forgiveness could not extend to a Republican vote for the presidency, which would be to give the government entirely to the Republicans. Americans were endorsing two negative coalitions in 1996, one against the majority of 1992 and one against the majority of 1994. None of this of course is to deny the importance of a good economy as an issue that worked strongly in Clinton's favor; and a bad economy could have been fatal for the President's cause. But in the end, it was the political situation that was decisive.

The Fall Campaign

One of the best pieces of evidence for the centrality of the political context to 1996 was the stability of the fall campaign. The election was largely set by March; the interregnum as a whole only solidified those tendencies already established. Both parties received the customary convention "bounce" in August, with Republicans closing the gap and

Democrats reopening it. By Labor Day, when Republican National Chairman Haley Barbour had believed voters would start making up their minds, most already had, and largely stopped gathering information.[4] The presidential and vice-presidential debates failed to ignite interest or change the direction of the campaign. Indeed, the campaign, on the surface, had no dynamic; the real dynamic had taken shape in the institutions of government over the previous year and a half. Consequently, throughout the fall campaign, there was very little movement in the standing of the candidates. Polls, though varying wildly, were consistent on at least one point: Clinton was ahead, Dole was behind, and Perot was barely noticeable. No variation occurred in the relative position of the candidates. Yet there was a fall campaign, and there was movement at the end that altered the margin of the presidential victory and that reversed the outcome of the congressional elections.

The 1996 race represented the second time in as many presidential elections that Bill Clinton succeeded to a remarkable extent not only in imposing his own themes but also in declaring off-limits potentially damaging opposition themes. In 1992, he set the focus on the poor economy—supposedly in its worst condition since the Great Depression—and in 1996 it was the good economy—supposedly in its best condition in 30 years. Republican "extremism" became the leitmotif in 1996, even though it took the form in many cases of merely doing what Clinton himself had promised in 1992. And in both years, at Clinton's insistence, "character" became widely scorned as a non-issue, a diversion from the real problems facing America, like school uniforms. Of course, this success was only partial, since it did not prevent Bush or, ultimately, Dole from raising the character issue, although for a long time that discussion was somehow considered within the polite media to be beyond the pale.

Throughout 1996 Clinton remained stubbornly "on message." The message had three parts: 1) Americans need a check against Republican "extremism" as demonstrated in their attempt to "gut" Medicare, Medicaid, education, and environmental programs, 2) Bob Dole is implicated in that extremism by his association with Newt Gingrich and the 104th Congress, and 3) the Clinton/Gore ticket offers a proven, positive, moderate (or even moderately conservative) alternative that will keep America on track and build the bridge to the twenty-first century. These themes were sandwiched from the bottom by the micro-issues and from the top by an overarching emphasis on "values."

In contrast the Dole campaign moved from issue to issue, never managing to "close the sale" on one before moving on to the next. Coming out of San Diego the economic plan was the focus. Yet emphasis on the plan soon came under fire both from social conservatives, who resented the subordination of moral issues, and many Republican Party officials, who believed that it was failing to resonate and nervously hoped for some other kind of initiative. While never dropping the economic plan, Dole at times gave it less attention, translating it from a broad blueprint for jobs, growth, and liberty into a simple Dole-speak appeal of "15% for everyone." The economic plan failed to ignite interest for three reasons: the economy continued doing well, Clinton succeeded in portraying it as a "risky scheme" that threatened prosperity, and its constituency at times seemed to be voters not doing well financially—a group otherwise not normally a core part of the Republican constituency.

Drugs became the next focus, driven by studies showing a large increase in drug usage among teenagers during the Clinton administration. But most Americans did not seem to believe the President could do much about that problem. The Dole campaign then accused Bill Clinton of being a "closet liberal," a charge based on sufficient evidence to be plausible but one against which Clinton had spent considerable effort inoculating himself. Then the campaign sent a variety of disconnected issues flying randomly across the national radar screen, from immigration to affirmative action to education. Finally, Dole settled on character—not questions of private life but of public character related to performance in office. This theme was unlikely by itself to bring victory. Americans already knew more than they needed about Bill Clinton's character, public or private, and most had already decided that it did not matter. But character did at least offer the benefit of mobilizing the Republican base, thus perhaps narrowing the gap with Clinton and helping to save Congress.

If that was the calculation, it proved correct. Shortly after Dole's character offensive began, the Democratic fundraising scandal broke open; it centered on revelations of Democratic fundraising irregularities involving the receipt of large contributions from foreign sources. The ethical standard of the administration and by implication the President's character were once again put in question. Pointing to this issue—and enjoying the luxury of following the major media rather than trying to lead it—Dole began to hammer his way back to respectability. And Ross Perot, whom Dole had shortly before helped to revive through a highly publicized appeal to make a deal and quit the race, also began to gain ground. A non-entity through most of the election season, Perot trained his sights on Clinton, buying five nationally televised "infomercials" on the last weekend before the election. Dole launched a "96-hour marathon" to end his campaign, visiting 20 states and travelling over 10,000 miles.[5] Dole's (and Perot's) gains in the last two weeks deprived Clinton of his cherished popular majority and, according to White House pollsters, deprived the Democrats of House control. One in six voters (17 percent) made their presidential decision in the last week of the campaign, with the gains being made by Dole and (especially in the last three days) by Perot. In fact, Bob Dole won the last week of the presidential race.[6] Had the final results been very close, the fundraising scandal might have led some to question the legitimacy of the outcome on the grounds that evidence was being directly hidden and sources were being silenced. In the end, of course, the margin was so substantial that none of this mattered, except for the lustre lost from Clinton's victory.

Turnout

When the votes had been counted, it was clear that voter turnout in 1996 had reached its lowest point since 1924, falling from 55.2 percent in 1992 to 48.8 percent in 1996. This decline was extremely broad, occurring in every state in the union. Fifteen states experienced record low turnout, and in eight states voters cast more ballots for senatorial and gubernatorial candidates than for President. Overall, ten million fewer votes were cast in 1996 than in 1992.

The decline in turnout was something of a surprise. Turnout in 1992 had gone up considerably over 1988, and there were hopes that a new trend had begun. Ross Perot, whose presence in 1992 had been widely considered partially responsible for the rise that year, was running again. And the National Voter Registration Act of 1993 (or so-called "Motor Voter Act") led to an increase in registered voters of an estimated 7–10 million.[7] The traditional argument that low turnout is the result of difficult registration procedures has been dealt a serious blow by the 1996 election.

Three explanations were offered for the decline in voter turnout. The first is that it was a result of citizen disaffection, alienation, and cynicism bred by attack ads and the influence of big money. Curtis Gans, head of the Committee for the Study of the American Electorate, argued that voters lacked motivation due to "misaligned political parties, inadequate civic education, self-seeking values, weak political institutions, television and cynicism."[8] If this interpretation is correct, there would be cause for considerable concern about the future of American democracy.

The second explanation was that Americans were generally satisfied with the political situation in 1996 and saw no reason to exert themselves. If conflict, crisis, and social stress lead to higher turnout, lower turnout may be due to the absence of a desire to alter the status quo. One of the nation's most prominent political analysts, Everett C. Ladd, interpreted 1996 to be "a status-quo election;" if his is a reasonable interpretation of what Americans wanted, then it may also be a good explanation of why so many failed to vote. If this diagnosis is correct there is little reason for undue concern about the rate of nonvoting.

The third explanation is that there was something peculiar to the 1996 presidential contest: it was uniquely uninteresting. There were many indications of significantly lower citizen interest. Compared with 1992, far fewer citizens claimed during the course of the campaign to be following it closely. In October 1996, only 39 percent of voters were willing to describe the election as "interesting;" in 1992, that figure was 78 percent. First-night television viewing of the national conventions fell by more than 20 percent for both parties, while the presidential and vice-presidential debate audiences were down by anywhere from one-fourth to one-half. Even election night results attracted the lowest audience share in 30 years.[9]

Disinterest may not have been an entirely natural or spontaneous result, but rather the product of certain distinct features of 1996. With Clinton commercials beginning to air in June 1995 and the general election campaign beginning by March 1996, the campaign may have continued too long to hold people's interest. The decline of media coverage of the campaign in the fall may have contributed. The Center for Media and Public Affairs reported that election coverage was almost 40 percent lighter in September 1996 than it had been in 1992, although it is not clear whether this lack of media attention caused lower voter interest or was the effect of it.[10] U.S. News & World Report editor James Fallows argued that the primary reason for media inattention was "the lack of perceived drama."[11] The lack of drama was likely contributed to by a proliferating number of polls that uniformly showed Bob Dole far behind Bill Clinton. Never before has a political event been so closely measured by technical experts with so little of interest to report. And what might have been of genuine interest to the public—namely the apparently large movement of public opinion in the final week—was necessarily missed by many of the polls, which did not take measurements at the very end. In fact, most of the final polls were off by a substantial margin. A CBS/*New York Times* final poll had the dubious distinction of being farthest from the mark, showing a difference of 18 points between Clinton and Dole; most other polls had a margin in the low teens. Only two polls, the Hotline/Battleground Poll and the Reuters/John Zogby Poll, "forecast" the final result. Perhaps coincidentally—or perhaps not—these were the two polls that had long shown a much closer race.[12]

If disinterest was the primary factor underlying the drop in voter turnout in 1996, neither gloom nor complacency for American democracy is justified. Instead, thought might be given to some of the institutional arrangements in the presidential selection system that may have unduly diminished any sense of drama. To pray for a crisis to save electoral turnout obviously makes no sense, but neither can anyone be pleased with prospects of holding national elections in which few participate. Politics does not exist to divert or to entertain, but any democratic process must take into account the need to sustain the public's interest under ordinary, non-crisis situations.

Election Results

A candidate's electoral strategy generally proceeds on four different levels. There must be a geographic plan to win the requisite number of electoral votes, a demographic plan to locate and win over identifiable groups of voters, an issues-and-thematic strategy to persuade the undifferentiated mass of voters, and finally—since presidential elections are always about specific persons—a plan to sell the personal qualifications of the candidate. These four levels are overlapping and interrelated, but they capture the different ways in which strategists try to grasp hold of the campaign. The election results are also best considered from this perspective.

Geographic results

Campaigns must account for the fact that American presidential elections are actually 51 local elections that must be approached at least somewhat independently. The geographic strategy consists of putting together a coalition of states with a majority of votes in the Electoral College. Normal incremental strategizing consists in beginning from the last election's electoral results and then asking where inroads can be made into the other party's base without sacrificing any of one's own. The Republicans faced what is now becoming an old dilemma: either aim to recapture California or else win a swath of states in the industrial Midwest. Dole went back and forth between these options and in the end, as the logic of geography closed upon him, tried to stay in California. The last-time victor must attempt to protect his base, and Clinton's geographic strategy all along was anchored in keeping California and then trying to add the big prize of Florida.

Regionally the 1996 election returns were highly consistent with 1992. Clinton won two states that he had lost in 1992 (Arizona and Florida) and lost three states that he won in 1992 (Colorado, Georgia, and Montana). The shift toward Clinton in Florida and Arizona was clearly helped by the Medicare issue, which had particular salience for these states with very large numbers of elderly voters. In Arizona as well, the mobilization of Hispanic voters for Clinton was a key factor. The shifts away from Clinton restored some (though not nearly all) of the pre-1992 Republican base in the South and Rocky Mountain West. The other 45 states and the District of Columbia voted the same way in 1996 as they had in 1992. Ross Perot's support was in some ways as unpredictable as he was. Never possessing a reliable geographical base, Perot showed a decline in strength across the board. Off ten percent nationwide from 1992, he experienced dramatic fall-offs in his home state of Texas (22 percent to 7 percent) and throughout much of the West: in California (21 percent to 7 percent), in Washington (24 percent to 9 percent) and in Colorado (23 percent to 7 percent).

Several regional distinctions could be observed in 1996. Clinton did best in the Northeast, winning (for the second time) the former Republican stronghold of New Hampshire. He carried every state in the region with more than 50 percent of the total vote, the only region where that was the case. Furthermore, four of his five most improved states in the two-party vote were in the Northeast (New Jersey, Rhode Island, Maine, and Massachusetts) and his top three state performances (excluding the District of Columbia) were from the Northeast: Massachusetts (62 percent), Rhode Island (60 percent), and New York (59 percent). Clinton also did quite well on the West Coast. Dole's strength was in the South and in the middle of the country, the agricultural Midwest and Rocky Mountain states.

The famed Republican lock on the West and South that won five of six elections from 1968–1988 is now clearly a vestige of history. It has given way to a new, bicoastal Democratic coalition with additional strength in the industrial Midwest. It is premature to declare this regional pattern a fixed feature of American presidential politics, but both the overall stability evidenced from 1992 to 1996 and the strengthening of Democrats in selected areas indicate that this will be the basic outline of the regional strategy for the next election.

Demographic results

Even if campaign strategies are formulated in the first instance with reference to states, ultimately it is people who vote. Having in mind some physical idea of different groups of people allows the campaign to craft specific messages that will appeal to various interests. In 1996 the most discussed demographic feature was the "gender gap," the difference between the candidate preferences of men and women. Bill Clinton (and Democratic candidates generally) were able to build a large lead among women voters, while barely holding their own or losing among men. This tendency was evident from polls taken throughout the campaign, and it was thus not only part of the campaign's output but part of its input, affecting the strategies and messages of the candidates. The pervasiveness of this appeal to women voters led some to identify the 1996 election as a watershed in what was called the "feminization of American politics."

There was much debate at the time of the adoption of the Nineteenth Amendment over whether men and women had different political attitudes and inclinations and, if so, what the political consequences of those differences might be. As matters turned out, women for decades after voted nearly identically with men, except that women's turnout rates were generally lower. Almost all discussion of the difference issue ceased until the 1980s, when a "gender gap" began to be noticed both in opinion surveys and voting behavior. The gap was generally spoken of as favoring Democrats, although in 1984 and 1988, at least at the presidential level, it seemed that Democrats had more of a problem with men than Republicans had with women. But even in these elections, the gap in presidential politics had always taken the form of pluralities of men and women both supporting the same candidate, but by different rates. Those differences ranged from modest to small. In 1984 Ronald Reagan received 62 percent among men and 58 percent among women; in 1988 George Bush won 58 percent of men's votes and 51 percent of women's votes; and in 1992 Bill Clinton had a plurality of 45 percent among women and 41 percent among men.[13]

Only in 1996 did the gender gap reach full-blown proportions in a presidential election. Not only was there a considerable difference between men and women voters, but a plurality of women supported, for the first time, a different candidate than the plurality of men. Clinton defeated Dole by a large margin among women (54 percent to 38 percent), while Dole eked out a narrow victory over Clinton among men (44 percent to 43 percent).[14] A similar phenomenon took place in the congressional elections, with Republicans winning 54 percent of men's votes and Democrats winning 55 percent of women's votes; indeed, the congressional gender gap was "purer" than the presidential gap because the two sexes were almost a mirror image of the other in their support for the two parties.[15] As with any large-scale political or social phenomenon, it would be a mistake to assume that the gender gap has a single underlying cause or that it can be traced to a single source. There are instead several possible factors at work. One is that, as a result of either biological nature or cultural conditioning (or both), women are more likely than men to value certain things and to viscerally abhor other things. Women may place a higher value on compassion, community, or continuity while recoiling from risk, aggression, and confrontation. Conversely men may be more likely than women to value independence and action and to disdain fuzzy sentimentality and appeasement of adversaries. As one popular author put, "Men are from Mars, Women are from Venus."

Some evidence for this proposition could be seen in the 1980s, when the gender gap had a connection with foreign policy issues and defense spending. Where men saw Ronald Reagan as a firm defender of America in a hostile world, many women saw him as unnecessarily belligerent. The arena for potential conflict has tended to shift in the last decade from the international order to the domestic order. "Belligerence" can be seen as taking the form of cutting people adrift from the protection provided by government on economic security issues like Social Security, Medicare, and welfare.[16] Education was another issue that seemed to resonate among women in this realm of values. Even among Republican women who have conservative views on many issues, the perception of confrontationalism has been an important factor in driving them away from some Republican candidates. In the Republican primaries, Pat Buchanan—easily the most inflammatory of the Republican candidates—suffered from a very large gender gap in his primary races with Bob Dole. House Speaker Newt Gingrich has likewise been damaged among Republican women by his association with a deliberate strategy of confrontation. Radicalism may also affront women's preference for stability, and in 1995 and 1996 it was Republicans who were seeking significant changes while Clinton stood for the "safe" status quo.[17]

A good case can be made that one of the keys to the widening of the gender gap in 1996—at least to the extent that it was driven by more-or-less visceral values—was the Oklahoma City bombing of April 1995. Of course, the entire nation was outraged by the terrorist act, but women may have been more likely to connect the bombing to the militias, the militias to the National Rifle Association, and the NRA to the Republicans. The Republican rhetoric of "revolution," already a bit disconcerting to those with an aversion to conflict, seemed dangerously similar (at least in form) to the overheated broadsides emerging from the militia movement.

If the inherent value structure of women is a necessary precondition for the gender gap, it is certainly not a sufficient explanation, for otherwise all men and all women would vote for opposite candidates. The gender gap clearly depended on short-term political factors to activate it and on the disproportionate mobilization of particular subgroups of women. There have been at least two such specific sources for the gender gap. The first was the subgroup of women identifying with feminist ideology. These women tend to be young, educated, relatively affluent, and more often than not single. Despite Hillary Rodham Clinton's problems with the nation as a whole—or perhaps because of them—she was a rallying point for this subgroup of women, who viewed her as the model of a strong, independent, and powerful modern woman. Supporting the first lady was an act of solidarity. On the whole, although abortion has been overstated as an issue driving the gender gap, in this subgroup it is a contributing factor.[18] Feminists, of course, had to set aside concerns about Clinton's personal attributes, most notably accusations that he was guilty of sexual harassment as governor of Arkansas. Ideological conformity proved more important than a strict conformity to feminist principle—a fact that frustrated Republicans but changed few votes.

The second source was a larger group, motivated not by ideology but by self-interest, consisting of women who were economically vulnerable and most interested in maintaining a strong system of government assistance. This group included poor women, divorced women, and single mothers, even middle-class women who looked ahead with concern to the prospect of caring for elderly parents.[19] Additionally, of the 24 million employees of government or related nonprofits, 14 million are women.[20] Indeed, women as a whole are more economically dependent on government, which contributes to their being consistently friendlier to federal government programs than men. Of course, there is no necessary conflict between this interpretation of voting based on perceived economic self-interest and voting for more government because of values that exalt community over independence. In the view of columnist Ellen Goodman, "Women seem to carry with them into the polling booth a complex view of the economy and caretaking that goes beyond 'jobs' and 'taxes.' It's a connected sense of family and community, a wide lens portrait of their self-interest and government's role."[21] Still, appealing to women in this second constituency requires a very different approach from appealing to the feminists, as the economically-disadvantaged single parents tend to be more fiscally liberal and more culturally conservative than most self-described feminists.[22] The importance of economic vulnerability to the gender gap leads to the caveat that over the years there has been not so much a gender gap as a "marriage gap." Dole was the strongly favored candidate among married couples as a whole, and he won an even split among married women, 44-44. This marriage gap may have as its source the relatively greater sense of economic vulnerability felt by single women, as well as a different value structure between the married and the unmarried. But even among married people there remained a significant gap, with married men far more likely than married women to support Dole.

Bill Clinton in 1996 was not simply the passive beneficiary of a gender gap, but he courted it assiduously, deliberately constructing a good part of his campaign around it. The Democrats, according to Ellen Goodman, "made a much more concerted and successful attempt to speak the female language" with issues like the v-chip and family medical leave.[23] And they were able to bridge the difference among the various subgroups that have been the source of the gender gap. The Clinton campaign had a pro-choice stand for the feminists; v-chips and government spending for the vulnerable; and the protection of the safety net and gun control for those concerned with community. Perhaps the best example of this strategy was Hillary Clinton's book *It Takes A Village*, as well as her highly publicized address to the Democratic national convention. Ms. Clinton was able to appeal to the economically vulnerable women, especially single parents, by promising the protection afforded by the "village." At the same time, she was able to cut into the support of traditional families and more culturally conservative women by assuring them that families were still part of the village.

A gender gap always has two sides: how women vote and how men vote. The size of Bill Clinton's margin depended on a combination of the two. While Clinton aimed much of his campaign at women and clearly benefitted from the support given him by women voters, an equally important strategic goal for him was to cut into Dole's support among men enough to roughly break even. At the beginning of 1996, the presidential race was close because Clinton already held a large lead among women and Dole held a large lead among men. What happened over the course of the campaign was that Clinton kept his large lead among women while Dole lost his large lead among men. This created a strategic dilemma for Dole of whether to try to cut into Clinton's female support or to try to regain his own lost male support and create a mirror image gender gap. The second alternative was perhaps a more difficult task and certainly one that was historically unprecedented for presidential contests. Dole chose the former, avoiding a highly polarizing strategy, but he was thus forced to fight largely on Clinton's terrain.

While much discussed, the gender gap was hardly the only demographic division of importance. Religious divisions have long been associated with party divisions, and in the last decade a large part of the difference has followed not so much the traditional denominational cleavages as the great cultural war between the strong church-goers, who have become increasingly Republican, and the more nominal members of each denomination and the "secular" voters, who are more Democratic. Yet in 1996 one of the traditional denominations turned out to be one of the key swing groups: Catholic voters. Catholic voters used to be a reliable part of the Democratic coalition before falling away in the 1970s and 1980s. In 1972, Richard Nixon for the first time won a narrow majority of the Catholic vote for the Republicans, while a large number of the Reagan Democrats came from Catholic voters. In 1984, Reagan accomplished the historic feat of winning Catholic voters by the same plurality as Protestants. Clinton in 1992 had regained the edge among Catholics with 53 percent of the two party vote. This figure jumped considerably in 1996 to 59 percent.

Unlike the appeal to women, however, this surge in Catholic support was not the result of an explicit Catholic campaign strategy by the Clinton campaign. If anything, Catholics as Catholics were more heavily targeted by Dole through his criticism of Clinton's veto of the partial-birth abortion ban. Instead Clinton's gain among Catholics was an incidental by-product of his success with other targeted groups and regions. Specifically, his gains among heavily Catholic Hispanics and among union households concentrated in the Northeast, Midwest, and West Coast probably accounts for the Catholic swing. Nor does it appear that Catholic voters are now any more attuned to the issue of abortion than Protestants as a whole, despite the position of the Church. Catholics became a crucial part of the Clinton coalition not by voting as Catholics but as members of other groups.

While there were only modest shifts in ethno-racial voting patterns from 1992, some important facts stand out. Bob Dole narrowly won among white voters, reducing Clinton's two-party share of the white vote from 51 percent in 1992 to 48 percent in 1996. This outcome repeated the elections of 1960 and 1976, when Democrats John F. Kennedy and Jimmy Carter won close elections despite having lost the white vote. A key to Clinton's victory was thus his vote among nonwhite Americans. While maintaining his 88-12 margin among blacks from 1992, Clinton expanded his percentage among Hispanics from the low 70s into the high 70s. More importantly, more Hispanics voted relative to the overall American electorate. Hispanics are the fastest growing minority group in America, and get out the vote efforts succeeded to the extent that Hispanics significantly increased their share of the electorate. There is considerable variation among different polls in their estimate of the Hispanic vote, but the Voter News Survey exit polls showed the national Hispanic vote jumping from 3 percent of the electorate in 1992 to 5 percent in 1996. In Texas, Hispanics as a share of all voters rose from 10 percent to 16 percent, and smaller increases were recorded in other key states like Florida and California. In some states, Hispanics may have been mobilized by local short-term factors like the Texas Senate campaign of Victor Morales and California Propositions 187 in 1994 (banning social services to illegal aliens) and 209 in 1996 (banning racial and gender preferences in government policy), though one-third of Hispanics voted for 209. California's Proposition 187 and provisions of the 1996 welfare reform bill may have triggered a broader Hispanic mobilization over the issue of immigration, and they may have associated Pat Buchanan's extreme anti-immigration rhetoric with Republicans as a whole.[24] There were also some indications that Immigration and Naturalization Service officials were speeding up the processing of citizenship applications to increase the pool of (presumably pro-Democratic) immigrant voters.[25] Among other groups, Clinton's two-party share of the union vote slipped slightly in 1996 but he retained a 2-1 margin and benefitted from significantly increased union turnout relative to the rest of the electorate.

Finally, there has been much talk in the last few years of the emer-

gence of a generation gap, or even more dramatically, of a metaphori-
cal "generational war." At issue is the rapidly growing set of federal
programs aimed at supporting retirees, which has increased the tax
burden on the working part of the population. In 1996, there were three
possible manifestations of the politics of age, but only two actually
came into play and the results were ambiguous. There was one obvious
appeal, helpful to President Clinton, that could be made to seniors: his
opposition to Republican proposals to reform Medicare. There were
two issues that could appeal to the young: the runaway costs of Medicare and other programs, which might have been used by Bob Dole,
and the "issue" of Dole's physical and mental age (what might be
called the "fuddy-duddy" issue), which could work in Clinton's favor.
In actuality, the "protection" of Medicare became a consistent Democratic campaign theme, and Dole's age became a subtle subtext of the
campaign. The obvious Dole counterpunch, appealing to the hard-
pressed young as the victims of redistribution to the old, never came
in any systematic fashion.

Both operative issues worked against Dole, though not necessarily
in predictable ways. Medicare was judged the second most important
issue in the campaign, trailing only jobs and the economy. Dole lost
the over 60 age group, and he lost the 18–29 age group by a greater
margin. Yet Dole lost every age category, and the over 60 group represented his smallest margin of defeat. Perhaps surprisingly, Bill Clinton's two-party vote percentages did not materially change from 1992
to 1996 among either the oldest or youngest voters. Nevertheless, Bill
Clinton's emphasis on Medicare succeeded in maintaining a plurality
among the elderly when the return of Perot voters favored Dole. At the
same time Clinton gained among the obvious groups by promising to
keep the money flowing, he was able to finesse the downside issue of
who (the young) was going to be paying for it. For the young, evidently, Clinton being "in touch with the 1990s" was a more salient
consideration. Whatever else one might say for Bob Dole, he was not
conspicuously a person who was in touch with the '90s.

Issues and the vote

Modern campaigns seek to mobilize vaguer constituencies that are
defined by their support of or opposition to certain policies. The candidates's objective is to discover (and perhaps create) issues on which
they have an advantage over their opponent, and to increase the sali-
ency of that issue and the size of the constituency concerned with it.

Candidates can win if they get the country to respond to "their" issues on their terms.

Exit polls indicated the degree to which Bill Clinton succeeded in dominating the terms of debate in 1996, as he had in 1992. Of the four issues adjudged by voters to be "most important" in 1996, three (jobs and the economy, Medicare, and education) were "his" issues. On only one, the budget deficit, did Dole have an advantage among voters, and Dole's preferred central issue—taxes—ranked only fifth in importance among voters. Clinton succeeded not only in promoting his own agenda, but also in deflating Dole's. By the end of the campaign, a more than 2-1 majority believed that Bob Dole could not cut taxes and reduce the deficit at the same time. As in many other respects, the top three issues of 1996 bore a striking resemblance to those of 1992: the economy, Medicare, and the deficit in 1996 versus the economy, the deficit, and health care in 1992. The shift from "health care" to Medicare did reveal, however, the extent to which Clinton had been put on the strategic defensive since 1992. Protecting an existing government program replaced creating a new one.[26]

As important as the issues that dominated the race were the issues that were absent. Republicans were deprived of two long-time issues, welfare and crime, when Clinton signed welfare reform and found himself endorsed by major police unions. And as an explicit campaign issue, foreign policy was even less of a factor than in 1992. The percentage of voters who considered it the most important issue moved from small to exiguous, falling from 8 percent to 4. Yet its true importance to the structure of the campaign was masked by this low number. The fact that no one cared much about foreign policy was an important triumph for President Clinton, who made a number of foreign policy stumbles early in his term and could have been badly hurt by a foreign policy crisis. Instead, his hand steadied and he compiled a number of diplomatic successes, which produced little positive gain for him politically but had the effect of neutralizing his earlier image of diplomatic incompetence. They thus contributed to Clinton's ability to hold his own in the fourth crucial realm of campaign strategy, presentation of the personal qualities of the candidate.

Personal qualities

As a "personal" office headed by one individual, the selection of the presidency always involves considerations that extend beyond matters of ideology or issues. In this area of campaign strategy, it is important for a candidate to convince voters that he is the sort of human being suited to be president. While Bob Dole clearly hoped to dominate this part of the debate owing to Clinton's ethical baggage, he ended up gaining only a small net advantage. Of the five different personal qualities voters considered, Dole had a clear advantage on only one.

The most obvious was the quality Dole referred to as "character," by which he meant honesty and integrity. On that score, Dole did indeed possess an advantage in public opinion that was fairly consistent throughout the race, even before he made "character" the centerpiece of his campaign in late October. On Election Day, one in five voters declared honesty to be the most important factor behind their votes, and they split 84-8 in favor of Bob Dole. Of all voters 54 percent said that Clinton was not honest and trustworthy and 60 percent offered the opinion that he had not told the truth about Whitewater. But honesty and integrity were only part of the so-called character question. Four other qualities came into play: empathy, vision, competence, and willingness to stand up for what one believes. On those four, Clinton held a clear advantage on the first two while the other two were essentially a draw. Clinton's greatest strength, a strength which helped to overcome his weakness on the honesty question, was his ability to "connect" with the day-to-day lives of American voters. A plurality of all voters said they did not believe that Dole understood their problems, including 77 percent of Clinton voters. One in ten voters even cited "caring about people like me" as their first priority in a President, and Clinton won a 72-17 majority among them.

Clinton also won big on the "vision thing," which was at least to some extent a form of the "fuddy-duddy issue" and hence a surrogate for the age question. Almost one in five voters placed a "vision for the future" as the most important quality driving their presidential vote; Clinton got 77 percent of their votes. On a similar kind of concern, one in ten voters wanted above all a President who was "in touch with the 1990s." Bill Clinton won an even larger majority among them, with 89 percent. Clinton was in the 1990s driving over a bridge to the next century in an Acura Legend, while Bob Dole was driving a 1946 Packard to a Brooklyn Dodgers game. Of course, to many Americans that was a strength for Dole instead of a weakness, but on balance Clinton held the edge.

In terms of competence and steadfastness, Clinton held his own to an extent that would have been surprising at any time before 1995. His foreign policy successes removed many doubts about his competence in that respect, and his White House operation made far fewer mistakes. His campaign, as in 1992, was a model of efficiency, presenting an unmistakable image of competence that at times stood in stark contrast with the Dole operation. The post-1994 Clinton makeover was successful in revising his image as a perpetual waffler without core beliefs, one of his greatest weaknesses in 1993–94. Central to this change was his veto strategy. Clinton also pointed to his support of controversial legislation (like the Brady Bill) as proof of his "character." On Election Day, Clinton actually held a slight lead (42-40) over Dole among the 13 percent of voters who believed that the most important quality of a president was willingness to stand up for his beliefs. Thus, on both competence and fortitude, Clinton managed to fight Dole to a standoff.

The most usual way of discussing presidential elections when an incumbent is running is to view the contest as a referendum on his stewardship in office.[27] This framework is useful—up to a point—for analyzing the 1996 election. Having run as John F. Kennedy in 1992, President Clinton ran for reelection as Ronald Reagan in 1996, posing the central issue in classic Reaganesque fashion: "Are you better off now than you were four years ago?" And the answer for many voters was "yes." Central to this judgment was clearly a favorable assessment of the performance of the economy. Dole scored better among voters who believed the economy was poor.

Viewing 1996 simply as a referendum, however, is clouded by two facts. First, there is the question of which of the two Bill Clintons was being judged: the liberal of 1993–94 or the moderate of 1995–96. Clinton offered himself in 1996 in a centrist image, all the while signalling that those on the left had no other alternative but to embrace him. The gambit was successful. As the electorate moved to the right from 1992 to 1996, Clinton won the same percentage of self-described conservative and moderate voters. At the same time, with his vision of increasing quantities of little government, he secured the overwhelming backing (72 percent) of the minority (42 percent) who preferred more government. Second, Clinton managed successfully to turn the election in part into a referendum not on his own stewardship, but on the stewardship of Newt Gingrich. Clinton's campaign was characterized by a negative element that was unusually strong for an incumbent seeking reelection and that more typically characterizes challenger campaigns. As in so many other instances Bill Clinton managed in both these cases to have it both ways. The election of 1996 both was and was not a referendum on the President, and each option was defined in a way that promoted his electoral advantage.

Outsiderism in 1996

The 1992 election introduced the dimension of outsiderism into American politics with a greater intensity than ever before. Outsiderism competed with the traditional factors of party and ideology, exerting substantial influence on the presidential and congressional elections and spawning the term limits movement. But even in 1992, there were questions about the helpfulness of this ploy. In the end extreme outsiderism in 1992 proved itself to be as much a liability as pure insiderism. A kind of outsiderism was again important in 1994, as Republicans seized control of Congress as the "country" party running against the Democrats as the "court" party.

In 1996 outsiderism was still present but played a far smaller role. In the Republican nomination process, outsiders in the persons of Pat Buchanan, Steve Forbes, and Lamar Alexander were major challengers to Robert Dole. But once Dole captured the nomination, the contest became a race between an incumbent President and a challenger who had spent more than thirty-five years in the United States Congress. Except for a brief moment after Dole resigned his position as Majority Leader and became Citizen Dole, neither candidate even suggested the theme of the outsider. Outsiderism also subsided considerably in the congressional elections. Incumbent reelection rates rose for the first time this decade. In comparison with 1992, third-party congressional activity fell and the pressure for term limits was reduced.

Only Ross Perot could claim the mantle of outsiderism in 1996, but it was with much less fervor and success than in 1992. Perot after all had been around for some time, had allowed his movement to be formed into a third party, and was accepting public funds from the federal government. Perot received less than half of his 1992 vote percentage and spent most of the campaign as either an oddity or a nonentity. In contrast to 1992, he was shut out of the presidential debates at the insistence of Bob Dole (a decision that many in the campaign later came to regret). Still, Perot's vote of 9 percent was considerable, and it is possible that another more plausible candidate running for the Reform Party might have gained more votes than Perot, who never fully recovered from his drubbing at the hands of Al Gore during the NAFTA debate. Perot's showing was also enough to guarantee access to federal funds again in 2000 (though at a reduced level), and pressure will likely grow within the Reform Party to broaden its reach and become less personalistic. Former Colorado Governor Richard Lamm, who challenged Perot for the Reform Party nomination in 1996, indicated after Election Day his intention to fight Perot for the future of the party.

After two consecutive elections with a respectable showing, it is no longer possible to speak of all of Perot supporters as simply "floating" voters. Many are just that, as evidenced by the very large number of Perot voters who claimed they chose their candidate to register a protest, and the large number of his 1992 voters who drifted away in 1996, either not voting or voting for other candidates. Yet there seems to be a hard core of Perot supporters representing perhaps 5 percent of the electorate. Exit polls indicated that about one-third of Perot's 1992 voters who came to the polls in 1996 voted for him again. Are these committed voters who are now no longer dealigned but aligned with the Reform Party? No answer can be given until another election has passed, with a Reform Party candidate other than Perot. The rise of outsiderism in 1992 was built on an intersection of institutional and structural factors, which opened the nominating process and modern campaigns to personalistic outsiders, and the popular acceptance of (or even demand for) outsiders, which resonated with the voting public. While the second has abated, it hardly disappeared, as evidenced by the Powell groundswell in 1995, Perot's 9 percent showing, and polls that indicated that more Americans thought there should be a third party in 1996 than in 1992.[28] Furthermore, the first set of factors— the structural openness to personalism—remains. If there should be another shift in public sentiment in favor of outsiderism, it will find the institutional ground still very fertile.

1996 and American Politics

The 1996 elections were unusually stable on the surface. But just below there were some important changes. In the area of new institutional features, there was the pioneering of the "permanent campaign," the advent of the five-month interregnum period between the nominations, and a relearning process after years of one-party government in the Congress of the real powers and potentialities of both the Congress and the presidency. The political developments of 1996 were even more striking. A succession of negative coalitions brought a new divided government that consisted of two mutually checking forces: one to block big government and the other to block or slow the reduction of big government.

The inclusion of these two negative coalitions inside the same government at the same time is the most powerful force shaping the politics of the new period. The return of a Republican Congress renders highly improbable any significant shift to the left, even if (as Bob Dole and other Republicans charged) this was the secret desire President Clinton harbored in his heart. The issues likely to prove central—budget balancing, entitlement reform, tax cuts, and cultural/social issues like affirmative action and immigration—are both potentially divisive and situated essentially on the Republicans' playing field. Thus, there will be either a return to gridlock or a continued move to the right by Clinton, who will seek to ensure himself a legislative record on which to secure his "place in history."

Another issue likely to occupy attention is campaign finance reform, driven largely by the DNC fundraising scandal at the end of the 1996 campaign. Although most attention will be focused on the role of foreign contributions (already illegal) and of large independent expenditures of party "soft money" (already constitutionally protected), some of the simplest questions about the integrity of the entire electoral process will likely go unanswered. For example, do we really want our campaign finance system to give an insurmountable advantage to an unchallenged candidate from one party (normally the incumbent) over the nominee of the other? The current system does this all fairly inside the law. Or do we want to give a large advantage to the billionaire candidate, who can spend without any limits, over the candidates who raise money under the system?

Both major parties face challenges. Republicans have the usual coalitional divisions among the different parts of the party, which is still a new feature for a party that has just achieved majority status within the Congress. But it is in thinking about a future majority for the presidency that Republicans need to be most careful. The striking similarity of the 1992 and 1996 presidential election results provides a clear warning that Democrats may be in the process of constructing a new and durable presidential majority coalition. Republican weakness in some regions (particularly the Northeast) and among some groups (women and Hispanics) is a cause for concern. While no great government initiatives will come from Bill Clinton, Republicans cannot discount the strategic danger posed by Clinton's formula of "lots of little government" Clinton clearly hopes over time to subvert the philosophical conservatism of Americans by stroking their operational liberalism.

The Democrats face a conflict between their old liberal wing (a liberalism of the heart) and the recent ploy to try to build a new majority status by moving right. If the last direction is assumed, Democrats have yet to formulate a coherent, positive, and principled philosophy that can stand apart from both knee-jerk negativism and simple "metooism." The intra-party debate over how to accomplish that has already begun and promises to be easily as divisive as any of the potential fights among Republicans. This debate will reflect all the ambiguities of Clinton's policies and his campaign, but without the President's easy virtue of spanning contradictions. In addition, Democrats will be living with a President in his second term, a situation that has proven notoriously difficult in this century. Even in the absence of great disappointment or disaster, Clinton will see his influence wane as his term runs out. Clinton has maintained his grip on power at times by extraordinary feats of political gymnastics, but he is neither widely loved nor deeply respected, as evidenced by his 49 percent vote share, which fell well short of the 60 percent average attained by the last four reelected Presidents. If a recession, a foreign policy blow-up, or an expansion of the scandals is added to the picture, Clinton's presidency will be in serious danger of having the bottom fall out.

Election analysis is often guided by a search for historical parallels. Democrats may hope that the new form of divided government has inaugurated a period of Democratic presidential dominance to rival the dominance held by Republicans from 1968 through 1988. And as the domestic public philosophy in the pre-Reagan years was defined more by Congress than by the Republican presidents, Republicans have hopes—if they can hold the Congress again in 1998—that a slow tide will move, and in fact is already moving, in their direction. In this view the deeper reality, despite the political stalemate, is that President Clinton is a Democratic President in a Republican or conservative period, in a way analogous to both Presidents Eisenhower and Nixon, who were Republican Presidents in a Democratic or liberal period. The parallel between Eisenhower's "Modern Republicans" and Clinton's "New Democrats" is striking; as with Eisenhower and Nixon the only path of leadership President Clinton may foresee is to accommodate himself to this era, moderating the reduction of government and winning some small victories for liberalism along the way.

In the last decade both parties have learned that it is possible to win by losing and to lose by winning. The balance today between the two parties remains quite close with both parties having a reasonable prospect of ending the government of two negative coalitions and instituting a program based on a more unified vision. In the meantime, governing can only take place by a form of stalemate or compromise. The division and ambivalence of the American people remains the central feature of our electoral politics and an invitation to the formation of negative coalitions that reinforce the incrementalist bent of our institutions. For now the decisive bloc of American voters, convinced with Madison that government is not inhabited by angels, seems content to insist with him that ambition be made to counteract ambition.

Notes

1. Based on 1996 polling data, political analyst Paul Starobin argued just before Election Day that voters were less "angry" than in 1992 or 1994, but had not totally overcome the anxiousness that characterized them in the early 1990s. *National Journal*, November 2, 1996, 2339–2342.

2. In a March 1996 *New York Times* poll, 46 percent of Democrats and 40 percent of Republicans said they would like to see a third-party candidate enter the race. Richard L. Berke, "With Dole Cashing In, Both Sides Say All Bets Are Off for Fall," *New York Times*, March 14, 1996, B11.

3. Charles Krauthammer, "It's the Campaign, Stupid," *The Weekly Standard*, November 18, 1996, 13.

4. Richard Morin and Mario A. Brossard, "Poll: Knew Early, Knew Enough," *Washington Post*, November 15, 1996, A1.

5. For an account of the campaign's last few days, see "Bridge to 2000: The Last Lap," *Newsweek*, November 18, 1996, 120.

6. CNN/TIME AllPolitics Vote '96, November 6, 1996.

7. *San Diego Union Tribune*, November 17, 1996.

8. *The Hotline*, November 8, 1996, 6. There is substantial academic literature arguing this case in general, for example Ruy A. Teixeira, *The Disappearing American Voter* (Washington, D.C.: Brookings, 1992); Stephen Ansolabehere and Shanto Iyengar, *Going Negative: How Attack Ads Shrink and Polarize the Electorate* (New York: The Free Press, 1995).

9. "TV Ratings, Final Chapter: Election is a Turnoff," *The Hotline*, November 8, 1996, 6.

10. Ibid.

11. Martin Walker, "Yawn Away From Victory," *The Observer*, October 6, 1996, T17.

12. For a presentation of the results of the polls in 1996, along with a thought-provoking discussion of their performance and the possible effects, see Everett C. Ladd, "The Pollsters' Waterloo," *Wall Street Journal*, November 19, 1996, A22.

13. See "What Voters Said Election Day," *The Public Perspective*, January/February 1993, 90.

14. The data presented here are from the CNN/Time poll. Poll figures in this chapter for the 1996 election are taken from either the CNN/Time poll or

the Voter News Service exit polls. The VNS poll can be found in *National Journal*, November 9, 1996, 2407.

15. "Who Voted for Whom in the House," *New York Times*, November 7, 1996, B3.

16. For an excellent discussion of the gender gap in the 1990s, particularly on the role of government questions, see Janet Clark and Cal Clark, "The Gender Gap: A Manifestation of Women's Dissatisfaction with the American Polity?" in Stephen C. Craig, ed., *Broken Contract? Changing Relationships Between Americans & Their Government* (Boulder: Westview Press, 1996), 167–182. Some analysts argue that in the 1980s, issues of welfare state maintenance were also critical, with the 1982 midterm elections serving as a watershed. See Steven P. Erie and Martin Rein, "Women and the Welfare State," in Carol Mueller, ed., *The Politics of the Gender Gap* (Newbury Park: Sage Publications, 1988).

17. See Danielle Crittendon, "What Does Woman Want?" *National Review*, December 9, 1996, 53–54.

18. That the gender gap can be explained to only a very limited degree by abortion could be seen in the Massachusetts Senate race, where pro-choice Republican William Weld suffered a 21-point gender gap.

19. Amy E. Schwartz, "Fallacy and the Female Voter," *Washington Post*, November 20, 1996, A19.

20. "The Marriage Gap," *Wall Street Journal*, November 15, 1996, A14.

21. Ellen Goodman, "Victory at the Gender Gap," *Washington Post*, November 16, 1996, A25.

22. See Clark and Clark, 177.

23. Goodman, "Victory at the Gender Gap," A25.

24. Some analysts go further, arguing that all recent efforts to reform immigration have contributed to an anti-Republican backlash among Hispanics. See Paul A. Gigot, "Anti-Immigrant Reckoning Comes Ahead of Schedule," *Wall Street Journal*, November 22, 1996, A14.

25. See William Schneider, "Massive Immigrant Vote for Clinton?" *National Journal*, September 14, 1996, 1986.

26. See CNN/TIME AllPolitics Vote '96, November 6, 1996; "A Loud Vote for Change," *The National Journal*, November 7, 1992, 2542.

27. See V. O. Key, Jr., *The Responsible Electorate* (New York: Vintage,, 1966); Morris P. Fiorina, *Retrospective Voting in American National Elections* (New Haven: Yale University Press, 1981).

28. In 1992, 53 percent said they wanted a third party; in 1996, 58 percent. James Toedtman, "A Third Convention: Perot, Lamm Vying for Reform Party's Approval," *Newsday*, August 9, 1996, A6.

Appendix 1

Presidential Vote by State, 1996

State	Clinton (D)	%	Dole (R)	%	Perot (I)	%	Electoral Votes
Alabama	664, 503	43	782, 029	51	92,010	6	9
Alaska	66, 508	33	101, 234	51	21,536	11	3
Arizona	612, 412	47	576, 126	44	104,712	8	8
Arkansas	469, 164	54	322, 349	37	66,997	8	6
California	4, 639, 935	51	3, 412, 563	38	667,702	7	54
Colorado	670, 854	44	691, 291	46	99,509	7	8
Connecticut	712, 603	52	481, 047	35	137,784	10	8
Delaware	140, 209	52	98, 906	37	28,693	11	3
District of Col.	152, 031	85	16, 637	9	3,479	2	3
Florida	2, 533, 502	48	2, 226, 117	42	482,237	9	25
Georgia	1, 047, 214	46	1, 078, 972	47	146,031	6	13
Hawaii	205, 012	57	113, 943	32	27,358	8	4
Idaho	165, 545	34	256, 406	52	62,506	13	4
Illinois	2, 299, 476	54	1, 577, 930	37	344,311	8	22
Indiana	874, 668	42	995, 082	47	218,739	10	12
Iowa	615, 732	50	490, 949	40	104,462	9	7
Kansas	384, 399	36	578, 572	54	92,093	9	6
Kentucky	635, 804	46	622, 339	45	118,768	9	8
Louisiana	928, 983	52	710, 240	40	122,981	7	9
Maine	311, 092	52	185, 133	31	85,290	14	4
Maryland	924, 284	54	651, 682	38	113,684	7	10
Massachusetts	1, 567, 223	62	717, 622	28	225,594	9	12
Michigan	1, 941, 126	52	1, 440, 977	38	326,751	9	18
Minnesota	1, 096, 355	51	751, 971	35	252,986	12	10
Mississippi	385, 005	44	434, 547	49	51,500	6	7
Missouri	1, 024, 817	48	889, 689	41	217,103	10	11
Montana	167, 169	41	178, 957	44	55,017	14	3
Nebraska	231, 906	35	355, 665	53	76,103	11	5
Nevada	203, 388	44	198, 775	43	43,855	9	4
New Hampshire	245, 260	50	196, 740	40	48,140	10	4
New Jersey	1, 599, 932	53	1, 080, 041	36	257,979	9	15
New Mexico	252, 215	49	210, 791	41	30,978	6	5
New York	3, 513, 191	59	1, 861, 198	31	485,547	8	33
North Carolina	1, 099, 132	44	1, 214, 399	49	165,301	7	14
North Dakota	106,405	40	124, 597	47	32,594	12	3
Ohio	2, 100, 690	47	1, 823, 859	41	470,680	11	21
Oklahoma	488, 102	40	582, 310	48	130,788	11	8
Oregon	326, 099	47	256, 105	37	73,265	11	7
Pennsylvania	2, 206, 241	49	1, 793, 568	40	430,082	10	23
Rhode Island	220, 592	60	98, 325	27	39,965	11	4
South Carolina	495, 878	44	564, 856	50	63,324	6	8
South Dakota	139, 295	43	150, 508	46	31,248	10	3
Tennessee	905, 599	48	860, 809	46	105,577	6	11
Texas	2, 455, 735	44	2, 731, 998	49	377,530	7	32
Utah	220, 197	33	359, 394	54	66,100	10	5
Vermont	138, 400	54	80, 043	31	30,912	12	3
Virginia	1, 070, 990	45	1, 119, 974	47	158,707	7	13
Washington	899, 645	51	639, 743	36	161,642	11	11
West Virginia	324, 394	51	231, 908	37	70,853	11	5
Wisconsin	1, 071, 859	49	845, 172	39	227,426	10	11
Wyoming	77, 897	37	105, 347	50	25,854	12	3
TOTALS	45, 628, 667	49	37, 869, 435	41	7, 874, 283	8	538

175

Index

About the Authors

James W. Ceaser is professor of government and foreign affairs at the University of Virginia, where he has taught since 1976. He has also held visiting appointments at Marquette University, the University of Basel, Claremont Mckenna College, the University of Bordeaux, and Harvard University. Professor Ceasar is coauthor with Andrew Busch of *Upside Down and Inside Out: The 1992 Elections and American Politics* (Rowman & Littlefield, 1993) and author of *Presidential Selection* (1979), *Reforming the Reforms* (1982), *Liberal Democracy and Political Science* (1990), and *Reconstructing America* (1997).

Andrew E. Busch is assistant professor of political science at the University of Denver. He is coauthor with James Ceaser of *Upside Down and Inside Out* and author of *Outsiders and Openness in the Presidential Nominating System* (University of Pittsburgh Press, 1997). He has also authored numerous book chapters and articles in journals including *Polity* and *PS*. He received his Ph.D. in government at the University of Virginia in 1992.